MURDER IN
LEXINGTON

MURDER IN
LEXINGTON

VMI, Honor and Justice in Antebellum Virginia

DANIEL S. MORROW

Charleston — London

THE
History
PRESS

Published by The History Press
Charleston, SC 29403
www.historypress.net

Front cover: Mary Evelyn Anderson Bruce (1835–1916). *Special Collections, Leyburn Library, Washington and Lee University*. Three unnamed VMI cadets from the class of 1854. *VMI Archives*. Lexington, Virginia, Washington College and VMI, Casimir Bohn lithograph, 1857. *Courtesy of the University Collections of Art and History, The Reeves Center, Washington and Lee University. Back cover*: Cadet Marcellus Newton Moorman (1835–1904). *VMI Archives*. Allen & Thurber pepperbox. *Courtesy of Alex Cudaback.*

First published 2013

Manufactured in the United States

ISBN 978.1.60949.896.2

Library of Congress CIP data applied for.

For Glenda and Alex

CONTENTS

CONTENTS

PREFACE

For nothing is lost, nothing is ever lost…And all times are one time, and all those dead in the past never lived before our definition gives them life, and out of the shadows their eyes implore us. That is what all of us historical researchers believe. And we love truth.
—*Robert Penn Warren,* All the King's Men

Born in November 1944, I was nearly two years old before I saw my father, Daniel Carter Morrow. He returned from service with the 83rd Infantry in Europe, went to work and moved to Danville, Virginia, the "Last Capital of the Confederacy." There he raised a family in which many of the values, good and bad, of 1854 Virginia would not have seemed strange.

Though he never knew it, he set in motion all the research that led to the publication of this story of the sad events of January 15, 1854.

He was named for his great-uncle, Robert Carter, who had served under Charles Edward Lightfoot in the Sixth North Carolina. Lightfoot was one of Cadet Thomas Blackburn's roommates at the Virginia Military Institute. An afternoon's search in the VMI archives for Lightfoot's friends and classmates led to the personnel file of Cadet Robert Preston Carson, a clipping of Charles Burks Christian's obituary and a provocative note scrawled in red across its face by an archivist long loved and lost.

Over time, most, if not all the overt expressions of the *worst* of the antebellum "values" have either disappeared, or have been justly suppressed to those dark corners of the heart and mind where such things sadly linger and dwell despite ourselves.

The *best* of those values, conscious and unconscious, no doubt drove my own arguably obsessive interest in the sad tale of Charles Burks Christian and Thomas Blackburn.

For all practical purposes, those values appear to be hard-wired, as experimental psychologist Jonathan Haidt and his students have so carefully chronicled. They are, I now believe, instinctive, extremely powerful and, more often than not, the driving force behind the stories we tell to explain why we think what we think, do what we do and say what we say, both in our own self-defense and in defense of those we love or admire.

Among the most important of them, along with their opposites, are loyalty, a sense of what harms others and ourselves, respect for authority, a sense of overwhelming awe and an innate sense of justice.

Arguably, they lie at the heart of all our codes of behavior, formal and informal; the stories we tell to explain them; the rituals we perform to reinforce them; and the sometimes self-destructive behavior they lead us to engage in, despite ourselves (or what we think ourselves to be).

All those values, instincts and behaviors—right and wrong, good and bad, just and unjust, harmful or redemptive, tragic and inspiring—are, I believe, embodied in the story of the events of January 1854, the trials that followed and the lives of the young men and women who lived through them.

They would not have been strange to my father's grandfather (who fought at Gettysburg) or to his son's grandson.

My only hope is to have done them justice.

ACKNOWLEDGEMENTS

When one publishes one's first book at a relatively advanced age, the list of people and institutions to whom one is indebted could well fill a second, and certainly more worthy volume.

Thus any list, including this one, is inevitably unjust and inadequate.

I am deeply indebted and grateful to all those stewards of a very special trust—the archivists, librarians and devoted enthusiasts—who have given their lives and labor to preserving and making accessible things worth remembering.

The institutions without which this work would have been impossible are listed in the bibliography.

I would be remiss, however, were I not to give special thanks to Diane Jacob and her colleagues and staff at the Virginia Military Institute, to John Jacob and his colleagues at the Washington and Lee University School of Law Archives, and Lisa McCown and her colleagues at Special Collections, Leyburn Library, Washington and Lee University. They have tolerated me and my questions for too many years to count, and they have never been anything less than gracious, forthcoming and committed to the very best traditions of their profession.

The following individuals provided advice, counsel, support and in many cases material assistance: Tim Alexander, John and Linda Bell, David Bruce, Tom Buckley, Childs Burden, Doug Cooper, Jolly DeGive, the Frederick S. Fisher family, Mrs. Carter Glass III, Jennifer Green, Alexandra Gressitt, Lee Hadden, Scott Hutchison, Janine Johnson, Marc Leepson,

Katie Letcher Lyle, Thomas Markham, Alma Walker McCarthy and family, Caroline Miller, the Robert H. Mollohan family, Jim Morgan, Barclay Rives, James Robertson, Catherine Coleman Seaman, Tom Vogel, Michael Wallace, Barbara Blackburn Wells, Betsy Wells, Alexander Williams, Richard Williams, Bradford Wineman, Lorna Wycoff and Liz Whiting.

The list of those to whom personal credit is due is as long as a lifetime.

The list that follows thus fails twice. It is too short and, for most who will read this work, will be either cryptic or totally meaningless. Too many of those named are gone. Others, no doubt, will have no idea why they are listed here. They are, however, special and each in their own way made this work possible. First and foremost, the two people to whom this book is dedicated, Glenda and Alex Cudaback. My parents, my sister Mary and, to paraphrase James Taylor, a holy host of others who made us who we were and are: John Hudson; Evelyn Hair; Eugene Stryker; Peggy Moran Morrow; Robert Albritton; John Witeck; John Selser; Joseph Blotner; John Snell; Peter Nelson; Karl Otmar Freiherr von Aretin, his family and his colleagues at the Institute for European History in Mainz; friends, clients and colleagues at WBTM; WCHL, Whitney Communications, the *Washington Post*, Cudaback Strategic Communications, International Data Group, Computerworld, the Smithsonian Institution, the Jamestown Exploration Company, Techonomy, the information technology industry and all those dedicated to its history and its future, the men and women of the Mosby Heritage Area Association and all those who touch or are touched by the newspaper that first began to serialize the story, the *Middleburg Eccentric*.

INTRODUCTION

In late 1853, nineteen-year-old Mary Evelyn Anderson—by all accounts one of the most beautiful women in Virginia—refused to walk to church with Lexington law student Charles Burks Christian. Christian soon confronted, stabbed and killed the man he believed to be responsible for her decision: her cousin, VMI First Classman Thomas Blackburn. This is the story of that deadly confrontation, how and why it happened and the trials that followed. The notions of duty, honor and justice associated with those events shaped an extraordinary group of men and women who would all too soon face the larger trials of the American Civil War.[1]

Part I

THE UNHAPPY HOLIDAY

OUT OF THE DARKNESS

James Woods Massie had heard the sounds before—the slash and snap of a heavy switch or cowhide lash and the echoes of hard blows striking home. It sounded, he said, like someone thrashing a slave—nothing unusual, it would seem, for a Sunday afternoon in Lexington.[2]

Massie said nothing about it to his three friends walking carefully in the dark along Nelson Street, on their way to late Sunday services at Lexington Presbyterian Church.

No one raised an alarm. It was dark. It was wet. It was Sunday, and whatever was going on in the shadows, it was none of their business.

By the time Massie's little group had walked another few paces, two men came tumbling out of the darkness behind them, locked in each other's arms, struggling in what one witness described as a "deadly silence."

Perhaps recalling rumors of slave unrest and the mobilization of troops in Lexington only a few years earlier, Massie handed his hymnal to a young law student and ordered him to lead the ladies of their company to the light and safety of Main Street.[3]

Massie then turned to face whatever might be out there in the dark. Hopelessly nearsighted, Massie could just make out two shadowy figures, both of whom were now rolling on the ground, their faces completely hidden, their bodies only dimly visible in the glow from the church windows behind him.[4]

Inside the well-lit Presbyterian Church sanctuary, the Reverend Dr. George Junkin, president of Washington College, was just beginning evening

Lexington Presbyterian Church as it appeared around 1880. Photograph by Michael Miley. *Special Collections, Leyburn Library, Washington and Lee University.*

services. His congregation numbered one hundred or more. Among them were the usual assortment of VMI cadets, Washington College students and bright young men from Judge John White Brockenbrough's Law School, many of whom, by their own admission, attended services less for religious reasons than to see or be seen by the young women in the congregation.

Junkin's family was also there: his wife, his three daughters and his new son-in-law Major Thomas Jonathan Jackson, a West Point graduate, Mexican war hero and now a struggling instructor at the Institute.

For the Junkin and Jackson families, the recent holiday season had been exceptional. Ellie Junkin, Major Jackson's new wife, was pregnant with their first child, though it is unlikely that either she or her husband were yet aware of her condition.

Ellie's younger sister, eighteen-year-old Julia, had walked to church that night on the arm of a tall, blond, popular and handsome VMI First Classman, Cadet Thomas Blackburn, by all accounts one of the most well-connected young men in Virginia. He was also something of a bad boy, having only recently returned to VMI following a court-martial for a notorious prank played on none other than Major Jackson.[5]

Blackburn was also related, or better said, formerly related, to another woman in the congregation: Sally Campbell Preston McDowell, daughter of the late governor of Virginia, James McDowell.

Blackburn's uncle, former governor of Maryland Francis "Frank" Thomas, had married Sally McDowell in her father's house in Lexington, despite her father's objections. She was half the age of her new husband. Within a year of their marriage, Frank Thomas divorced her. In the process, he published a pamphlet outlining his reasons for doing so. Among them were incest and abortion.[6]

Before Sally Campbell Preston McDowell heard benediction that night, her one-time nephew, Cadet Tom Blackburn, would be killed by Charles Burks Christian, a law student who believed Blackburn had insulted him.

THE MISTRESS OF COL ALTO

Tom Blackburn's erstwhile aunt, Sally Campbell Preston McDowell, was thirty-two years old in 1854, divorced and on the eve of her second marriage.[7]

On the day before Tom Blackburn was killed, she had marked the eighth anniversary of her shocking and all-too-public divorce. Because of it, McDowell had been a social outcast for a dozen years, ever since her legal separation from Frank Thomas in 1842. She was living at Col Alto, her late father's house, within walking distance of the Presbyterian Church on the corner of Nelson and Main Streets in Lexington.

Were she not divorced she might well have been one of the most prominent and powerful women in two states. Her father James McDowell, Lexington's favorite son and the first Virginia governor born west of the Blue Ridge Mountains, died in 1851. Her mother, the late Susanna Smith Preston, was the daughter of a U.S. congressman and a niece of Patrick Henry.

McDowell was barely fifteen when she began her relationship with Tom Blackburn's uncle Frank, then a U.S. congressman from Maryland. She had met him in Washington, where she was learning to be a proper lady at Miss English's Female Seminary in Georgetown.

While a student, McDowell had lived with her aunt, Elizabeth Preston McDowell, the wife of the powerful senior senator from Missouri, Thomas Hart Benton.

Frank Thomas boarded in the same house as the Bentons. Apparently smitten at first sight, he courted McDowell for four years, from 1837 until she finally agreed to marry him in 1841.

Col Alto, the McDowell House. Home of Blackburn's aunt, Sally Campbell Preston McDowell. *National Register of Historic Places.*

Thomas's cause may have been helped by McDowell's best friend, cousin and friendly rival Jessie Benton, who, like Sally, was young, beautiful, popular and involved with an older man unpopular with her parents. In 1841, three months after McDowell married Frank Thomas, Jessie Benton would marry John Charles Fremont, an officer, explorer and soon-to-be national hero eleven years her senior.

Frank Thomas later claimed McDowell seduced him, and that her aunt Elizabeth Benton helped.

Thomas's enemies (McDowell's father first among them) insisted he was insane. Frank replied that if he were insane, McDowell had driven him to it.

Yet, despite its unhappy ending, the Thomas/McDowell marriage had begun well. Before their first anniversary, Thomas had won a hard-fought election and with his new wife had celebrated both victory and his inauguration as governor of Maryland.

During the campaign, however, Thomas had often been away from home, sometimes for days, sometimes for weeks at a time. Rumors apparently fed suspicions, and only months after his inauguration, Thomas accused McDowell of having an affair with his law partner, Robert J. Taylor, who also happened to be McDowell's first cousin.

When, shortly thereafter, McDowell miscarried, Thomas let it be known that he believed she had aborted the ungodly product of an incestuous relationship, both of which were not only sins but also crimes in the state of Maryland.

Thomas soon filed for divorce, which could only be granted by a special act of the state legislature. To support his case before the Maryland assembly, Thomas published a pamphlet outlining in detail his charges against Virginia governor McDowell's favorite daughter. He then distributed the pamphlet to every member of the Maryland State legislature and to every member of the United States Congress.

The McDowells replied by starting their own divorce proceeding in Virginia. The result, after five years of personal, legal and sometimes physical confrontation, was an unprecedented double divorce, each granted by a full vote of the plaintiff's respective state legislature. The proceedings, and thus all of Frank Thomas's embarrassing allegations, became the talk of Washington, Maryland and Virginia.

By January 1854, however, McDowell's life had begun to change. Eight years after the final divorce decrees, and after well over a decade of shame, religious discrimination and largely self-imposed isolation in Lexington's strict southern Presbyterian society, Sally Campbell Preston McDowell had fallen in love again. The man she loved, loved her and had asked her to marry him.

Courtship was difficult for a divorced woman in mid-nineteenth century Virginia. Marriage was even more difficult, both legally and socially. For McDowell and her beloved, both devout southern Presbyterians, it was also a religious nightmare.

McDowell's fiancé, John Miller, was an active Presbyterian minister. Under church law, her divorce meant that she could only remarry if she could prove that Frank Thomas, the former governor of Maryland, had been unfaithful to her before he had filed for divorce.

Sally Campbell Preston McDowell, divorced wife of Tom Blackburn's uncle Francis Thomas, former Maryland governor. *Courtesy of Louise Minor Sinclair.*

24

Under the circumstances, McDowell would have noted, no doubt with more than passing interest, the arrival of Frank Thomas's nephew, Tom Blackburn, at VMI in the fall of 1850.

Sally McDowell had known Tom Blackburn since he was a child. She knew and by all accounts was especially fond of Blackburn's parents, who had sheltered and cared for her while she recovered from the loss of her baby.

In a town with a free white population of just over 1,100 souls, it would have also been virtually impossible for her to miss hearing about Blackburn's escapades at VMI in the years that followed.

She may have also noticed his arrival at church on the night he was killed. He was tall and blond, wearing the dress-blue "walking out" uniform coat reserved for senior cadets, escorting the Reverend George Junkin's nineteen-year-old daughter, Julia.

Perhaps she also noted Blackburn's early departure, accompanied by another singularly handsome young man, a law student with a none-too-savory reputation of his own: Charles Burks Christian.

3

THE INVITATION

When Tom Blackburn left Julia Junkin and walked out of the Lexington Presbyterian Church to meet Charles Christian, those who knew the men assumed they were off to settle an earlier "difficulty" over another young woman, Blackburn's cousin, Mary Evelyn Anderson.

Anderson was a striking eighteen-year-old brunette, a "famous beauty" from Fincastle, a valley town some forty miles south of Lexington.[8] Her father, Francis Thomas Anderson, was a prominent lawyer and state legislator who would later become rector of Washington and Lee. Her uncle, Joseph Reid Anderson, was the founder of Tredegar Iron Works in Richmond.

Mary Evelyn Anderson had been invited to Lexington by her aunt Evalina Moore, a determined matchmaker with a keen eye for the opportunities presented by the Christmas and New Year's holidays in a town blessed with no fewer than three all-male institutions of higher education.

Anderson immediately attracted the attention of most, if not all, the young men at VMI, Washington College and Judge John White Brockenbrough's law school. Among them was Charles Burks Christian, one of Judge Brockenbrough's law students. Later events would reveal that Christian also caught Miss Anderson's eye.

Christian was older (nearly twenty), had a neatly trimmed mustache, wore jackets in the new "English" style and, perhaps best of all, was one of Brockenbrough's "bright young men."[9]

He had grown up in Amherst County, a long thirty miles southeast of Lexington, on the far side of the Blue Ridge. His father had died when he

Mary Evelyn Anderson Bruce (1835–1916). *Special Collections, Leyburn Library, Washington and Lee University.*

was only ten, leaving a young widow to care for Christian and his three younger sisters.

Like Anderson's cousin Tom, Christian enjoyed a reputation as a bad boy. Shortly before entering law school, he had been expelled from Richmond College, formerly a Baptist seminary almost universally referred to as the Baptist College. He had reportedly threatened to shoot the school's president.[10]

On Thursday, December 22, 1853, Christian attended a Christmas party at the home of John White Brockenbrough. The judge lived in a large house, which also served as his law school, situated on the southwest side of Washington Street, just across from the Washington College campus and the home of its president, George Junkin.

Though it was probably not the first time Christian had seen Mary Evelyn Anderson, it was the first time he had seen her closely. He was clearly smitten.

Never shy, Christian prevailed upon Robert White, a friend and fellow law student who was living in the Brockenbrough house, to introduce him.[11] White obliged, and once formally introduced, Christian wasted no time.

As Anderson later told a jury, "Very soon after being introduced," Christian asked if "I had company to church the next Sunday night."

"I told him I had not," Anderson testified. "He then asked me if he might call for me."

She agreed on the spot. After all, she later testified, Christian had been introduced to her properly, by a "gentleman," in his own home.[12]

Despite Charles Burks Christian's reputation as something of a bad boy, not only Anderson's guardians but Lexington society in general considered him "a gentleman" as well.

The Christian and Burks families were well known and respected in Lynchburg, Campbell, Bedford and Amherst Counties. His cousins on his widowed mother's side (not least among them the nine sons of Bedford County's Martin Parks Burks) would become some of the state's most distinguished jurists, teachers and soldiers. And young Christian, by all accounts, had already been invited into the homes of some of Lexington's finest families.

But he was not wealthy. The only son of a widowed mother, Christian said he had come to Lexington with a purpose: to learn a profession and then practice it well enough to care for his mother and his three still-unmarried sisters.

Though considered something of a man of the world in Lexington, friends of the family later insisted he had only really been away from home once before, while a student in Richmond. From Richmond, Christian had moved to Lexington to study law under Judge John White Brockenbrough.

Judge Brockenbrough was already well on his way to becoming a legend. He was barely forty years old when President James K. Polk appointed him judge of the United States Court for the Western District of Virginia in 1846.

On October 31, 1849, Brockenbrough opened his own private law school in Lexington, the Rockbridge County Seat and the home of Washington College and the Virginia Military Institute. By 1852, he was a member of the Washington College Board of Trustees.

By 1854, his record on the federal bench was not only respected, but by some standards, perfect. Not one of his decisions had been reversed on appeal, and none would be for years.

As a result of his growing reputation, and no doubt the steady stream of relatively well-to-do young men through Lexington's schools, Brockenbrough had no trouble attracting students. By 1854, at age forty-eight, he was well on his way to running what would become the largest private law school in Virginia.[13]

Charles Burks Christian's life would soon depend on Judge Brockenbrough, and the people who visited, lived, studied and worked with him in the house where Christian first met Mary Evelyn Anderson.

4

A BLOW TO THE HEART

On Friday, December 23, 1853, just a day after their first meeting, Mary Evelyn Anderson found herself once more in Christian's company, at a holiday fair staged by the new rector of Lexington's Grace Episcopal Church, the Reverend William Nelson Pendleton.

Forty-six years old, Pendleton had graduated from West Point with the class of 1830. He would later rise to the rank of brigadier general and command the artillery of the Confederate Army of Northern Virginia. His only son, Sandie, a Washington College student in 1854, was both talented and popular. He would later serve on the staffs of Confederate generals Stonewall Jackson, Richard Ewell and Jubal Early.[14]

The senior Pendleton's Christmas Fair was, by all accounts, one of the most eagerly anticipated events of the 1853–54 social season in Lexington. As VMI Cadet John Howard Sharp remembered it more than half a century later, "All the beauty and fashion of Lexington" were to be there and best of all, the VMI cadets were allowed to attend.[15]

The occasion demanded nothing less than spit and polish, boots and brass, and haircuts and shaves for all those who could afford the one or were old enough to need the other.

Thus, early on Friday morning, Sharp's friend Thomas Blackburn found himself surrounded by VMI cadets, Washington College and Brockenbrough law students, waiting for service at the barbershop in Mr. Edwin Porter's Lexington Hotel, conveniently located not far from the Rockbridge County Courthouse on Main Street.

Lexington, 1870. Crowds gathered at the former Porter's Hotel. Photograph by Michael Miley. *Special Collections, Leyburn Library, Washington and Lee University.*

Despite what one guest described as its "narrow and uncomfortable quarters," Porter's was one of the most popular boardinghouses in Lexington. Reverend Pendleton, his wife and young Sandie Pendleton had lived there for four months while the Episcopal Parish House was undergoing repairs. Major Thomas Jackson had boarded there too, along with VMI Professor Thomas Hoomes Williamson and his wife. So had Junius Fishburn, a Washington College professor who, like Jackson, would marry one of George Junkin's daughters. Charles Harrison, another of Brockenbrough's students and best man at Major Jackson's wedding, had also been a guest.

Indeed, at any given time one could expect to find an interesting mix of fifty or sixty boarders at Porter's, including large contingents of young lawyers and most, if not all, of Brockenbrough's law students.[16] It was, thus, not altogether surprising for Blackburn to find Charles Burks Christian seated in Porter's barbershop ahead of him.

Christian was five feet, eight inches tall, dark-haired and fair-skinned. A friend of Blackburn's described him as "a small dudish black-eyed, black-haired, good looking man with a well-cared-for black moustache." He was twenty years old and seen as "boyish in appearance, but not delicate...rather thick-set and muscular."[17]

The barber, in the time-honored tradition of his trade, no doubt played to the audience of young men waiting in his shop and at one point, according to John Howard Sharp, remarked, *sotto voce*, that Christian was "a regular lady killer, etc."

Christian reportedly quipped in reply, "I can seduce any woman in Lexington."[18]

In antebellum, strait-laced, Presbyterian Lexington, the very word "seduction" was, if not taboo, not a word to be used lightly—and certainly not a word to be tolerated when applied by another man to a female member of one's own family.[19]

Sharp claimed that Blackburn overheard the remark. If so, he chose not to confront Christian, said nothing and returned to the VMI barracks. There, Sharp said, he "brooded" over what he had seen and heard "for some time" before heading back into Lexington, to Grace Church and Reverend Pendleton's Christmas Fair.

Soon after arriving at the fair, Sharp remembered, Blackburn found himself "not a little surprised to see...Miss Anderson on the arm of Christian and promenading with him."[20]

Anderson later swore that Christian's behavior at the fair was boorish and "ungentlemanly" and his attentions "very disagreeable."[21]

A.G. Strayer, a law student and a good friend of Christian, remembered seeing Christian and Anderson together at the fair but admitted he couldn't say whether "Christian's attentions were either disagreeable or very acceptable" to her, because he himself had been too busy, "engaged in talking to another lady."[22]

Whatever the case, Anderson's less-than-twenty-four-hour-old agreement to "walk out" with Christian "was not mentioned that night." She later swore she had already decided not to walk out to church with Christian well before Tom Blackburn said one word about him and had said so to her aunt Evalina Alexander Moore and to VMI professor Lieutenant Daniel Truehart on the carriage ride home from the fair.

Blackburn was soon made aware of Christian's behavior, however, and appears to have discussed at length both Anderson's "promenade" and Christian's remarks about "seduction."

Less than twenty-four hours later, early in the morning on Christmas Eve, Blackburn marched out of the VMI barracks, past Superintendent Francis Henney Smith's quarters, past the VMI Porter's Lodge, to the nearby Samuel McDowell Moore house to speak to Anderson.

Mary Evelyn Anderson would later testify that she thought Blackburn called on her that day only "to apologize for allowing Charles Christian to annoy me with his attentions." Instead, Blackburn told her that he had already left the fair before he became aware of Christian's boorish conduct.

By all accounts, he did not tell her about the incident in the barber shop or about Christian's use of the word "seduction." Anderson reportedly never spoke the word in public, and Blackburn, as a gentleman, may well have never spoken the word in her presence.

Whatever the case, it is clear that Blackburn and Anderson talked at some length about Christian, and whatever Blackburn said to her confirmed Anderson's determination not to "walk out" with him to church or anywhere else. Blackburn then advised her, she said, to make her intentions absolutely clear by writing Christian a note, formally canceling their Christmas Day "engagement."

The Moore House, between Washington College and VMI. Detail from Casimir Bohn lithograph, 1857. *University Collections of Art and History, The Reeves Center, Washington and Lee University.*

At some point during their conversation, Anderson's uncle, Samuel McDowell Moore, walked in and Anderson asked his advice. Moore agreed completely with Blackburn's suggestion that she make her intentions (or lack thereof) clear, in writing.

As soon as Blackburn left for the barracks, Anderson thus dutifully penned a one-line note to Christian. For some unexplained reason, however, she waited until the next day, after she had returned home from morning church services, to send it.[23]

Christian thus received Anderson's note on Christmas Day, in the presence of his friends, just hours before he was due to walk to church with someone he and his law school friends believed to be the most beautiful woman in Lexington.

Anderson's rejection was thus not only totally unexpected, but it was also humiliating—and apparently deliberately so.

The note contained fewer than a dozen words:

Miss Anderson declines going to church with Mr. Christian this evening.[24]

5

DESPAIR AND INDIGNATION

If Christmas Day 1853 was less than merry for Charles Burks Christian, the day after must have been worse.

On Monday, December 26, Anderson's aunt Evalina Moore threw a party in her niece's honor. Although Christian had been received cordially in the Moore house on previous occasions, this time he was pointedly not invited. Neither, it would seem, did conversation at the party enhance Christian's reputation, something that did not long escape his attention or, apparently, that of anyone else in Lexington.[25]

Christian's reactions were predictable and excruciatingly proper.

"A few days afterward," Anderson later testified, Christian "called at my Uncle's and sent in his card to me."

Anderson's first reaction, she said, was to send a "servant" to tell Christian she couldn't see him, despite the embarrassing and obvious presence of "another visitor in the house."

Anderson's aunt intervened, however, and took it upon herself to deliver the bad news to her niece's now thoroughly confused suitor, who by at least one account had actually come fully prepared to propose marriage. Christian, humiliated once more, left without seeing Anderson.[26]

That evening, Alfred Strayer, one of Christian's law school classmates, called on the Moores. He told them that Christian's friends and fellow students had all heard that Christian had gone to the Moore house that day and that "Miss Anderson had denied herself to him."

Evalina Moore did her best to smooth over the incident, telling Strayer "that Christian was a very pleasant and fluent gentleman and she would be happy for him to continue his visits to her house" regardless of the opinions of her young niece.

Later that evening Strayer told Christian what he had heard at the Moores'.[27]

By Friday, December 30, 1853, Christian's dander was up, and he dispatched a note of his own to Anderson, a document that, much to the family's embarrassment, became a critical and widely publicized piece of evidence in a murder trial.

Reproduced in newspapers all over Virginia, the note was, on its surface, pure soft sentimentality, barely cloaking a hard core of understated high dudgeon.

Mary Evelyn Anderson's aunt, Evalina Alexander Moore (1812–1860). *Moore, Memories, 16.*

Lex. Dec 30, 1853

Miss Anderson,

Being induced by my exalted opinion of your refined feeling to believe that you would not wantonly wound the feeling of any gentleman, and being myself the unhappy victim of your mal-treatment, I must conclude that you had an apparent cause. And failing in my attempted interview with you on last evening, I deem it necessary in justice to my reputation as a gentleman, to find out the mysteries of the matter, and to clear my self of all imputations incompatible with the character of a gentleman, and the strict rules of courtesy.

Then, I ask it of you, as a last favor, to tell, if any there be, [t]he cause that actuated you to do so illiberal an act.

And if there be a calumniator so base, so envious as (with his own vile fabrication) to break the friendship heretofore existing between us, do tell me, and I will bring the culprit to justice and prove to you and the world that I am innocent; and that such a deed is beneath the dignity of those principals of honor that was the care of my aged parents to instill into my youthful bosom, and my constant endeavor to practice.

But if the said causes are not the work of slanderers, but phantoms of your own creation, causes germinating in your own breast, say so, and all is well.

I write not these lines in order to place myself in status quo, for it is done,
the die is cast; the Rubicon is crossed; but I write with the vain hope of
proving to you and the world that I could not treat any lady otherwise than
strictly courteous and respectful.

And in closing these lines, I bid you an affectionate adieu, invoking the
blessings of heaven, and hoping that your path may be strewn with flowers
while sojourning in this world of care. So: Vale, Vale (formosessima puella)
Aeturni Vale!

Peace to thy heart, though another's it be,
Health to thy cheek, though it bloom not for me.
Your humble friend,
Chas. B. Christian

Christian's description of himself as a "gentleman" and of his unknown detractor as a "calumniator" were the moral equivalents of a tossed gauntlet. Though Christian could not possibly have known it at the time, his postscript was even more damaging:

PS
You will please answer, addressing me through box No. 101, or return this
epistle, and close the sad drama forever.
C.B. Christian
Friday Morning, in confidence[28]

The phrasing of this apparently gracious postscript would resonate with most of the leading families of Lexington in a way Christian could not possibly have imagined, and with Tom Blackburn and his family in particular.

It reprised almost exactly the phrasing of a note which Tom Blackburn's uncle Frank had sent to Sally Campbell Preston McDowell in 1842, a note that had led directly to an oft-recounted physical confrontation between the Maryland governor and McDowell's father, Virginia governor James McDowell, at a stagecoach station in Staunton, Virginia.[29]

Anderson later testified that she "hastily" read Christian's note aloud to her aunt and then announced her intention to burn it. Instead she listened to her aunt, who suggested, "Keep it! It is a curiosity!"[30]

Unfortunately for Charles Christian, the note was long remembered and too-often discussed by Anderson's aunt Evalina Alexander Moore. She was, after all, born an Alexander, Sally Campbell Preston McDowell once wrote, and "You might as well proclaim things thro' a trumpet as confide them to an Alexander."[31]

Nevertheless, according to Anderson, for a short time, Christian's note passed out of her mind and into her dresser drawer "until the morning of the 14th of January, 1854."

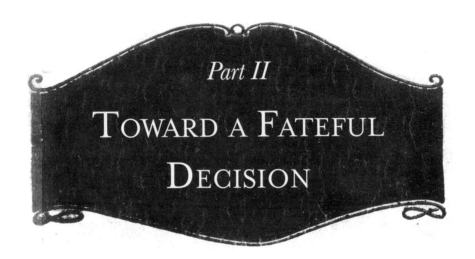

Part II

TOWARD A FATEFUL
DECISION

6

THE GATHERING STORM

On Saturday morning, January 14, 1854, Cadet Tom Blackburn walked once more across the VMI parade grounds to Samuel McDowell Moore's house. He arrived to find Mary Evelyn Anderson and her Aunt Evalina entertaining his classmate, former roommate and close friend, Alexander Broadnax Bruce.[32]

"Sandy" Bruce was one of the most eligible young bachelors in Virginia, if not the entire South. He was the third son of James Coles Bruce of Berry Hill in Halifax County, a planter, land speculator, heir to a large chain of successful country stores and the owner of more slaves than there were free white citizens of Lexington. Though rich and handsome, Bruce was by no means the sharpest blade ever drawn from a VMI scabbard. He stood dead last in the class of 1854 with little to no hope of improvement.[33]

When Blackburn arrived that morning, the group gathered in the Moores' parlor was discussing mail: letters written, letters received and how important they were to young men and women away from home.

When Blackburn started to describe a letter he had "written recently," Evalina Moore interrupted to ask if he had seen the "very ridiculous" letter Charles Burks Christian had written to Anderson. It was, she said, absolutely "calculated to produce laughter."

Blackburn asked if Christian had, indeed, written to Anderson. Anderson reluctantly admitted it was true.

Moore suggested she show Christian's letter to Blackburn and Sandy Bruce, just for fun. Anderson refused.

The Samuel McDowell Moore House, Mary Evelyn Alexander's home for the 1853–54 holiday season. *VMI Archives.*

Moore "didn't think there would be any harm in showing it, as it was something rich." Anderson, again, refused, insisting the letter was really "nothing."

Blackburn and Bruce were now both insisting she show them the letter.

When Anderson complained that she really didn't feel like going "all the way upstairs" to fetch it, Moore offered to send a "servant." Anderson gave in, went to her room, fetched the note and gave it to her cousin Tom to read.

Blackburn read the letter quietly to himself, she later testified, except for some "Latin sentences" that he read aloud. As he read he "smiled several times." Sandy Bruce agreed that Blackburn read only the Latin passages aloud but swore he laughed at every single line, in English or Latin.

When Blackburn finished, Moore, who had set the entire dramatic reading in progress, thought to remind Anderson that Christian had written to her "in confidence."

Later Anderson said she had "no thought" that the note "contained anything that would create a difficulty" between her cousin and Christian or anything that her cousin could "take exceptions to." At the time, later testimony would reveal, she believed that the "calumniator" whose name Christian had demanded was not Tom Blackburn at all, but another cadet she had known for about a year and a half, James White Humes of Abingdon.[34]

Humes would later testify that he had heard that Christian "had made an engagement with Miss Anderson to escort her to church" at least a week before Blackburn was killed. He told Blackburn "immediately," he said, not only about the "arrangement" but also about rumors that Christian already considered himself "a suitor" of Miss Anderson. It was at that point that Humes advised Blackburn to keep Anderson away from the man, on the grounds that "Christian's reputation so far as I was acquainted with it was not such...that it would be to his cousin's credit to go to church with him."

As for who, if anyone, should take up the matter of "calumny" with Charles Burks Christian, Humes was certain of at least one thing: It was not to be Cadet James White Humes. "I considered Blackburn more responsible to Christian than I was," Humes later testified, noting that, in fact, he did not consider himself "responsible at all."[35]

THE BLACKBURN FAMILY

Tom Blackburn's family defined him and, arguably, would kill him.

Tom Blackburn's mother and Mary Evelyn Anderson's father were first cousins, thus Blackburn and Anderson were "kissing cousins," second cousins, too closely related by nineteenth-century Presbyterian standards for a romantic relationship, though apparently distant enough for some in Lexington to consider Blackburn a possible suitor of Anderson.

Blackburn's father, Richard Scott Blackburn, was a physician, a successful farmer and part owner of a canal-boat freight business in Harper's Ferry. There were eight children in the Blackburn household in 1854 and another on the way. Thomas was the first of the Blackburns' children, born on September 11, 1834, at Spring Grove, near Ripon, Virginia (now Rippon, West Virginia), just off the main road between Berryville and Charles Town.

The Blackburn family was one of the most distinguished in the United States, linked closely not only to newly prominent "western" families like the McDowells of Virginia and Thomases of Maryland, but also to some of the most prominent old line eastern Virginia families, including the Washingtons and the Lees.

Blackburn's great-great-grandfather, Colonel Richard Blackburn, had been a member of the Virginia House of Burgesses, an architect and a soldier. He designed and built his own home, Rippon Lodge in Fairfax County and designed the first Mount Vernon and the original "Falls Church."

Cadet Tom Blackburn's father, Richard Scott Blackburn (1809–1867). The original painting has been lost. *Photograph courtesy of Clarke County Historical Society.*

Colonel Blackburn's son, Lieutenant Colonel Thomas Blackburn of the Second Virginia, fought beside the first president and was wounded at Germantown while serving as aide-de-camp to General Washington.[36]

In 1785, Julia Ann Blackburn, Tom's great-aunt, married General Washington's favorite nephew, Bushrod Washington, later a Supreme Court justice. She lived with him for many years as mistress of Mount Vernon, and both are buried on the grounds.

In 1811, Dr. Blackburn's first cousin, Jane Charlotte Blackburn, married John Augustine Washington, a grand-nephew of the president. At her death in 1855, she became the second Blackburn to live, die and be buried at Mount Vernon. Her son, also named John Augustine, would later serve as aide-de-camp to another relative by marriage, General Robert Edward Lee of nearby Arlington Plantation.[37]

For all the ancestral baggage he carried, or perhaps because of it, Richard Scott and Eleanor Thomas Blackburn's eldest son was, by all accounts, "very popular among the Cadets and liked by everyone."[38] He stood out in any crowd. He was almost six feet tall, weighed about 165 pounds, was "powerfully and finely developed—not fat, but muscular." In January 1854, a Lexington physician would testify he had "seldom seen such a man for his age."[39]

Not all Tom Blackburn's family ties were assets. The most problematic (and impossible to ignore in Lexington) was, of course, his mother's brother, Blackburn's notorious uncle Frank Thomas, divorced husband of Sally Campbell Preston McDowell and the former governor of Maryland.

Unfortunately for both Blackburn and his former Aunt Sally, Frank Thomas had emerged from a post-divorce, self-imposed, seven-year exile in 1853 to re-enter Maryland politics and run, once more, for the governorship.

Given that the salacious details of the Thomas/McDowell divorce cases still smoldered in Lexington, Uncle Frank's re-emergence and fiery new brand of politics fanned new flames. He campaigned with a passion, damning slavery and all his former Democratic Party friends and affiliations. Despite his reputation in Virginia, Frank Thomas was still an articulate and talented politician. He missed being re-elected governor of Maryland by barely more than a thousand votes.

In Lexington, Thomas's shocking new antislavery rhetoric, coupled with his defection from the Democratic Party, no doubt re-opened many old wounds and inflicted a few new ones: personal, political, practical and religious.

Indeed, it is not surprising that Tom Blackburn found himself fairly often in a fight, given the foul reputation of his uncle and the general disposition of young southern "gentlemen" in the mid-nineteenth century to take physical exception to attacks on their honor, whether real or perceived. Blackburn would, of course, be especially sensitive to remarks reflecting on the reputation of the women in his family or anyone questioning his willingness to defend them.

Indeed, during his four years at VMI, Tom Blackburn's biggest problem was, arguably, Tom Blackburn.

As an underclassman, he had already developed a reputation among the students, college faculties and the townspeople of Lexington for both his drinking and his readiness to solve problems with his fists, sometimes with the help of a willing "posse" of fellow cadets.

Blackburn was said to have led just such a posse (some said as many as thirty strong) after a local "cow drover" who had reportedly "abused a young Cadet." As one witness described it, the cadets forcefully administered "that justice which the heartless drover denied to the boy."

Cadet George Baylor Horner, one of Blackburn's roommates in 1851–52, swore that he had seen Blackburn in at least three "difficulties" during their time together at the Institute. One of them, he said, pitted Blackburn against "a man at least a third larger than himself." In that fight, Horner swore, Blackburn "fought fair" and "did not resort to rocks or weapons of any kind" even though he "got the worst of it."[40]

Just after Christmas in 1852, VMI commandant Francis Henney Smith informed the Blackburn family officially that one of Tom's drinking incidents had brought "great discredit to the Institute."[41]

Smith's warning apparently had little effect. In 1853, at the end of Blackburn's junior year, he was court-martialed and dismissed from VMI for participating in one of the most famous pranks in the history of the Institute, involving the man who was arguably its most famous professor.

The prank began innocently enough. One long, dark January night, Blackburn and John Moncure Robinson of the class of 1855 tied Blackburn's cousin, Cadet James Edward Towson, to a chair. They leaned the chair (and Cadet Towson) against the door of the room in the new VMI barracks occupied by professors Thomas J. Jackson and Lieutenant Thomas Harris. Blackburn and Robinson then banged "violently" on the door, ran away and hid to watch the fun.

Jackson himself opened the door, and Towson tumbled in. Unfortunately for Blackburn and Robinson, the major's sense of humor, such as it was, did not extend to pranks or hazing.

After seeing to the release of Towson, Jackson promptly asked a few questions and filed charges against both Blackburn and Robinson for "abusing" their fellow cadet and "disrespectful conduct to a superior officer."

Both were tried before a Garrison court-martial in late January 1853, with Blackburn confidently pleading "not guilty" to all charges and specifications. During the hearing, Blackburn staged a vigorous (if, at

Major Thomas J. Jackson in 1853.
Tom Blackburn from time to time
emulated his Napoleonic pose.
VMI Archives.

times, gratuitously insulting) defense on his own behalf.

Though already standing trial for "disrespectful conduct," Blackburn did not hesitate to bait Major Jackson during cross-examination. "Have you ever, by word or action, given me any cause to be disrespectful?" Blackburn asked Jackson at one point. Jackson, an awkward and notoriously untalented teacher, had of course been the butt of barracks-room jokes since his arrival on the VMI campus some three years earlier. Jackson replied to Blackburn with five words: "Not that I know of."

Blackburn's "summation," taken down verbatim in the VMI court-martial reporter's tight script, filled nearly nine large pages.[42] Despite those efforts, (or more likely, because of them), on January 24, 1853, the court found Blackburn and Robinson guilty on all counts and dismissed them from the Institute.[43]

Blackburn, of course, immediately appealed to his family's friends and relations on the VMI Board of Visitors. His reinstatement took less than a month. On February 8, 1853, the VMI Board ordered the court-martial reversed, and both Blackburn and Robinson were reinstated.[44]

Blackburn's classmates demonstrated their opinion of the affair (and of Major Jackson) by promptly electing Blackburn to the Board of Managers for the July 4, 1853 graduation day Military Ball, the last he would attend.[45]

Cadet Robinson never returned to VMI. His father, a Sorbonne-trained civil engineer, requested that his son be allowed to resign, citing fears he would not be able to "redeem his lost time in his studies so as to pass his annual examination."[46] In 1889, Robinson was granted an honorary degree from the Institute, having served as an engineer and staff officer in the Confederate army and as president of both the Baltimore Steam and Packet Company and the Richmond, Fredericksburg & Potomac Railroad.[47]

James Edward Towson, the cadet Blackburn and Robinson had tied to the chair, would later serve as part of the honor guard that accompanied Tom Blackburn's body home.[48]

A Fateful Decision

According to Samuel McDowell Moore, Tom Blackburn left the Moore house on Saturday morning, January 14, 1854, convinced that he was "bound to inform Christian" that he had advised Mary Evelyn Anderson "not to walk with him" to church.

In a note to her father, Moore credited Blackburn's "chivalrous disposition" for the decision, though it was, in fact, a decision defined and shaped not only by Blackburn's "chivalry," but also by the outspoken advice and unspoken demands of his family, friends and peers.[49]

Blackburn's friend James White Humes took some pride in being the first to tell Blackburn that a man of unsavory reputation had made "advances" toward his cousin. Humes believed he was honor bound to tell Blackburn and that Blackburn was honor bound to do something about it.[50]

Humes was not alone, however. Blackburn shared room thirteen of the "new" VMI barracks with four other popular cadets, all insistent that Blackburn do the "honorable" thing.

Two of the roommates, Charles Edward ("Charley") Lightfoot and Robert Preston ("Kit") Carson, were seniors, VMI first classmen like Blackburn himself.

Lightfoot was First Captain of the Corps, the highest-ranking cadet officer. Like Blackburn, he was well-known, well-connected and very popular and had come perilously close to dismissal from the Institute. Unlike Blackburn, Lightfoot's problems did not take the form of one or two big things, but many small ones: demerits, ninety-nine of them, just one short of automatic dismissal. Despite (or perhaps because of) those dubious achievements, Lightfoot's classmates had elected him and his recently court-martialed roommate to the Board of Managers for the 1853 graduation ball.[51]

Kit Carson had the best grades in room thirteen. He would finish third in the class of 1854, just behind James Lane and Richard Taylor. Carson was also one of a large contingent of cadets from Abingdon, Virginia.[52] Among his Abingdon friends was James White Humes, who not only told Blackburn that Christian had made "unwelcome" advances toward his cousin, but also told Christian that Anderson had become vocal about her dislike of him.[53]

George Buck of Berkeley Springs was room thirteen's junior, or second classman. Carson described him as "a nervous, cracked-voice sort of a fellow" who, when asked his name, "invariably answered, 'G. Buck, by Gad.'" Buck, like Carson, was bright and brave. After graduating from VMI, he would go to medical school and, during the Civil War, serve as lieutenant colonel of the Thirty-seventh Virginia.[54]

The youngest roommate was Cadet Hiram Claiborne Burks, one of the Burks of Bedford County and a third cousin (once removed) of Charles Burks Christian. Like Blackburn and Lightfoot, Burks was always in trouble. After only a year and five months at VMI, he would be dismissed for "excessive demerits."[55]

As Tom Blackburn walked from the Moore house to the VMI barracks, he asked Sandy Bruce for advice about what he should do, especially about the passage he had just read in Christian's letter to his cousin describing him as a "calumniator."

Bruce, of course, hadn't read the letter and had only heard Blackburn read aloud a few selected passages (in Latin, by all accounts). Bruce also had no idea what Christian meant by his demand to know the name of his "calumniator" until Blackburn either explained the passage or defined the word for him.

"After a little consultation," Sandy Bruce later testified, he and Blackburn "concluded" that Blackburn had "better see Christian" and tell him Blackburn was, indeed, "the gentleman" who had advised Mary Evelyn Anderson to stay away from him.

Soon thereafter, Blackburn and Bruce reached the VMI barracks and went their separate ways.

After returning to room thirteen, Blackburn ran into Richard Taylor and, without revealing any confidences, sought Taylor's advice. As Taylor remembered it, Blackburn bent his ear, "endeavoring to plague me because a young lady whom he said I was in love with up town had sent some message

Berry Hill, Alexander Broadnax Bruce's home in Halifax County, Virginia. *Library of Congress.*

or something to him." Only later would Taylor discover what Blackburn was really talking about.

Kit Carson ran into Blackburn in the VMI barracks sometime between noon and 1:00 p.m. Blackburn spoke frankly to Carson, telling him right away that he'd seen a letter from Christian to Anderson in which Christian had referred to him as a "calumniator." Blackburn, Carson said, had already "determined to go and tell Christian" that "he had advised his cousin."[56]

Later, around 2:00 p.m., Blackburn found Humes and G.B. Horner of Warrenton finishing dinner at the VMI mess hall.

"Fellows, you are the very ones I want to see!" he said as he entered the side door of the building. His tone apparently prompted Horner, who had roomed with Blackburn in 1851, to ask him if something were wrong.

Blackburn warmed himself at the mess hall stove and told his story one more time, describing Christian's note as "the most ridiculous thing he ever read." For "delicious nonsense," he said, "he had never seen its equal."

Blackburn then asked Humes and Horner if they thought he ought to go to town to confront Christian, man to man.

51

Humes, who had spoken to both Blackburn and Christian about the affair, encouraged Blackburn to see Christian immediately. "I did not think it a matter in which a fight was to be feared," Humes later testified, but "justice and honor demanded that Mr. Christian, if he desired it, should know the name of the man who had done him an injury."

Humes also warned Blackburn that if he did not shut him up about it, or take some notice of it...[Christian] would make the whole affair, and his cousin's name in connection with it, a subject of town gossip."

After listening to Humes, Blackburn appeared ready to seek out Christian right away. Horner, however, warned him not to be hasty, especially about going into Lexington alone.

Horner "knew" he said, "that if Christian resented the communication made by Blackburn, he would strike him." Indeed, Horner later testified, it was his belief that Christian would either strike a blow the moment Blackburn told him "he was the calumniator," or he would "resent it in some other way," perhaps by sending Blackburn a formal challenge.

Horner convinced Humes, who now argued that if Blackburn confronted Christian, especially "in the presence of others" he might "have a difficulty with him." Humes also noted that "if this happened among or in the presence of Christian's friends," Blackburn might well "need some assistance." With that, Humes and Horner told Blackburn that "if he could wait" they "would go with him."

Blackburn took them up on their offer, and as soon as his two friends finished dinner, the three cadets set off "with the expectation and purpose" in Horner's words, "to put it to Christian...either to act the coward or the man of courage."[57]

Blackburn had gone to the Moore house that morning wearing only his tight-fitting navy-blue "furlough coat," a uniform only VMI first classmen were allowed to wear off campus. Perhaps because the weather had turned colder, Blackburn and his friends stopped by room thirteen in the barracks to pick up Blackburn's long, gray overcoat, modeled on those worn by West Point cadets. Buttoning only the cape to keep it in place, Blackburn set off with his friends across the parade ground toward Lexington in search of Charles Burks Christian.

The trio's first stop was McDowell's Hotel, where Christian was a boarder. A "servant" was sent up to fetch him and quickly reported that Christian was "out."

At Horner's suggestion, the cadets next checked Moore's Hotel, a popular hangout just up the street. Christian wasn't there either.

Blackburn, Humes and Horner were now not only frustrated but also openly expressing hopes that when they finally found Christian he would take offense at Blackburn's "revelation." Horner admitted their only real "fear" at that point was that Christian would be too "obtuse" to understand that he had been insulted and would avoid a fight.

It was in that frame of mind that the three cadets returned to McDowell's, with Blackburn, according to Horner, walking with his hand stuck in the breast of his overcoat, in the style of the Emperor Napoleon, "as was his habit."

Christian, they soon discovered, had been at McDowell's Hotel the entire time.[58]

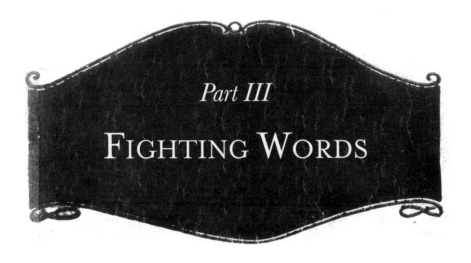

Part III

FIGHTING WORDS

THE "INTERVIEW"

B lackburn, Humes and Horner were "within a few paces of the front
door leading to the bar-room" at McDowell's when Horner spotted
Christian standing in the doorway with Edward Alexander Langhorne, a
seventeen-year-old VMI cadet from Cloverdale, Virginia.[59]

Christian had been at McDowell's all morning, he later told classmate
Robert W. Winn, and was still in his room when the servant sent to find him
told him some cadets were looking for him. When he went downstairs to see
who was calling, Blackburn and his two friends had "disappeared."

Christian's first instinct was to look for them in the bar, which also served
as the hotel office. There he found Langhorne and Cadet Joseph Peterson
Gilliam of Dinwiddie Court House.[60] The two had just left VMI on their
way to dinner at George's in Lexington and remembered seeing Humes and
Horner at the VMI mess hall.

After dinner, they walked from George's to the McDowell's Hotel bar,
where they had a drink, talked and watched the street for passing girls.
Both later claimed Christian was at the bar when they arrived. Whatever
the case, Christian, Langhorne and Gilliam were soon sitting together,
talking and drinking.

Christian knew Langhorne fairly well. Neither of them had been in
Lexington very long, and since their arrival they had met periodically in
Langhorne's room so that each might "see some of his countrymen."[61]

As they talked, Langhorne noticed that Christian was carrying a heavy,
black, silver-headed walking stick. He asked to see it, and Christian handed it

over, apparently without a second thought. Impressed, Langhorne passed it to Gilliam, and Gilliam, equally impressed, said he gave it back to Christian.

Christian later insisted the conversation in the barroom had been a set-up, cleverly contrived by the two VMI cadets to disarm him, and that while they talked, his heavy cane had simply "disappeared."

Planned or unplanned, the timing was perfect. Just as Blackburn, Horner and Humes arrived back at McDowell's, Langhorne noticed two "young ladies" on the street outside and called Christian to the window to see if he knew who they were.[62] By the time Christian reached the window, the girls had "disappeared" into John Blair Lyle's popular bookstore. Christian and Langhorne were still waiting for them to reappear when Blackburn, Humes and Horner walked up.

Cadet Horner later testified he didn't remember seeing any "young ladies" at all, though he clearly remembered seeing Langhorne and Christian standing together at the door of McDowell's bar.

"There is Christian," he said.

Blackburn removed his hand from the breast of his furlough coat, walked straight up to Christian and, according to Horner, said "in a respectful tone" that he wished to see him, "or something to that effect."[63]

Christian said something in reply that none of the cadets seem to have remembered, then walked down the steps of the hotel and followed Blackburn into a "passage" next to the hotel entrance. As he walked, Blackburn buttoned his blue furlough coat tight around him. Several witnesses swore Christian was carrying his silver-headed cane.

Despite Blackburn's "respectful tone," Hugh Laughlin, the bartender and clerk, said he knew there was going to be trouble. Both Blackburn and Christian "seemed excited" as they approached each other, and Laughlin just didn't like the look of it. When they vanished into the passageway, Laughlin said he too made it a point to disappear, "up the alley towards the stable," as one Richmond newspaper reporter put it, to avoid "being a witness."[64]

Blackburn's friend, Humes, on the other hand, relaxed. As soon as he saw Christian was alone, he said, he knew there would be no fight.

While Blackburn and Christian talked, Humes and Horner stood guard—Humes standing close to the open door to the passageway Horner about six feet away.

After what everyone remembered as a very short conversation, Blackburn turned to leave. Just as he reached the door, Horner thought he heard Christian say, "Sir, I honor you for your noble principles." Blackburn,

Three unnamed VMI cadets from the class of 1854. *VMI Archives.*

he remembered, said only "Good evening, sir," or "Good evening, Mr. Christian" before emerging from the passageway, smiling.

When Humes and Horner asked Blackburn what had happened, Blackburn, "in an ordinary tone of voice," said, "Just as I expected, he has not enough courage to strike a child."

Pressed for details, Blackburn said he told Christian to his face that he was the "traducer or calumniator" that Christian had denounced in his note to Anderson and that it was he who had advised Anderson not to accompany him to church. If Christian wished to know why he advised his cousin to avoid being seen with him, Blackburn said, he would be happy to tell him.

When Christian asked why, Blackburn told him he did not have "a very good reputation in Lexington," and that, as a result, he "did not wish to see his cousin with any such man."

Blackburn also confirmed what Horner had thought he had overheard, namely that Christian had said he "honored" Blackburn's "noble principles."

With the dreaded "interview" now over and done, Horner returned to the VMI barracks while Blackburn and Humes set off, apparently in fine fettle, to "call on some ladies."

Humes later claimed that little or nothing more was said of the matter that day. While he and Blackburn were waiting for "ladies" at McDowell's, Blackburn said he was "satisfied." Nevertheless, later that evening (or maybe the next day) Blackburn told Humes "if he were challenged by anyone he would fight him from a revolver down to a pop gun."

As for Cadet Horner, he said he felt only contempt after Christian failed to respond with either a blow or a challenge to Blackburn's insults. "Mr. Christian's conduct dishonored him in my estimation, and in the estimation of every honorable man," Horner later testified. "I did not think Christian a coward previous to that time but thought his character blasted and gone forever by his conduct at that time."

Christian, apparently shaken, returned to the bar, met Cadets Langhorne and Gilliam and asked both to go up to his room with him. Langhorne did so while Gilliam remained downstairs in the bar. Once Langhorne and Christian were alone, Langhorne asked his friend "what was the matter between him and Blackburn?"

Christian said that it was "something he could not speak of" and then asked Cadet Langhorne "what sort of a fellow Blackburn was."

Langhorne replied that he'd only been at the Institute a short time and frankly "did not know much about him."

With that, the conversation ended.

As Langhorne left Christian's room and headed back to the bar, he thought he heard Christian say that "the affair was not done with yet."[65]

THRICE-TOLD TALES

Tales of Christian's "interview" with Tom Blackburn began to seep out of McDowell's Hotel and evolve almost as soon as the cadets left the bar.

Hugh Laughlin, the bartender who had hidden rather than see something he'd rather not see, later remembered seeing Blackburn and Christian emerging from the hotel passageway.

"Both looked changed," he testified. "Both seemed to be in better humor and looked satisfied."[66]

Laughlin appeared to have been at least half right. Almost as soon as he got back to the VMI barracks, Tom Blackburn told Cadet Robert Carson all about the affair. Christian, he said, had admitted that Blackburn was "acting properly" or "doing his duty," and that he even "admired him" for his "noble principles." According to Carson, Blackburn was smiling as he told the story and seemed to be genuinely in "good humor."[67]

Richard Taylor said that he also heard that Christian was "very frightened and seemed glad to get out of the scrape." He also agreed that, when all was said and done, "Everybody thought all parties were satisfied."[68]

Years later, Cadet John Howard Sharp claimed that Christian's remark about Blackburn's "noble principles" had been "told all around." As he remembered the story, Christian said, "I admire you, Mr. Blackburn, for the course you took under the circumstances and would have done just as you did."

Blackburn, Sharp said, "coldly made no reply" to Christian's remarks, but "with a sneer turned his back on him and left him."[69]

Humes told cadets Robert McKinney, Edward Alexander Langhorne and no doubt a number of others congregated in Cadet Richard Taylor's room that he believed the matter "had been adjusted."[70]

Cadet Ned Langhorne, however, disagreed. A young man with a particularly fine-tuned sense of personal honor, Langhorne knew both Christian and Blackburn and had been with Christian at McDowell's Hotel both before and immediately after the confrontation. Langhorne insisted that Christian, far from being mollified or intimidated, had said quite clearly to him that "the affair was not done with."[71]

At Samuel McDowell Moore's house, the initial accounts of "the interview" appear to have produced a universal sigh of relief. Moore's fourteen-year-old daughter, Sallie Alexander, remembered that everyone was delighted to hear that Blackburn and Christian had shaken hands and "parted friends." Blackburn, she wrote in her memoirs, had admitted to Christian "that he knew nothing personal about him" and "had only heard about him from hearsay."

Sallie had no doubt heard that version of the story from the man who would eventually marry Mary Evelyn Anderson, Cadet Alexander Broadnax Bruce.[72] Blackburn had talked to Bruce soon after the confrontation on Saturday

evening, as Bruce was on his way to visit Anderson. Blackburn, well aware that Sandy Bruce and not Charles Burks Christian would be walking Anderson to church on Sunday, asked Bruce to tell her "he had taken some notice" of the affair with Christian. According to Bruce, Blackburn didn't go into detail and "made no mention" of how Christian had conducted himself.

After talking to Blackburn, Bruce, like most of his fellow cadets, seemed to think the "affair" was over and said as much to Anderson and the Moore family.[73]

But it was clearly not over for Christian.

At some time between 3:00 and 4:00 p.m. on Saturday, January 14, Christian walked into J.M.

Cadet Alexander Broadnax Bruce (1833–1906) would marry Mary Evelyn Anderson in 1855. *Courtesy of the Frederick S. Fisher Family, Westover Plantation, Charles City County, Virginia.*

Pettigrew's store.[74] There he picked out a "six-barreled revolver," one of several pistols Pettigrew later claimed Christian had been "considering" for "a month past."

When Pettigrew asked Christian how he intended to pay for it, Christian told him, "he was looking for money every day," and would pay "when he got it."

Pettigrew, a well-known Lexington merchant and one of the directors of the local bank, later swore he had no idea that Christian "had a difficulty with any one." He let him take the pistol on credit.[75]

Christian, of course, knew something about pistols. He had already used one to threaten the president of the "Baptist College" in Richmond. His selection of the six-barreled pepperbox (and perhaps the notion that he might be able to get away with using it) may well have been inspired by something he knew about recent events at the University of Virginia.

On December 23, 1853, the day before Mary Anderson refused to "walk out" with Charles Christian, the governor of Virginia formally ratified a decision he had made on December 6 to pardon a former University of Virginia student from Amherst County, a nineteen-year-old "graceless scamp" named John Singleton Mosby, for using just such a weapon to shoot George R. Turpin, a fellow student.

The Mosby case was remarkably similar to Christian's, and one of his lawyers was Alexander Rives, the father of Cadet Alexander Rives Jr. of the VMI class of 1857.[76]

Turpin, like Blackburn, was tall, handsome, "athletic," popular and, by all accounts, something of a bully. Mosby heard from third parties that Turpin had made insulting remarks about him and sent him a letter asking for an "explanation." When Turpin made fun of the much smaller Mosby and his "challenge," Mosby felt compelled to defend his "honor."

When Turpin showed up for a meal at Mosby's boardinghouse, Mosby spotted him, borrowed a pepperbox and waited for him on the stairs outside. Though Turpin was unarmed, some witnesses claimed he "charged" Mosby, who drew his pepperbox, shot and wounded him.

Three of the best lawyers in Charlottesville defended Mosby in Albemarle County Circuit Court, pleading self-defense. After two days, a divided jury agreed to find Mosby guilty of only one charge, "unlawful shooting," and sentenced him to six months in jail, a $500 fine and payment of court costs.

In his own eyes—as well as those of his strongest supporter, his mother, and most of his fellow Virginians—Mosby had behaved honorably and lived to see his behavior ratified by the governor's formal pardon.[77]

On January 14, 1854, some three weeks after Mosby's pardon, Charles Burks Christian pocketed his own pepperbox and quickly returned to his room in McDowell's Hotel. There, shortly after 3:00 p.m., he showed up in William Robert Winn's room. Another law student, William M. Morris, showed up a few minutes later.

Winn and Morris appear to have been the first to hear Christian's version of his encounter with Blackburn, Humes and Horner. It was also, apparently, the first time Christian told anyone the complete details of what he considered an unbearable and now terribly public humiliation at the hands of Mary Evelyn Anderson.

John Singleton Mosby (1833–1918) in 1851. *Courtesy of University of Virginia Visual History Collection (prints 10478). Special Collections, University of Virginia Library.*

Winn and Morris reacted predictably, though perhaps not in precisely the way Christian might have preferred at the time.

"I asked why he did not knock Blackburn down," Winn later testified.[78]

Morris, equally shocked by what he considered a blatant insult, asked why he "didn't pitch into him?"

Christian had three good reasons. First, he said, the taller and heavier Blackburn "could whip six of him." Second, he believed that Blackburn was armed. And third, there were several other cadets present at the "interview" while he "had not a friend" in sight.

The more he talked about it, the more Christian appeared to believe he had been set up. It was a "pre-concerted affair," he told Winn and Morris. While he was in the office (and bar) at McDowell's, he said, "one of the cadets" had taken his heavy silver-headed walking stick "out of his hands." There were also, he said, several cadets standing about the door of the hotel, "some of whom came up with Blackburn."

Morris said he believed that, under the circumstances, there was but one response possible for a gentleman. "Christian had been basely slandered...He would either have to challenge Blackburn or encounter him in a street fight."

Christian replied that a formal challenge was out of the question. For one thing, the VMI commandant "kept his cadets under such tight scrutiny" there would be no way for Blackburn to get away to engage in a formal duel. Dueling was also illegal in Virginia, and Christian, who had just bought his new pistol on credit, insisted he had no money to set up a challenge in "some place like North Carolina" unless he could himself get "away to Richmond or Lynchburg" for a loan. As for a simple street fight, Christian once more made himself absolutely clear. "Well," he said to Morris, "you wouldn't let Blackburn beat me to death, would you?"

Morris, now worried that Christian might well do nothing at all, told his friend that if it came to a street brawl, he would "pull him off if I saw him on you."[79]

KNIVES AND PISTOLS

While Morris tried to convince Christian to call Blackburn out, William Robert Winn continued to suggest face-saving alternatives.

Perhaps, Winn suggested, Blackburn wasn't really the problem. After all, if Mary Anderson "had heard from a reliable source anything derogatory" to Christian's "character as a gentleman," Winn suggested "she could not be blamed" for writing the note that Christian found so humiliating. And if Blackburn had heard from "any credible source" that Christian was an inappropriate companion for his cousin, Winn reasoned, as "a near relation, he might be excused" for advising her not to be seen with Christian. Finally, he continued, if either or both those things were true and Blackburn were the gentleman he claimed to be, "justice to Christian and himself" would compel him to give up the name of "Christian's calumniator."

There was thus absolutely no need, Winn insisted, for another face-to-face confrontation. Why not simply write a note, he suggested, "asking Mr. Blackburn for his information."

Winn's idea pleased Christian who, still leery of confronting Blackburn directly, asked Winn and Morris to draft a note for him. Winn demurred, insisting that Morris was much the better writer. Morris, no doubt flattered, retired, pen in hand, to his room.

While waiting, Winn reiterated what seemed to him to be the critical question in the affair: Did Blackburn's remarks indicate he had said something negative about Christian based "upon a mere rumor" or was

Blackburn "responsible for the slander himself?" Christian admitted he wasn't sure and retired to his own room to think about it.

In the meantime, Morris finished his draft. Leaving the freshly inked document on his desk to dry, he headed back to Winn's room, arriving just as Christian returned from his meditations. When Morris told him the draft was finished, Christian rushed off to read it.

With Christian out of the room, Winn asked Morris the same question he'd put to Christian: Had Blackburn defamed Christian on his own, or was he merely repeating something he'd heard from someone else? They were discussing the matter when Christian returned, praising Morris's draft note, and insisting that Winn and Morris deliver it immediately to Blackburn.

After talking to Winn, however, Morris was having second thoughts. He put Winn's critical question once more to Christian. Christian replied that he really had no idea whether Blackburn or someone else was the original source of the slander.

Hearing that Christian was still in doubt, Morris retracted his draft. "If you understand Blackburn to be responsible for the slander that is not the note," he told Christian. "It would be a farce to carry it."

Christian, who still seemed to have no real desire to face Blackburn again, continued to insist "it would be best to have Blackburn's statements in writing."

Winn, however, was now having none of it. He repeated the advice he had given Christian earlier: "Go to Blackburn and ascertain the fact whether he was as responsible for communicating the slander."

As for the slanderous remarks themselves, Morris chimed in, if Blackburn insisted that he was only passing on things that he'd heard others say, "then he would be honor bound to give up the name" of their author.

Christian's alternatives could not be clearer, Morris added. "If Blackburn should say he was responsible for the calumny itself," Christian had three choices: "to challenge him," to "tell him what he thought of him and take the consequences" or "to back out and prove himself a coward."

Backed into a corner, Christian surrendered, promising Winn and Morris he would face Blackburn again. "If Blackburn said he was the author of the slander," Christian swore, "he would tell him that he was no gentleman; and if Blackburn assailed him, he would defend himself as circumstances required."

According to Winn, Christian also swore he would not initiate an attack on Blackburn, but would only defend himself "as best he might under the circumstances."

At that point, Winn and Morris went for a walk, leaving Christian, once more, to his thoughts. As they walked, VMI Cadet William C. Mason, who had himself reportedly "had some difficulty with Blackburn," fell in beside them.[80]

At around 7:00 p.m., just before sundown, Winn, Morris and Cadet Mason stopped by the room of Taliaferro Stribling, another of Judge Brockenbrough's law students.[81]

Christian was there too, closely examining percussion caps for the two pistols he was now carrying: his new pepperbox and an older, significantly more accurate, single-shot, rifled-barrel weapon.

When Winn appeared, Christian looked up and asked if he could "borrow his knife." Winn, Christian had learned, was the proud owner of not just any knife, but a truly extraordinary weapon he had sworn never to lend to anyone.

"It belonged to my brother," Winn told the group in Stribling's room. "It was a Bowie knife that he carried with him in traveling through the Western States."

Six-shot, .36-caliber Allen & Thurber cap and ball "Pepperbox." *Courtesy of Alex Cudaback.*

Several students then asked to see it. Winn agreed, and the entire group trooped off to his room for a look. There, Winn opened his trunk, removed the Bowie knife and laid it on his table for everyone to admire.

The boys took turns handling it, examining its inch-and-a-half-wide blade, feeling its edge and weight. Christian, according to Winn, was the last to hold it. "I told him to hand it [back] to me," Winn said, "but he remarked in a careless tone, 'Why, Winn! I believe I will keep it anyway!'" slipping the weapon "into the waistband of his pants" and walking out of the room.

Later that evening, Christian stopped by Winn's room to discuss new rumors he was hearing about Blackburn's behavior since the fateful "interview" at McDowell's Hotel.

"Winn, what do you reckon?" Christian complained, "That rascal is adding insult to injury. He is going about the street calling me a coward."

Christian didn't say where he'd heard the rumors. When pressed by Winn, he said only from "a friend."

At that point Winn asked Christian to give him back his Bowie knife. Christian demurred. "He said he did not intend to use it except *in extremis*," Winn said.

> *He was afraid when he should meet Blackburn that he would have a crowd of Cadets about him, and if he had no weapons to defend himself, and none of his friends were present, the Cadets would beat him to death—that he wanted to keep the knife to protect himself against numbers.* [82]

Christian probably clinched the argument, however, by simply asking Winn to go with him into the street in search of Blackburn. Winn "declined on the plea of business," but let Christian keep the knife.[83]

Friendly Advice

S hortly after he talked William Winn into letting him keep his Bowie knife, Christian ran into Andy Moore, a law school classmate and friend, on the steps of McDowell's Hotel. At Christian's request, they immediately went back into the hotel and up the stairs to Christian's room, where Christian anxiously asked if Moore had "heard of his difficulty."[84]

Moore, the son of Rockbridge County's chief prosecutor, Commonwealth's Attorney David E. Moore, should have been an excellent source. He was Mary Evelyn Anderson's third cousin, the nephew of Samuel McDowell and Evalina Moore and a frequent guest in the Moore house. He also knew and liked Tom Blackburn.

Moore said he had no idea what Christian was talking about.

Christian told Moore the whole story: that Tom Blackburn had seen a note he had written to Andy's cousin; that Blackburn had admitted that he had personally advised her not walk with Christian to church; and when asked why, had told him he thought Christian's character "bad or infamous."

Moore's first reaction was to ask "how in the world" Christian had "kept his hands off" Tom Blackburn.

Christian said he saw that Blackburn "had his hand in his breast as he advanced towards him" and was probably armed.

Moore, who knew Blackburn as well as he knew Christian, laughed at the notion, telling Christian it was Blackburn's "habit to carry his hand in that manner."

No matter, Christian argued. He believed that his recent and highly unsatisfactory encounter with Blackburn was no accident but a "pre-concerted" affair.

"There were a good many Cadets standing 'round," he told Moore, and "a Cadet had taken his cane from his hand" just before Blackburn arrived.

When Moore said he wished he had been there, Christian clearly thought Moore meant he would have "taken up for him" against Blackburn.

Moore replied that that wasn't what he meant at all. As a friend of both Blackburn and Mary Evelyn Anderson, Moore said, if he'd been there, he might have "settled the matter to the satisfaction of both."

When Christian asked how Blackburn was related to Anderson, Moore was more supportive. Blackburn was only her third cousin, he said, a relationship he thought "was rather far out" for Blackburn to be giving her advice about walking out with Christian.

Indeed, upon reflection he thought it rather "officious" of Blackburn to give such advice to his cousin. After all, he said, Mary Anderson "was under the care of Mrs. Moore" who had often "seen Christian at parties and had opportunities to judge of his character." As far as Andy Moore was concerned, if Mr. and Mrs. Moore considered Christian a man of bad character, "it was their business to advise her," not Tom Blackburn's.

When Christian worried aloud about whether or not he really had a bad reputation in Lexington, Moore both reassured and ribbed him. His name, he said "was never mentioned, except in ridicule of his moustache."

When Christian finally asked Moore what he thought he should do, Moore replied, "I would go to Blackburn and ask for an explanation, and if he refused to give it, I would fight him."

This was clearly not what Christian wanted to hear. He complained, Moore later testified, "Mr. Blackburn was much stronger than he and could 'whip him.'"

Moore retorted, "I would cane him."

When Christian hesitated again, arguing, "Blackburn was armed and would kill him," Moore was dismissive. If that were indeed the case, he told Christian, he should arm himself, and, if necessary, "wing him."

Christian then showed Moore he was already wearing Winn's bowie knife and carrying two pistols, though he was a little unsure of just how he should be wearing them. Opening his jacket, which Moore described as a modern "sack coat rather than a close-fitting cutaway," Christian revealed Winn's Bowie knife still stuck "in the waistband of his pants, running across from right to left."

Bowie knife. Captured from John Brown at Harper's Ferry, 1859. *Virginia Historical Society.*

Moore laughed and, speaking with absolute authority, told Christian that "Bowie knives are generally carried behind."

Christian complained that with a sack coat on, it might be difficult to get at the knife quickly if he wore it "behind." The pockets of the coat, on the other hand, seemed perfectly adequate for carrying the pistols.

The conversation continued for what seemed to Moore to be an hour or two, with much discussion of Christian's newly acquired weaponry. Christian showed Moore bullet molds, noted he had been "running balls for his new pistol" and complained that he had been forced to buy a good many caps in order to find some that would fit. When he offered Moore a box of the extra caps, Moore declined, saying he "had no use for them."

When Moore got up to leave, Christian promised that he would confront Blackburn in the street. He hoped, he said, that Moore would be there to back him up, just in case Blackburn's cadet friends might "double on him."

Moore told Christian to let him know where he intended to meet Blackburn, promising to do what he could to help if the VMI cadets tried to gang up on him.[85]

Later that night, Christian met with another group of law students gathered in Robert E. Seevers's room.[86] Christian asked the same question he had asked Andy Moore just hours earlier: what, if anything, had they heard of "the affair"?

A.G. Strayer, a friend so close that Christian had confessed to him that he wanted to marry Mary Evelyn Anderson, said he had only "heard a whisper of it." He then asked Christian to tell the group what he knew.

Christian rehashed his version of events for at least the third time that day, announced his intention to seek Blackburn out that very night and flashed his pistols and borrowed Bowie knife.

Strayer immediately pointed out that there was little to no chance of finding Blackburn at that hour and if Christian went about the streets of Lexington armed with deadly weapons, he was "liable to indictment."[87]

After "reviewing the laws of the State of Virginia," Christian replied, he had found a provision that made it clear it was "his privilege" under the code to arm himself when he had a "reasonable cause to believe that he would be attacked."

As for the practicalities, he assured his friends he was a crack shot, especially with his single-shot rifled-barrel pistol. With it he could put five shots "in the space of a dollar," he boasted, and anyone he shot at "would be a goner." Almost as an afterthought he added that, of course, he fully intended avoiding that circumstance if at all possible.

Technically, Christian observed, he had given Blackburn fair warning at the conclusion of their "interview" at McDowell's Hotel earlier in the day. His last remarks to Blackburn on that occasion, he swore, were, "All right for the present. I will see you again."

Blackburn, he said, had replied only: "Very good, Sir."

As far as Christian was concerned, "I will see you again," meant Blackburn "had reason to expect trouble."[88]

All this, of course, stood in sharp contrast to the stories circulating around the grounds of VMI, where Christian was both damned as a coward and credited for expressing his admiration of Blackburn's "noble principles."

Strayer, ever the lawyer, still thought it foolish for Christian to carry a knife and pistols on the street and repeated his advice to stand down. He "had no doubt," he said, "that Christian and Blackburn could settle their differences amicably."

When Strayer asked pointedly if Christian "did not desire such a [peaceful] termination" of the affair, Christian replied, "Certainly," but reminded Strayer "his character had been assailed."

When Strayer said he didn't consider the insult "sufficient reason to take notice of the matter," Christian asked, "what would he consider sufficient?" Why, he wondered aloud, would "Blackburn or anyone else" make such remarks about him? "He had always acted as a gentleman," Christian insisted, and, after all, he was "of as good a parentage as Mr. Blackburn or Miss Anderson."[89]

Seevers told Christian he still thought that, until Blackburn had been given a chance to either apologize or explain himself, the time was not right for a challenge.

Christian agreed, repeating his conviction that a formal challenge was out of the question in any case. In order to fight a real duel, he and Blackburn would have to go somewhere that allowed it. He had no money, he said, and could not get away to Lynchburg or Richmond, where he could get some.

Nor did he believe Blackburn could get any money from the Institute to allow him to travel to a place that would allow a formal duel. His options, it seemed, were thus limited.

At the first opportunity, Christian said, he would ask Blackburn to explain himself. If there were to be a fight, it would be a street fight, not a formal duel, and Christian would use his weapons only in self-defense. With those thoughts in mind, according to both Seevers and Strayer, Christian retired for the evening.[90]

Most of Christian's law school classmates and most of Blackburn's friends still appeared to believe that, for one reason or another, the "affair" was over. As one witness later told the Rockbridge County Circuit Court, by the time Christian was through reviewing his options and explaining his intentions, even his fellow law students "thought him too much of a coward to go through with it.[91]

Part IV

THE ENCOUNTER

SUNDAY MORNING JITTERS

Early Sunday morning, January 15, 1854, William Brosius, Sam Conn and David Curry ran into Christian as he was leaving the barroom office of McDowell's Hotel. Instead of his trademark heavy black silver-headed cane, Christian was carrying a "hickory cane," usually found under the arm of George Washington Lurty, one of Christian's law school classmates. Christian had "liberated" Lurty's stick in much the same way he'd "borrowed" William Winn's Bowie knife, picking it up after he saw it lying unattended in B.D. Chenoweth's room.[92]

When Brosius grabbed Lurty's cane from under Christian's arm and began to wave it around like a saber, Christian revealed that he was doubly prepared for trouble. He reached under his coat, pulled out his "borrowed" Bowie knife, assumed a defensive position and called out to Brosius, "If that is what you are for, come ahead!"[93]

Brosius was apparently shocked both by the size of the blade and Christian's decision to carry such a thing on the streets of Lexington on a Sunday morning. When he asked Christian why he carried such a knife, Christian, perhaps realizing his mistake, told Brosius the knife did not belong to him, that he was carrying it "for another man" and tried his best to re-sheath it.

According to Brosius, Christian had a hard time getting Winn's Bowie knife back into the sheath, now strapped onto his belt in the small of his back under his loose sack coat. After several tries he finally had to ask for help. Sam Conn obliged.[94]

Later, witnesses reported, Christian flashed the knife again as he walked out through the tavern yard on his way to services at the First Presbyterian Church. One swore he heard him tell "old Mr. Dall, the stage driver, that he intended to use it that night."[95]

After crossing the street and entering the church, Christian climbed the stairs to the balcony. There he found a seat beside Andy Moore, directly across from the upstairs gallery reserved for VMI cadets.

Christian's chances of finding Tom Blackburn at the Presbyterian Church were, at best, slim. Sharp said Blackburn "rarely attended inside of a church." Some thought Blackburn might be "skeptical" of revealed religion. Others, especially the more devout southern Presbyterians, may have noticed that Blackburn had been attending "Sabbath Classes" taught by the highly suspect Episcopalian, VMI's Colonel Francis Henney Smith. On this particular Sunday, however, Blackburn showed up at Lexington Presbyterian, climbed the stairs to the balcony and took a seat with his fellow cadets in the gallery across from Christian.

Dr. George Junkin—doctor of divinity, president of Washington College and father-in-law to Blackburn's erstwhile nemesis Major Thomas J. Jackson—was preaching that morning on predestination.

Some thought Blackburn was there for the sermon. Others thought Blackburn less interested in Dr. Junkin's topic than his youngest daughter, Julia, with whom he had just established a new "walking out" relationship.

In any case, Blackburn was spotted almost as soon as he sat down. "There is your friend," Andy Moore whispered to Christian, pointing out Blackburn sitting almost directly across from them.

"Yes, I see him." Christian replied, then smiled and, according to Moore, said nothing more for the rest of the morning service.[96]

From the cadet gallery, John Howard Sharp, sitting near Blackburn, was watching Christian. He noted that Christian's infamous mustache was gone, Christian was "clean shaven" and he was "looking daggers" at Blackburn.

Reverend George Junkin (1790–1868), president of Washington College. *Special Collections, Leyburn Library, Washington and Lee University.*

Blackburn, by all accounts, took no notice of Christian at all.[97]

Earlier that morning, Blackburn, Sandy Bruce and several other cadets had walked together to church from the VMI barracks. Bruce seemed worried. After muttering aloud to no one in particular that Christian "would challenge him yet," Bruce turned to Blackburn and said, "If he did, I reckon I will have to act as your second." Blackburn, he said, simply laughed and told him there was, "no danger of anything of that sort coming to pass."[98]

As the morning services drew to a close, Christian rushed past Andy Moore and out of the sanctuary. There he waited for Blackburn, posting himself just outside the main doors on one end of the church's long, columned, front portico.

Andy Moore had just caught up with Christian when Blackburn emerged on the opposite end of the portico. When Christian saw him, he hesitated and asked Moore "if he should go and see him then."

Moore told him "no" in no uncertain terms. It was, he said, "neither the proper time nor place."

Christian seemed relieved, let the moment pass and went back to his hotel, where he soon received an unexpected caller wearing a VMI uniform. [99]

Cadets Edward Langhorne and Algernon Stith Cousins had spent Sunday afternoon cruising the streets of Lexington, killing time until they could meet two "young ladies" who had agreed to let themselves be escorted to evening church services.

Langhorne, who had grown up in Amherst County and was distantly related to Christian, clearly still believed they were friends. Completely unaware of Christian's suspicions that he had conspired with Blackburn to steal his silver-headed cane, Langhorne asked Cousins to wait for him, then climbed the stairs to Christian's room "to brush his hair."

When he knocked, Christian let him in and, as soon as Langhorne entered the room, asked him if he noticed anything "different."

"I saw he had cut off his mustache," Langhorne later testified, and, "I noticed the cane he had was not the same he had the day before."

Christian then proceeded to grill Langhorne about the preceding day's "difficulty" with Blackburn.

Langhorne said he "knew all about it" and proceeded to recount the story of Christian's now infamous "interview" with Blackburn with reasonable, if embarrassing, accuracy.

Having heard Langhorne recount the tale of his backing down in front of Blackburn, Christian then asked if Blackburn were coming to church for evening services. Langhorne said he didn't know, combed his hair, went back downstairs to the bar and waited with Cousins for the arrival of their dates for church.[100] They were still there when Christian came down just before "supper time."

On his way out, Christian asked the two to come with him. When they declined, Christian headed for the Compton house, directly across the street from the church, where some of Judge Brockenbrough's law students were boarders. At Compton's, Christian found his classmate J.W. Woolfolk and several other law students gathered in Woolfolk's room.[101]

In what appeared to be a desperate last-minute effort to find support, Christian recounted, once more, his version of his confrontation with Blackburn. Woolfolk asked Christian why he "did not knock Blackburn down" then and there.

Christian, once more, said it was only because "he had no friends present" and thought the meeting had been "pre-concerted among the Cadets." He also repeated his belief that Blackburn was armed, claiming that "when he approached him he had his right hand in his bosom."

In an effort to debunk the now well-circulated story that he had not only backed down but had also praised Blackburn's sense of honor, Christian insisted that he had told Blackburn to his face that "he would see him another time."

His plan, Christian said, was to ask Blackburn the next time he met him to either tell him who was defaming him or, failing that, demand a personal apology. If Blackburn refused both, he told his law school friends, "he would tell him he was no gentleman, or that he had acted rascally." If Blackburn struck him, he told the group, he would follow Andy Moore's advice and "cane him."

Christian then asked for help, saying "he would like for witnesses and several other of his friends to be present so that if he should get into a fight with him, he would have fair play." Otherwise, Christian said, he feared, the cadets would "double on him."

He had intended to confront Blackburn that very morning, he insisted, and would have done so had not Andy Moore prevented it. In retrospect, however, he supposed, it was just as well, for "if he had gotten into a fight he would have had the whole Corps of Cadets upon him."

Young John Compton, the son of the owner of the boardinghouse, had been listening while Christian spoke. When he heard Christian say he "would have the whole Corps of Cadets upon him," Compton agreed. "The Cadets fight for each other," he said, and proceeded to retell the story of the ill-fated cow drover who had fallen victim to Blackburn and the "spirit of the Corps."

As Woolfolk later told the tale, Compton warned them all that the cadets fought for one another "like dogs."[102]

SUNDAY EVENING: THE CHALLENGE

CHRISTIAN

Christian left his law school friends at the Compton house at dusk.[103] J.W. Woolfolk had asked him to stay for supper, but Christian declined, returning instead to his room at McDowell's before leaving for church and the much-discussed and long-dreaded confrontation with Tom Blackburn.

Glancing into McDowell's bar on his way up to his room, Christian spotted cadets Langhorne and Cousins. They were where he had left them about an hour or so earlier, still waiting for their dates to church. Christian invited them both up to his room, where they talked until the first bells rang for evening services. Langhorne and Cousins rushed out to collect their ladies.

"About 15 minutes before the second bell rang for church," Christian went to B.D. Chenoweth's room where he was soon joined by William R. Winn.[104] Christian told Chenoweth and Winn he was "going over to the church," where he "thought he would probably see Blackburn," and all but begged them to go with him "in the event of a difficulty."[105]

Both declined, telling Christian they "thought the occasion unsuitable to say anything to Blackburn."

Chenoweth later swore that he had been more than emphatic, telling Christian "positively" that he would not go with him "to confront Blackburn on a Sunday at church."[106]

Winn agreed, telling Christian "it would prejudice him in the eyes of the community to say anything to Blackburn at church." What's more,

Winn warned, Blackburn "might be with a lady," and if that were the case, Christian shouldn't even think of confronting him.[107]

Christian told his friends that unless he acted immediately, he might not be able to see Blackburn for another week, during which time the cadet would most certainly further tarnish his reputation. Chenoweth dismissed the notion. Christian he, noted, could easily find Blackburn on Monday at the Institute.[108]

Christian replied that if he did, he would have 150 cadets on top of him. On the other hand, if he met Blackburn at church, he might only have to face thirty or so and he would have some of his own friends around to protect him.

By that time, it must have been clear to Christian that, despite his best efforts, none of his friends were ready to stand with, around or anywhere near him on that particular Sunday evening.[109] Reacting, no doubt, to the distinct chill permeating Chenoweth's room, Christian stood close to the fireplace and, speaking to no one in particular, muttered something about going.

Winn, perhaps feeling guilty, suggested Christian go upstairs and try once more to talk Bill Morris or some of the other law students into going with him. Whatever decision they reached, Winn said, he would support Christian, though he still preferred going to see Blackburn any day but a Sunday.[110] At that point Christian left the room, apparently without saying another word.

Winn told Chenoweth he hoped and believed that, at the very least, he'd talked Christian out of a Sunday confrontation.[111] Christian, however, had made up his mind.

Rather than approaching Morris, Christian played his final card, trying to convince his friend and classmate A.G. Strayer to go with him. According to Strayer, Christian was still asking for help, still explaining his plan to confront Blackburn and demand an "explanation," when the last church bells began to ring.

Christian said no more, jumped up, told Strayer "he must go" and left for church.[112]

BLACKBURN

For Cadet Thomas Blackburn, most of Sunday passed quietly.

He rose early and, unusually for him, attended morning services at the Presbyterian Church. If he had noticed Charles Christian sitting across from him in the balcony, he apparently didn't mention it to anyone. After morning services he went straight back to the barracks, apparently without incident.

James White Humes ran into him in the VMI mess hall and later swore Blackburn did not say a word about Christian and apparently had "no thought that Christian might attack him." Humes also swore that when Blackburn left for church later that evening he was "without question, unarmed."[113]

Cadet John Sharp saw Blackburn about an hour before everyone left for church and, he said, warned him to "look out for Christian." Apparently much to Blackburn's surprise, Sharp also told him that he had "observed Christian at church" that very morning. Christian's mustache, he said, was "clean shaven" and he had caught him "looking daggers" at Blackburn across the sanctuary.[114] Blackburn reportedly "hooted" at Sharp's warning, telling him Christian was "a d____d coward and would not fight."

With that, the talk in the mess hall appears to have turned to women, with Blackburn teasing Richard Taylor for trying to alienate the affections of Miss Julia Lewis,[115] his friend Sharp's latest heartthrob. After everyone had a good laugh at Sharp's expense, Blackburn left the mess hall to attend one of Colonel Smith's "Sabbath Classes."[116]

The cadets in Smith's class that Sunday insisted that the colonel, a devout Episcopalian, explain the Presbyterian doctrine of predestination. Smith declined, telling the class he wasn't in the habit of introducing such "vexed questions" into his classroom. The cadets insisted, protesting that Dr. Junkin "had preached a sermon on the subject in the morning."

Smith gave in, did his best to outline his views on the subject and in the process apparently quoted a friend of the Blackburn family, the Reverend Richard Hooker Wilmer, an Episcopal priest who would later become his church's only bishop in the Confederate states.

"As soon as I mentioned his name," Smith later wrote to Blackburn's father, "your son's countenance brightened up and he said, 'I knew him very well, he used to be our pastor—and he was one of the finest men I ever knew.'"

Smith concluded by telling the boys opinions about predestination really didn't matter in the end, "For unless we each repented of our sins and believed in the Lord Jesus Christ, we could none of us hope to enjoy the blessedness of the redeemed in Heaven."

The class ended around 3:00 p.m. It was the last time Colonel Smith would see Blackburn alive.[117]

After Smith's class, Blackburn returned to his room to dress for evening services at the Presbyterian Church. He was escorting Miss Julia Junkin to church that night, meeting her at Reverend Junkin's house on the nearby

Washington College campus. After Blackburn cleaned up and changed clothes, he realized he had twenty minutes or so to kill. He set off to wait in the room shared by cadets Sandy Bruce and G.B. Horner.[118]

Both Bruce and Horner were still getting dressed, and Blackburn talked and joked with the two as if nothing unusual were afoot. Bruce later swore the "affair" with Christian wasn't even mentioned.

When it was time to go, Blackburn left Bruce and Horner to fend for themselves and set off for the Junkin house alone, wearing his caped cadet gray overcoat and under it his distinctive blue furlough coat.[119]

From the barracks he headed straight across the parade ground, past the Moore house to the Junkins' to collect Julia, eighteen, and by all accounts "bright, energetic, amiable and very pretty."[120] Her father, who had preached that morning, would be preaching again at evening services.

At the Junkin house, Blackburn, no doubt, would also have run into Professor Jackson, who had been living in the Junkin house since August with his new wife, Dr. Junkin's eldest daughter, Ellie.[121]

The Junkin-Jackson House on the Washington College campus. *Special Collections, Leyburn Library, Washington and Lee University.*

Dr. Junkin and his wife, Junkin's brilliant middle daughter Margaret, Professor Jackson and his wife and "the entire Junkin clan" thus formed something of a family parade to evening services, with Blackburn and Julia Junkin bringing up the rear.[122]

Blackburn, they remembered, was wearing "kid gloves" and his "heavy army overcoat buttoned well up."[123] Julia Junkin remembered that she and Blackburn discussed predestination as they walked.[124]

When Blackburn and Julia Junkin arrived at the church, Cadet John Howard Sharp was there ahead of them, seated alone on the "front stone steps as the flock was gathering." Not far away were cadets Thomas Philip Mathews of Watkins Church and Robert M. McKinney of Lynchburg.

As Blackburn and Julia Junkin entered the church vestibule, Matthews and McKinney fell in a "few paces" behind them. According to Matthews, Blackburn and Miss Junkin had just passed through the inner vestibule doors and into the church sanctuary when Blackburn stopped and muttered something. Neither of the two could remember what he said.

Cadet John Howard Sharp lagged behind. He later testified that Charles Burks Christian then "waylaid Blackburn at the church door" touching him on the shoulder and asking "to speak with him for a moment." Christian's voice, he said, was "polite, but serious." Another witness described it as "constrained." Another noted Christian's face was pale and that he was clearly "agitated."[125]

Blackburn apparently hadn't noticed Christian when he entered the church and was clearly surprised when Christian tapped him on the shoulder. Despite the surprise, witnesses insisted, Blackburn never lost his composure, did not seem at all afraid and "readily assented" to Christian's request for an "interview," replying with a bow and the words, "Very well, Sir."[126]

As he left Julia Junkin's side, Blackburn handed her a book, perhaps a Bible or hymnal he had been carrying for her. "You know better how to use it than I do," he told her.[127]

That said, Blackburn turned and followed Christian out of the vestibule, onto the front porch of the church, down the front steps and onto Lexington's main street.

Christian walked on Blackburn's left, wearing his sack coat buttoned up to the throat, with Lurty's hickory stick under his arm and both hands in his pockets.[128] When cadets Matthews and McKinney saw that Christian was carrying a stick, both said they thought seriously about following the two young men, just in case there was a fight.

They didn't. Instead, they stayed on the porch and watched as Blackburn and Christian disappeared around the corner. Both later told Samuel McDowell Moore that, at the time, they weren't all that worried. Blackburn, they said, seemed well able to take care of himself, and Christian, they all knew, was a coward.[129]

Thus, as Matthews and McKinney watched, Charles Christian and Tom Blackburn walked north to the corner of Main and Nelson, turned right and headed east down Nelson Street, quickly disappearing from view.

A short distance down Nelson Street, "about the length of the church to where a pair of cattle scales stood," Blackburn stopped and reportedly asked Christian, "Haven't we gone far enough for our interview?"

They had, indeed.[130]

A Violent Scuffle

On Sunday evening, January 15, 1854, at some time between 5:45 and 6:15 p.m., James Massie "was going to church in company with a lady."[131] The sun had set, the moon had not yet risen and it was very dark. It was also wet, Massie said, and the "damp seemed to add to the darkness."[132] Massie and his friend kept to the sidewalk, walking west on the north side of unpaved, wet and muddy Nelson Street.

Just as they passed the front doors of the Baptist church, to their left on Nelson Street, they noticed the light falling from the second story sanctuary windows of their destination, Lexington's First Presbyterian Church on the south corner of Nelson and Main. The light was dim, but bright enough to cast a glow on White's Corner, directly across Nelson Street from the church.

Because the ground floor windows of the Presbyterian Church were shuttered, most of Nelson Street was very dark. The Lexington Engine House and a nearby open-topped shed protecting a set of hay scales, Massie said, were in deep shadow.

Massie and his lady[133] had reached a point about halfway between the two churches when Massie heard "a little scuffle, just at or about the Engine House door." He and his friend, he said, paid no attention until a new and louder noise stopped them in their tracks. Massie described the new noise as the "sounds of licks or strokes in quick succession, and more like a whip than a stick." Though he claimed he wasn't personally "familiar with the sound of a stick when used in striking anyone," the peculiar noise, Massie said, sounded like "someone was whipping a Negro with a cowhide."

Massie then noticed another couple, Thomas Benton Taylor and a lady, standing about fifteen yards farther west, down Nelson Street. They too had been stopped short, he thought, by the sudden explosion of sound from the shadows. Massie immediately hurried his lady along Nelson Street toward the Taylor couple and what seemed to be the relative safety of the glow from the church windows.

As soon as they reached the light, Massie said, "the strokes ceased and a tolerable violent scuffle ensued." The sounds of that "violent scuffle" went on for what seemed to Massie almost thirty seconds. Given the muffling effect of the mud in the street, Massie later observed that the scuffle "may have been more violent than I supposed" at the time.

It was clearly violent enough, and loud enough, to attract the attention of seventeen-year-old James Lindsay Kirkpatrick as he crossed the street from the Presbyterian Church to White's Corner.[134]

An unidentified VMI cadet seated near Cadet John Howard Sharp on the stone steps of the church also heard the commotion. The cadet, most likely William Alexander Thompson of the class of '57, jumped up and ran immediately toward the sound of the fight, shouting as he ran, "There is someone whipping another. Do you not hear the licks?" Sharp later claimed he heard nothing himself, but followed the other cadet.[135]

In the meantime, the nearsighted James Massie was squinting into the darkness where he could see, dimly, two men struggling on the ground. They were about fifteen or twenty feet away from where Massie stood, about a yard off the sidewalk and into the street. Massie could just see the tops of their heads, dimly lit by the glow from the church windows.

They struggled in silence, Massie later testified, "locked in a close embrace, their heads close together...no noise, no blows...entirely quiet."

Fearing that they might be hurting each other, Massie told a bystander, probably Cadet Thompson, that he "would go back and separate them." Thompson offered help, but Massie, instead, handed him his Bible and asked him to stay behind and watch over the ladies.

By the time Massie looked back down Nelson Street, the combatants were on their feet again, still holding on to each other. One he described as a "low and heavy-set figure" dressed in dark clothes. The other was wearing what appeared to be an overcoat, standing face-to-face with his shorter antagonist, with "his half front and left side" toward Massie.

Massie ran toward them. He was only a yard or so away when he saw the shorter figure give the taller "a violent shove with his right hand, which seemed to have hold of his coat collar."

White's Corner, 1870. The steps of the Presbyterian Church are on the right. Michael Miley Photograph. *Special Collections, Leyburn Library, Washington and Lee University.*

The man "staggered some three steps and fell heavily," Massie said, "like a drunken man," with his head toward Main Street, in a line with the cross street, about ten feet or so from where he had been "pushed."

Standing near the corner of Nelson and Main Street with Thompson and the ladies, Benton Taylor also saw both men rise from the muddy street, one of them shove the other violently and one of them fall.

After the taller man fell, his opponent "sprang actively to the sidewalk," ran straight toward Massie, then stopped directly in front of him. They looked straight into each other's eyes, according to Massie, but "exchanged not a word."

Massie said he didn't recognize the man at the time, even though later he realized he "knew him very well and had been in his company several times."

"I could see that he was a white man," Massie later testified, "genteelly dressed, with a sort of sack overcoat on, buttoned in front."[136]

When Massie turned to look at the man still down in the muddy street, the man who had shoved him ran again, this time straight toward Thomas Benton Taylor, stopping a yard or so away from him, "as if expecting some word or action on Taylor's part."

Taylor recognized Charles Burks Christian immediately, he said, but neither of them spoke a word to each other. As the two stood in silence, Christian turned to look back down the street in the direction of his fallen antagonist. As he turned, the light from the church windows fell on his face and Taylor saw it was covered with blood, "chin to brow."[137]

Christian then turned and ran again, passing directly between James Kirkpatrick and the two ladies he was guarding at the relatively well-lit corner of Nelson and Main, White's Corner. As soon as Christian ran by him, Taylor said, he gathered up the women Massie had placed in his charge and took them to the church. Once they were safely in the vestibule, Taylor headed back to Nelson Street.

Cadets Mathews and Sharp also reached the corner just as Christian ran by. Both later testified they saw "a man running, who afterwards proved to be Christian."

"He ran to his hotel," they said, "scarcely a block away."[138]

16

Stepping Up, Stepping In

When Jim Massie finally reached the side of the man who had gone down, he found him lying "slightly twisted" on his left side, with his head resting in a deep rut in the Nelson Street mud.

He was still alive.

"He made no moan or groan," Massie later testified, "but there was a gurgling, snuffling noise made in his breathing...like a man with his mouth and nose full of something."

The lower half of the downed man's face was covered in blood, Massie remembered. In the shadows it looked "black, as though he wore whiskers."[139]

"Hoping to prevent him from strangling in his own blood," Massie grabbed his right arm and pulled until his head was out of the rut. Massie then "called to him and asked who he was," but "he gave no sign of consciousness."[140]

"I believe some one is killed here!" Massie muttered to whomever might be listening, and then began to shout, "Help! Help!"

A "tall gentleman in citizen's clothes" was the first to reach Massie's side. When he asked what was the matter, Massie said he told him, "'Some man is killed here!' or something to that effect."

Much to Massie's distress, the "tall gentleman" at that point made "an exclamation of horror and ran off."[141]

Massie turned again to what he now saw was a very badly wounded man and tried to get him to sit up. Only then, he said, did he notice the distinctive cloak and brass buttons of the victim's overcoat and realized at once the man was a cadet.

As soon as he could see his face, Massie said, he "recognized the features of Cadet Blackburn," whom he "knew very well."

"A tall cadet and another gentleman then came up," Massie said. "I informed them that I believed some one had killed Cadet Blackburn, and requested them to go for a physician."[142] The unidentified cadet immediately set off for the nearby home of Dr. Patrick H. Christian.

Another "gentleman" wearing the dark blue uniform and cap of a VMI musician was next on the scene.[143] Though never precisely identified, he was, no doubt, A.V. Bancker, the VMI drummer, or one of his two sons. In 1854, the three comprised the entire VMI "band," having been hired some

James Woods Massie (1826–1872). Massie would become the Commonwealth's key witness. *VMI Archives.*

five years earlier to replace "Mike" and "Ruben," two slaves who had provided martial music for the corps of cadets during its first decade.[144]

The VMI musician recognized Blackburn immediately, "and stooping down near him called his name loudly several times."

"There was no answer," Massie later testified, though Blackburn was still alive and "the gurgling sound continued."

The uniformed musician then took Blackburn by the shoulders while Massie hung on to his right arm. Together they dragged him a few yards, onto some hay scales. By that time, by Massie's account, "some dozen persons had gathered around."

No more than two or three minutes had passed since Massie had seen Blackburn shoved, stagger and fall. For a short time, some said three to five minutes, the wounded cadet lay bleeding atop the hay scales. He was there, still alive, when Benton Taylor returned from the church and the "tall cadet" returned with Dr. Patrick H. Christian.[145]

Dr. Christian, thirty-six, was a native of Amherst County and second cousin to the man who had just stabbed Tom Blackburn. When Dr. Christian reached Blackburn's side, he was lying on the scales, breathing "slowly and heavily" with blood "oozing from mouth and nostrils."

After what seemed to Massie to be another four or five minutes, Dr. Christian suggested that Blackburn be taken to his office. Massie didn't think Blackburn would make it that far and suggested he be taken, instead, to the "counting room" of White's store, just a few steps away, on the corner of Nelson and Main.

With Massie leading the way, Benton Taylor and several others helped carry Blackburn, first into a relatively sheltered area behind White's store, and then toward the counting room door.

Just as they arrived, Massie ran into one of White's employees, a "Mr. Gold," who was just leaving work, locking the counting room door behind him. Massie convinced Gold to unlock the door and stepped inside the counting room. As soon as he looked around, Massie realized the space was much too small for Dr. Christian's or Blackburn's needs.

Instead, he had Tom Blackburn placed "on the cellar cap by the counting room door," in an area "separated from the street by a high fence, gated, and protected from the elements by a shed roof."[146]

The area was not well lit, and someone dispatched a cadet to McDowell's Hotel to fetch a lantern. At the hotel, Hugh Laughlin gave the cadet a lantern that hung at the front door and then followed him to White's store. As soon as he saw Blackburn, Laughlin later testified, he thought Blackburn was dying.[147] Massie, by that time, was dead certain.

The bleeding cadet lay helpless on the sloping cellar door, Massie said, "his mouth and nose full of blood...gasping...his eyes set."

The arrival of the lantern settled the matter for Dr. Christian. When he finally got a good look at Blackburn, he quickly came to the same conclusion as Laughlin and Massie.

"I saw a wound on his neck, on the left side, immediately below the ear, and directly in the course of the carotid artery," Dr. Christian later testified. "I saw that Mr. Blackburn was dying, and believed that his death proceeded from cutting the carotid artery."

Dr. Christian, nevertheless, went through the motions of trying to save the boy's life, asking that "stimulants be brought, and that another physician and instruments should be sent for."

He later admitted that he did so, not because he "thought they would be of service," but because he "thought it proper."[148]

First Aid

Two of Blackburn's friends and roommates, Richard Taylor and Cadet First Captain Charles Edward Lightfoot, had both arranged to escort "young ladies" to evening services on Sunday, January 15. One of them, apparently the object of the affections of both Taylor and Cadet John Howard Sharp, did not appear, and Taylor was reduced to tagging along with Lightfoot and Lightfoot's date for the evening, identified only as "Miss May."

Taylor, Lightfoot and Miss May had just reached Doctor Patrick Christian's door when Massie's "tall cadet" arrived, breathless, to tell the doctor "there was something the matter at Mr. White's down the street."

According to Taylor, the group, "thinking that a child or somebody was sick," at first, "paid no attention to it." As soon as they had reached the northwest corner of Main Street, diagonally across from the church, however, Taylor "saw a light and some one or two of our fellows on the fence."

He immediately ran ahead, across Main Street, to White's Corner to see what was the matter. A cadet, probably John Howard Sharp, told him "Blackburn has been stabbed." Taylor was shocked.

I knowing of the difficulty between Blackburn and Christian and thinking the students [of Brockenbrough's law class] *and cadets were going to fight and not dreaming that Blackburn was anything more than scratched and was still fighting over the fence or in fact scarcely knowing what I thought, ran back and told Lightfoot that some of our*

The streets surrounding Lexington Presbyterian Church. Detail from Casimir Bohn lithograph, 1857. *University Collections of Art and History, The Reeves Center, Washington and Lee University.*

> *boys were in difficulty & to carry Miss May in church, she begging us to keep cool and not fight.*[149]

With Miss May safely on her way to church with Lightfoot, Taylor ran back across Nelson Street "and jumped up on the fence."

"Oh God," he wrote his father the next day, "can I ever forget what a sight. There was a classmate, with whom but a few hours before I was laughing and joking with, in his dying struggle, I was perfectly paralyzed."

Blackburn's wounds were, indeed, shocking. The Richmond *Dispatch* reported, "A large quantity of blood was found in the street near the hay scales. It looked to be as full as if a large hog had been killed."[150]

Dr. James Jordan, who had been attending services in the Presbyterian Church, soon joined Dr. Christian at Blackburn's side. Jordan quickly confirmed his colleague's diagnosis. "The only wound I observed was in the left side of the neck," Jordan later testified. When he probed the wound with his finger he found that "it extended entirely across to the right side, passing by the back of the windpipe and terminating against the angle of the jawbone on the right side." He "made no further examination that night," he later testified, "but observed the body and admired its fine development and its fine proportions."[151]

Dr. H.G. Davidson joined doctors Christian and Jordan after Blackburn had been moved to the "cap" of White's cellar door. The crowd, he later remembered, had already grown so large he had to fight his way through it to reach Blackburn's side. When he got there, Blackburn was still breathing, but it was clear there was nothing he could do.[152]

Dr. John W. Paine, the fourth physician on the scene, arrived at about the same time as Dr. Davidson. He also quickly decided there was nothing he could do, and watched helplessly, he said, as Blackburn, "gave a few gasps and died."

Paine later swore he thought the wound in Blackburn's neck was even "more speedily fatal" than a knife-wound to the heart.[153]

Surprisingly detailed and accurate descriptions of what had been done to Blackburn began to circulate almost immediately. Samuel McDowell Moore wrote to Mary Evelyn Anderson's father that night, telling him "there were two stabs in the head and one in the neck" and that one of them "severed the artery and probably his windpipe."[154]

Rumors also began to circulate that Blackburn had been stabbed in the back, accounts later confirmed by the physicians who examined the body formally for a Rockbridge Court of Inquiry.[155]

The bloody horror of the scene appears to have made it impossible for some to tear themselves away. Richard Taylor abandoned his perch on the fence only after Blackburn "breathed his last." He was one of five cadets still there.[156]

Jim Massie also stayed until the end.[157] Even though he knew Charles Burks Christian well, Massie later swore he still had no idea that he was the man who had just killed Tom Blackburn. The man he saw run by, of course, had no moustache.

Then, Massie remembered, someone "called for Mr. Jordan, the Mayor, and said that the person who committed the offence [sic] had been followed to McDowell's Hotel."

Massie, having done his best for Blackburn, now joined Mayor Jordan, en route to McDowell's Hotel, in pursuit of someone they both believed to be a murderer.[158]

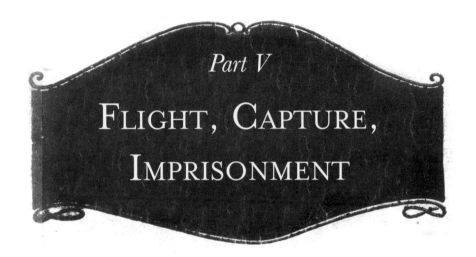

Part V

FLIGHT, CAPTURE,
IMPRISONMENT

CHRISTIAN'S FLIGHT

Tom Blackburn, covered in blood, somehow managed to stand up, look at the man who had stabbed him and take several steps before falling on his face in the mud of Nelson Street.

Charles Christian apparently didn't know what to do. He ran after a fashion, stopping and starting several times as he fled the scene.[159]

Steps away from Blackburn, he stopped to face Jim Massie, paused, said nothing and ran on. A few steps later he stopped again, this time in front of Benton Taylor, who recognized him. Christian then sprinted on, tossing aside Lurty's stick and the Bowie knife he had borrowed from William Robert Winn as he ran.

Passing young James Kirkpatrick and the two ladies in his care, Christian rounded the corner of Nelson and Main and ran past Cadet John Howard Sharp, among others, as he made for the shelter of his hotel room.

At McDowell's Hotel, he clattered up the stairs and burst into B.D. Chenoweth's room. He had left that room only twenty minutes or so earlier.

Both Chenoweth and Winn, the owner of the fatal Bowie knife, were still there.[160] Christian's hair, they said, was "very full of blood." There was blood on his face, mud all over the back of his coat, mud on the back of his trousers and blood all over the front of his shirt and on his shirt sleeves.

"What is the matter?" they shouted in unison.

Christian tossed his pepperbox and his single-shot rifled pistol on Chenoweth's bed and told his friends he had just "had a fight with Blackburn."

Chenoweth asked if he'd shot him.

"No," Christian said. The blood was all Blackburn's. The cadet had bled on him, Christian swore, after he had cut him "in the face" while Blackburn was holding him down and choking him.

Christian then asked Winn and Chenoweth to go "see if Blackburn was hurt seriously." He hoped not, he said.

Winn demurred. Noting the angry VMI cadets already in the streets, he suggested that Christian go to his own room and clean up. Christian agreed,[161] and Winn went with him. Once inside Christian's room, they locked the door behind them.

No sooner had Christian begun to wash away some of the mud and blood when someone knocked at his door. Winn opened it. Standing in the hall was a VMI cadet, most likely William Alexander Thompson, a friend of Christian's from Amherst County. Christian, "with hands uplifted," asked Thompson, "How is Blackburn? Please go and see if he is hurt!" Thompson, without entering the room, turned and ran off to see.[162]

Robert Seevers, one of Christian's law school classmates then "burst in." Christian begged him to go check on Blackburn as well. Seevers also disappeared.[163]

With at least two friends dispatched for news of Blackburn, Christian appeared to regain at least some of his composure and began to tell his friends what he remembered. According to Winn, Christian said that he had simply gone to church and when he arrived "in the vestibule…saw Blackburn standing with two Cadets."

Blackburn, Christian told Winn, gave him "a scornful look, tapped him on the shoulder and said that he wished to have some private talk with him." Thus, as Winn remembered the story, it was at Blackburn's request that he and Christian "went out and proceeded up the cross street."

When they got "near the Baptist Church," Christian continued, Blackburn called him out, saying that if he "had anything to say to him he had as well say it there." Christian's goal, he swore, was only to find out if Blackburn was personally "responsible for the slander" against him, or "for only advising his cousin upon rumor."

Thus, Christian said, he "asked Blackburn to explain what he meant by his remark at their former interview that he was responsible for the communication made to his cousin."

Blackburn told him "he would give no explanation or apology," Christian said, "but that he was responsible for all he had said or done."

Brockenbrough law school student, trial witness and later congressman John James Davis (1835–1916). *Wikipedia.*

When Christian told Blackburn "he was no gentleman," he claimed Blackburn snapped back at him, "Don't repeat it, sir!"

Christian replied, "You know it is true."

It was at that point, Christian insisted, that Blackburn "rushed on him." Christian "gave back several paces" as Blackburn came on, and then "struck at him with his stick." Blackburn bulled his way through the assault, "got hold" of Christian and "took his stick from him."

As Winn remembered Christian's account of the fight, Blackburn then "tripped him, fell upon him, and choked him violently." At that point, Winn later testified, Christian said he "cut him with the knife, attempting to cut him in the face, to make him loose his grasp." His "only object," Christian told the group, was to make Blackburn let go, "not to kill him."[164]

Christian had just finished telling his story to Winn and Chenoweth when William Morris[165] and Taliaferro Stribling,[166] two of the law students whose advice Christian had sought a day earlier, burst into the room.

Christian, who claimed he still had no idea Blackburn was dead, immediately asked both if they knew anything.

"No," they said.

Christian replied that he hoped he hadn't hurt Blackburn, then repeated for Morris and Stribling the story he'd just told Winn and Chenoweth.

Morris later testified that, given Christian's early indecision about standing up for himself, he was frankly "gratified when he first heard about the fight." Still unaware of Blackburn's condition, Morris immediately advised Christian to apologize, "to express regrets" not only because he believed Christian was truly remorseful, but also because there were cadets everywhere and no one could predict what they might do.

At that very moment, a VMI cadet banged on Christian's door. Happily for the gathered law students, it was Edward Langhorne, probably the last person to have talked to Christian before he set off for church and his deadly confrontation with Tom Blackburn.[167]

Langhorne had walked a young lady to church that evening but had not stayed for services. Instead, he later testified, he had chatted for a while with some cadets on the church's front portico, and then walked back to Christian's room at McDowell's Hotel. By the time Langhorne got back to the hotel, he said, he found "several law students on the steps of the passage" upstairs, a situation he found "unusual."[168]

When Langhorne tried Christian's door, he "found it locked." That too was "unusual." When he knocked. Winn opened the door.

According to Langhorne, Christian was standing there with his coat still in his hands. "There was blood and mud on Christian's coat," he said. "His face was also very bloody, and his shirt, the left sleeve, very bloody." Langhorne also remembered that Christian "had not pulled off his vest" but when he did so there was "blood on the bosom, near the collar."

Christian, Langhorne said, seemed "greatly excited" and asked immediately about Blackburn. He received only puzzled silence in reply from the seventeen-year-old cadet.

When Christian asked for a second time, "How is Blackburn?" Langhorne told him he didn't know. Indeed, Langhorne appeared to be completely unaware that there had been a fight.[169]

Langhorne then asked his blood-covered friend, Christian, where he was hurt. To Langhorne's apparent amazement, Christian replied, "Nowhere."

Christian then told Langhorne about the fight, said he had cut Blackburn "in the face," and demonstrated for Langhorne's benefit just how and where. The blood Langhorne saw on his face and clothes, Christian speculated, "must have come from Blackburn's jaw."[170]

Hearing another knock at the door, Christian asked if it were Phillips, presumably Martin Phillips, a friend who would later accompany him to jail and stand as a witness at his trial. Instead it was Robert Seevers, one of the law students Christian had dispatched to check on Blackburn's condition.

Seevers reported that Blackburn was dead or, as Cadet Langhorne remembered it, would die "in a few minutes." Seevers then suggested "strongly" that Christian run for his life.

Those words were barely out of Seevers's mouth when Winn, still acting as doorkeeper, heard ominous sounds out in the hall, "the noise of steps," as Winn put it, "coming up the stairs."[171]

Fear, Panic and More Advice

B lackburn was dead.

The sound of footsteps had been heard on the stairs.

There was near panic among the young men gathered in Christian's room.

Cadet Langhorne claimed he told Christian, still bloody from the fight, that it might be well for him to get out of his own room, go to someone else's, clean up and change clothes.[172]

Winn and Morris remembered things slightly differently. Winn recalled that Christian's first reaction to the news of Blackburn's death was to immediately plead self-defense, and that it was he, Winn, who suggested that Christian go to A.G. Strayer's room to clean up and change.[173]

Morris thought that it was about this time that Christian asked another law school classmate, Hampden Zane Shriver, to find an "officer of the law" and tell him Christian wanted to give himself up.[174]

Whatever the case, at the sound of steps on the stairs everyone fled Christian's room. Langhorne ran back down to the street to check on Blackburn. Winn went back to his own room. Christian went with Morris and Robert Seevers to A.G. Strayer's room, diagonally across the hall from his own.

Once they were there, Morris again told Christian "he ought to express his regret." He said that Christian again swore "he did not intend to hurt Blackburn."

Morris then made the obvious suggestion that it might be well to tell their law professor what had happened. Christian agreed. Morris and Seevers then set off to find Judge John White Brockenbrough, leaving Christian alone for the first time since the stabbing.[175]

According to Morris, it was only after he and Seevers were on their way back from their mission to find Judge Brockenbrough that they ran into their classmate, B.D. Chenoweth, and heard that Blackburn was, without question, dead.

While Christian was alone in Strayer's room, washing up and changing clothes, Andy Moore knocked on the door.[176] Moore, too, had walked a young lady to the Presbyterian Church that night and noticed the growing crowd at White's Corner. When he went to investigate, someone told him Blackburn had been killed.[177] Moore said he "at once concluded that Christian had killed him," and set off for Christian's room at McDowell's.

Along the way, Moore met "two ladies," headed in the same direction who asked him if he knew what was going on. Moore told them what he had heard and accompanied them to McDowell's Hotel. Once he had dropped them off, he said, he went straight up to Christian's room and found no one there.

Knocking on the door of Strayer's room, just across the hall, he found Christian, still on his feet, "washing his face, his coat and vest off, his shirt still bloody."

Main Street, 1860. Porter's Hotel is on the right, two doors south of the trees that mark Courthouse Square. *VMI Archives.*

Moore, the law student son of a lawyer, immediately advised Christian "to burn everything that had a drop of blood on it and *shove*."

At that point, Moore later testified, Christian told him "he had done it in self defense and would give himself up."

Moore clearly believed Christian still didn't understand the seriousness of the situation. He pointed out, once more, that Blackburn was not merely wounded, but dead.

Although Christian had already been told by Seevers that Blackburn was either dead or dying, at hearing the news from Moore, "He threw up his hands and exclaimed, 'Great God! No! Andy!'"

Though Moore was both a friend and distant relative of Blackburn's, he was clearly touched by what seemed to him to be Christian's genuine horror at what he had done. Acting on what he later described "as a mere impulse of mercy" Moore said, he recanted, told Christian that Blackburn was not really dead and fled the room.[178]

Christian finished cleaning up, changed clothes, left Strayer's room, crossed the hall and went back into his own room to wait for the authorities.[179]

William Winn soon found him there. No doubt surprised at Christian's abandonment of all attempts at concealment, Winn asked Christian what he was going to do.

Christian told Winn he had sent "Hammy" Shriver to fetch the authorities, "that he was going to surrender himself—that he had sent for the officer."

Shriver then knocked on Christian's door. He was accompanied, however, not by the mayor and a posse, but by a lawyer, another of Christian's friends, Sam Houston Letcher, an 1850 graduate of Judge Brockenbrough's law school, and a member of one of Lexington's most prominent families.

Unable to find the mayor or the sheriff, Shriver had stumbled across Letcher in the crowd at White's Corner. Letcher, by chance, had been at McDowell's Hotel when the cadet sent to fetch a lantern arrived. When the cadet told him about "the trouble" near the Presbyterian Church, Letcher followed him back to the scene. There, someone told Letcher "a Negro" had stabbed Blackburn.[180] Then he heard Massie say "the murderer" had run to McDowell's Hotel.

At that very moment Shriver arrived on his mission to "fetch the authorities" and told Letcher the "murderer" was none other than Charles Christian. Letcher, with Shriver in tow, then rushed back to McDowell's Hotel, apparently reaching Christian's room just ahead of Mayor Jordan and his hastily assembled "posse."

In the interval, Letcher gave Christian the same "legal" advice Andy Moore had given him. "I remarked that it was a very sad affair, and he [Christian] was conscious of his own guilt or innocence, and if he was guilty, he had better take the back door—i.e. he had better fly."[181]

Christian, now firm in his conviction that he shouldn't run, replied, "No! I could not help it!"

When Letcher asked him to explain, Christian rehearsed his story one more time.

> *I asked him* [Blackburn] *to explain, and he would not do it. I told him it was a rascally act and he was no gentleman; he then rushed upon me, and I tried to keep him off with a cane; he grappled with me; took the cane from me; threw me down and choked me till I could not halloo. I drew the knife when I was gasping and cut him to make him let go.*[182]

As Christian spoke, Letcher noticed that his comb and brush were covered with blood and that that there were still traces of blood on his face and on his right hand.

Christian then asked Letcher, "how Blackburn was."

Letcher replied he was either dead or dying, becoming at least the third person to do so. Letcher later remembered that Christian "grew paler and said, 'God, forgive me! I did not intend to do it! I would change places with him.'"

When Letcher asked about the knife, Christian told him it was a Bowie knife and that he'd thrown it away, "in a ravine, near the pumps."

Letcher's last words of advice were to "keep silent and say nothing—not even to his best friend."

The "authorities," in the form of Mayor Jordan, Jim Massie and others, then appeared at Christian's door.[183]

THE ARREST

M ayor William Jordan was inside the Presbyterian Church on the evening of January 15, he said, when "his attention was arrested by a noise in the vestibule." When Jordan went to investigate, he noted the time: around 6:10 p.m.

Jordan had just stepped out of the sanctuary and into the church vestibule, he later reported, when someone told him "a Negro has killed a Cadet."

When the mayor stepped out onto the front portico, he saw the crowd at White's Corner, ran down the church steps and pushed his way through the crowd onto Nelson Street. When he reached the fenced enclosure at White's Store, Jim Massie told him Blackburn was dead and that "the person who had committed the murder had gone into the hotel." Jordan immediately began to assemble "a small group of men" to serve as a posse.[184]

While he was doing so, an unnamed VMI cadet approached Blackburn's friend and roommate, VMI First Classman Richard Taylor, president of the class of 1854 and apparently the highest-ranking cadet then on the scene. Taylor asked him what he wanted, and the cadet handed him a bloody knife and a stick, found, he said, "behind the church where the fight took place."

"I could scarcely hold the knife in my hand," Taylor wrote his father that night. "It was a long wooden handle[d] butcher knife and clodded [*sic*] with...blood and flesh."

Taylor clearly had no idea what to do with either weapon. He looked for "a magistrate," he said, could not find one, and for some reason gave the knife to a "student" (most likely William Houston Barclay of Washington

College) and the stick to "a citizen" named Pole (probably John Gwynn Pole or someone in his family). "There was great dread," Cadet Taylor later testified, "lest the law students should get them and hide them."[185]

Mayor Jordan was apparently unaware of the discovery of Christian's knife and stick when he, Jim Massie and the "posse" set off for McDowell's.[186]

The posse's first stop was the barroom, which also served as the hotel office. The clerk on duty, presumably Hugh Laughlin, told them he had seen no one. Massie suggested that "the culprit" might well have avoided the office by entering the hotel through what he described as "the upper passage, about four doors above the bar-room and fronting on Main Street."

At Massie's suggestion, Mayor Jordan posted a guard at the "upper passage" door and another in the backyard of the hotel, cutting off all escape routes.[187] Jordan and Massie then led the rest of their men back through the hotel bar and into the adjoining hall.[188] The hallway opened onto a covered passage, which led to the hotel dining room. From the dining room, a narrow flight of stairs led up to the second story and into a small chamber. From there, a second flight of stairs led to the third floor.

The pitch-dark halls, stairs and passageways branching off landings soon brought Jordan's pursuit to a dead halt. As Massie put it, the mayor wasn't about to blunder around in the dark in hot pursuit of a murderer, so he simply "stopped, in order that we might get the Clerk or Landlord to pilot us through the house." The hotel clerk sent a servant upstairs with a light.

Mayor Jordan's posse then moved carefully by lantern light up the first flight of stairs. In the "chamber" at the top of the stairs, Jordan and his men ran into a "Mr. Barclay," clearly William Houston Barclay, to whom Cadets Taylor and Cousins had given the bloody knife and stick found at the crime scene. Behind Barclay were "several persons on the steps leading from the upper passage to the upper story."

Barclay told Jordan, Massie and their men that Christian wanted to give himself up and that he had already sent his friend Shriver to find the mayor.

It was at that point that the near-sighted and somewhat night-blind Massie finally realized that he knew the man he had seen running from the scene of the stabbing. He turned to Mayor Jordan as they stood at the foot of the stairs, he said, and told him, "Christian is the man."

Jordan then ordered the servant carrying the lantern to lead the posse to Christian's room, which, Massie noted, "was but a few doors from where we then were."

When the group reached Christian's door, Mayor Jordan either opened it himself, or knocked, and was let in immediately.

Massie, in the hall behind Jordan, could see only part of Christian's room at first. He later swore that one of the people he saw inside was Shriver, the man Christian had sent to find the mayor and had brought back Sam Houston Letcher instead.

Shriver, Sam Houston Letcher, W.M. Morris and Robert E. Seevers were, indeed, all in Christian's room. Shriver had just returned from his futile search for Mayor Jordan at the crime scene. Given what Barclay had just told Mayor Jordan, however, Shriver's presence in the room did not look good for Christian.

When Mayor Jordan stepped through the door, Christian moved immediately to meet him.

Christian "had on pantaloons and a clean shirt and seemed to have been washing," Massie later testified. "His hair was brushed up, and his manner was excited and embarrassed. His expression was concerned and anxious."

Still holding a towel, Christian spewed out in rapid succession a confession, an explanation and a plea of self-defense. "Well, Mr. Jordan, this is an ugly scrape into which I have gotten; but I could not help it," he said. "I asked him to apologize, and he would not do it, and I told him he was no gentleman."

Jordan remembered vaguely that Christian was beginning to explain that the fight was "the only way in which I could extricate myself" when someone, probably Sam Houston Letcher, told him to say no more.

At that point, or perhaps when Jordan or Massie began to search him for weapons, it dawned on Christian that he was about to be taken to jail. At first he protested, telling the mayor that he "preferred" to remain at the Hotel, "under guard if need be." Jordan told him that would be impossible. Christian offered to post bail.

Mayor Jordan said, "Put on your clothes, Mr. Christian, and go with me."

Christian, now resigned to his fate, replied, "Certainly, Sir."

They were about to leave the room when Shriver noticed there was still blood on Christian's face.

Mayor Jordan let him finish washing. While Christian stood at the washbowl, Jordan remembered, he "asked several times if Blackburn were dead," saying that "he hoped he would not die; he would not have him die for all the world."

Whether Christian was really hoping against hope that Blackburn was alive, or just setting up a defense, would be left for a jury to decide.

Without further comment, Mayor Jordan and Martin Phillips led Christian away. Although the jail was close by, just off Main Street on Courthouse

Rockbridge County Jail. *VMI Archives.*

Square, Jordan and Phillips took Christian there by a "circuitous route" in an effort to avoid a confrontation.

Morris, who had followed the group to the front door of the hotel, later testified that "a great crowd" had already gathered. Spotting Cadet G.B. Horner in the crowd, Morris took him aside and told him Blackburn was dead. Horner, he said, "stamped his foot and uttered some exclamation of grief or indignation," though apparently, "not of surprise."

Horner then told Morris, "Miss Anderson had gone with Cadet Bruce to church."

Morris told Horner that, under the circumstance, "he had better get her home." While Horner ran to the church to warn Sandy Bruce and Mary Evelyn Anderson, Morris headed for the jail.[189]

CALMING THE CORPS

As Tom Blackburn breathed his last not ten yards from the Presbyterian Church, Mary Evelyn Anderson and Julia Junkin were both still waiting in the sanctuary.

When Anderson heard Blackburn was dead, she stood up and walked out into a crowd already so thick on the streets that it was almost impossible to move.

Cadet Richard Taylor watched. "It was awful to see her," he wrote. "What my first feelings [were] I can scarcely describe. I felt as if I could see the author of that deed burned to a crisp."[190]

Most, if not all the Corps, agreed. "The unlooked-for suddenness and violence of the death," Colonel Smith later reported to his Board of Visitors, "immediately attracted to the scene of the tragedy all the cadets who were in the church and most of those who remained at the Institute."[191]

According to Taylor, the cadets "who now came pouring up with one accord, cried for vengeance" and believed themselves both ready and able to "take the author of this dreadful, dreadful deed from the jail where they had lodged him."

"But, thank God," Taylor wrote two days later, "better feelings soon came and we who were at first so excited endeavored to calm those who now came up panting and crying death to the cowardly villain."[192]

Those who sought to prevent the Corps from dragging Charles Christian to the nearest tree had a difficult task ahead of them. Among them were the Institute's commandant, Colonel Francis Henney Smith; one of the

VMI superintendent Francis Henney Smith (1812–1890). *VMI Archives.*

Institute's founders, Major John Thomas Lewis Preston; and by at least one account, Major Thomas Jonathan Jackson.

Colonel Smith was reportedly at home, still in his robe and slippers, recovering from pneumonia when word of the affair in Lexington reached the grounds of VMI.[193] One of those who brought him the news was Cadet Walter Browne Botts, a first classman from Fredericksburg who knew Blackburn well and had served with him on the Military Ball Committee during graduation week the preceding summer. According to John Howard Sharp, Botts had at least part of the Corps in marching order and on the way to Lexington well before Colonel Smith reached the barracks.[194]

Smith later testified he arrived at White's Corner "some 25 minutes after the deed was committed." There he found Blackburn's body "still lying on White's cellar door."

"Groups of Cadets were standing about," he testified, "some convulsed in sobs, others, as if consulting with each other, in little knots." Smith quickly came to the conclusion, he said, that it would be "proper to remove them at once from town to the Institute, to preserve peace."[195]

Some witnesses remembered Colonel Smith stopping at least one group by grabbing a cadet by the throat and ordering him put under arrest. The sight reportedly froze the other cadets in their tracks.[196]

Cadet John Howard Sharp remembered that Smith had "tried to stop us near the Exchange Hotel" but "we paid no heed to him" and marched on.

In Sharp's account, "Stonewall Jackson showed himself in the middle of the plank road a few seconds farther on & commanded us to halt, we did so."

Jackson, he wrote, told the cadets "the law of Va. must prevail, that the murderer must be tried by the Courts, & he would see that able counsel was employed to prosecute." Major Jackson then ordered the cadets on the scene to "form up, 'about face' and march back to the Institute."

The words and actions Sharp attributed to the man who became "Stonewall" Jackson, however, are much more likely to have been those of the late-arriving Colonel Francis Henney Smith.[197]

Whatever the case, someone standing near Blackburn's body, probably Colonel Smith, sent Hugh Laughlin, the hotel clerk, off to fetch a horse and wagon. When Laughlin returned, it was clearly Colonel Smith who ordered Blackburn's bloody corpse placed on the wagon and driven back to the grounds of the Institute.[198]

It was a brilliant decision. In what Smith himself later described as "a commanding voice," he told his cadets, "Young gentlemen, we must stick to the body!"[199]

According to Cadet Taylor, Smith's instinctive call on the Corps to protect its own had the desired effect. "By and by," Taylor wrote, "the cadets were quieted by the exertions of many of the citizens of the place and professors and when his remains were carried down they were persuaded to follow him, a mournful, mournful crowd."[200]

The press reported that "the stunned and angry Cadets formed up behind the one-horse wagon bearing young Blackburn's body" and, led by Colonel Smith and the other officers, "followed the wagon down the plank road, up to the Institute."[201]

According to Smith, every cadet remaining in the town marched back to the Institute with Blackburn's body. When the "mournful crowd" reached the VMI barracks, Smith, still fearing that "in the excited state of youthful feeling...violence might be attempted," wisely gave the cadets orders that no soldier, and certainly no cadet who was a friend or classmate of Tom Blackburn, could possibly refuse.

Smith ordered the cadets to take Blackburn's body to "Church Harbor," Major John Thomas Lewis Preston's empty classroom. Once there, they were to stand guard over it, following "positive orders that no individual should be allowed to touch it, or to interfere in any manner with the person or dress."[202] The Corps followed orders.

Cadet Sharp was one of those who stood watch.

I was one of the sentinels in that room of death that cold night, with the wind blowing a hurricane seeming to tear the tin off the roof of the arsenal while the rats were ever present in that black yard. I stood for 2 hours in the presence of death with a flickering light from a taper in oil to present the gruesome picture.[203]

With Blackburn's body under guard and most, if not all, his cadets back on the grounds of the Institute, Smith ordered the beating of the long roll, the signal to assemble the Corps. The cadets not posted with the body fell in again and were marched to an empty classroom.

There, Smith reported, "I addressed them upon the melancholy event which had just transpired," and "told them how deeply I sympathized in their affliction."

He also told the boys how he "desired specially to guard them against allowing any thought of vengeance to enter their minds; that their youthful feeling under so great wrong, might prompt them to such a course; but mature reflection would make them ever regret any act of violence; that the offender was then in hands of the law."[204]

Perhaps, as Sharp remembered, Smith then reprised a promise that Major Jackson had made earlier that evening in the middle of the plank road. More likely, all on his own, Smith gave his word to his cadets, promising to pursue a course that would eventually cause him to face charges of malfeasance and misuse of public funds and shatter a long and personal relationship with Judge John White Brockenbrough.

"It was the duty of every good citizen to confide in [the law's] faithful administration as the supreme arbiter," Smith told the cadets.

So that "their minds might be relieved from all apprehension on this point," he then swore to them that "as the Superintendent of the Institute, standing *in loco parentis*, not only to them but to the deceased, I should consider it my highest duty to see that a fair and impartial trial should be had before the courts of the country."

He then "begged them to retire to their rooms" and "reflect upon the uncertainty of human life as exhibited in the sad issue then before them."

"Every cadet," he later told his Board of Visitors, then "promptly repaired to his room."[205]

Not all the cadets, of course, really did so. Richard Taylor and Sandy Bruce slipped away for half an hour to toll the Institute's bell.[206] Taylor was Blackburn's friend. Bruce was not only a friend, but also the cadet who had helped coax Mary Anderson to allow Blackburn to read Christian's ill-fated note. He was also the man who would later marry her.

The slow tolling bell "sounded very solemn on the still midnight air," Taylor wrote, "and as I thought that the young man whose spirit had just winged its flight to its creator and whose sad requiem we were then performing, but a few hours before was sitting next to me in church and afterwards was in our room talking and joking."

With their boys now safely back in the barracks, Colonel Smith and Major Preston walked back into Lexington to see Mayor Jordan, "with a view of seeing whether the prisoner was securely lodged in jail, and discovering, if possible, the weapons in his possession."

The two officers, no doubt from force of habit, would have fallen into step on the way, with Smith setting the pace, marching unconsciously to the cadence called by the slow tolling of the Institute's bell.

In Lexington, Smith and Preston ran into Mayor Jordan just as he was returning to McDowell's Hotel from the county jail. Smith asked Jordan if he had already conducted a search for weapons.

Jordan, embarrassed, replied that he had "entirely overlooked it."

Smith and Preston then accompanied the mayor to Christian's hotel room. With William Winn, B.D. Chenoweth and several other of Christian's friends watching, the three men carefully searched the room. They found no weapons, Smith recalled, "just some bullets, bullet-molds, and percussion caps under the foot of the bed."[207]

Then one of the trio noticed Christian's trunk, tried to open it and found it locked. Mayor Jordan went back to the jail to see if Christian had the key. He did, and when Jordan returned, the trunk was opened and thoroughly searched.

Inside they found the clothes Christian had been wearing during the fight. They were "very bloody," Mayor Jordan noted, and there was "a great deal of mud on the back of his coat."

No weapons were found, of course. Neither Winn nor Chenoweth said a word to the searchers about the missing weapons, even though Christian had dropped both his pistols in Chenoweth's room and had used the Bowie knife he had borrowed from Winn. The two law students also knew that Christian had thrown away the hickory stick he had borrowed to replace his beloved silver-headed cane.

Their search finished, the mayor, Colonel Smith and Major Preston left the hotel and headed for Christian's jail cell.[208] Winn went with them.[209]

Once they were gone, Chenoweth retrieved Christian's pistols from his own room, slipped back into Christian's room and left them there, he said, for "some later search party" to discover.[210]

CHRISTIAN IN CUSTODY

C hristian had been in jail for an hour or more when VMI Commandant Francis Henney Smith arrived with Mayor Jordan, Major Preston and Christian's law school classmate and friend William R. Winn.

Christian hadn't expected to go to jail. He had offered to "give security for his appearance" and clearly believed he should have been allowed to wait for arraignment in his hotel, under guard, if necessary, as befitted a "gentleman."[211]

When he discovered that growing crowds of VMI cadets were apparently calling for his life, however, his attitude seemed to change. He was afraid, and to make matters worse, "several Law Students" who had stayed on at the jail as informal bodyguards were now talking about going home for the night. Most, indeed, had already left when Smith, Preston, Jordan and Winn walked in.[212]

Thus, there was more than one good reason that, much to Colonel Smith's surprise, Christian "stepped forward and shook him by the hand." Clearly happy to see the colonel, Christian told Smith he was sorry about what had become "a bad affair."

Smith was equally surprised, he later testified, at Christian's immediate and apparently heartfelt confession: "I had rather it had been me that died than Blackburn."[213]

The colonel, of course, had no way of knowing that Morris had already advised his law school classmate that it would be wise to express just such regrets.[214]

Nor, it would seem, was Smith aware that minutes earlier Judge John White Brockenbrough had been part of the informal bodyguard protecting Christian. Brockenbrough, Christian's law professor, would become one of his student's most staunch defenders, both in and out of the courtroom. Whether or not Brockenbrough had seconded Morris's advice was never made clear.

What was clear, however, was that he was thinking both as a defense lawyer and teacher when he came to the Lexington jail to visit his imperiled student. Little escaped him.

Judge John White Brockenbrough (1806–1877). *Lewis F. Powell, Jr. Archives, Special Collections, Leyburn Library, Washington and Lee University.*

Witnesses were important. Noting that Christian was hurt, Brockenbrough asked the jailer, Thomas Littleton Perry, to check him over while he and several law students watched. Morris sat on the bed beside Christian during the process. Winn, Sam Houston Letcher, John James Davis and possibly others were also on hand.

Perry later testified Christian was "spitting blood against the wall of his jail cell." Upon closer examination by lantern light Perry also said he found scratches "on his neck just under the left jaw," and noticed "a general redness of the neck, but no bruises."[215]

Law student John James Davis remembered seeing "impressions of fingers" on Christian's left jaw, in "two or more" places and "one on the right." They appeared to be the kinds of marks a right-handed man would have made if he had slapped Christian, and then backhanded him across the face.[216]

William Winn later swore that he was absolutely sure the blood on the jail house wall actually came from the wounds on Christian's throat, rather than from his mouth, noting that he had seen Christian "rinse his mouth frequently at his room and after he went to jail."

When Perry finished his examination, Brockenbrough apparently went home. Much to Christian's chagrin, the rest of his friends from the law school also began to talk about leaving for the night. Christian begged for someone, anyone, to stay the night with him.

William Morris volunteered and asked his newly arrived classmate William Winn if he would stay with Christian while he went back to his room to collect a few things for his upcoming all-night vigil. Winn agreed, Morris left and Winn took the opportunity to take a closer look at Christian's injuries.

He found, he said, ruptured skin or scratches on Christian's cheek and ear and marks on Christian's throat. "It was very red," Winn remembered, "and fingers had been impressed upon his neck."

When Winn told Christian that it seemed to him "Blackburn came near fixing him," Christian replied that, indeed, "he was nearly out of breath" when he struck at Blackburn with his knife.[217]

At that point Morris returned to the jail, ready to spend the night standing watch over Christian. Winn and Sam Houston Letcher then went home, leaving Christian alone with his thoughts and Morris. Morris later testified that during the night Christian tried to draw him "into conversation about the affray" but he "discouraged him from doing so, and advised him not to talk about it."

Christian protested. "I cannot say any thing against myself, consistent with the truth, calculated to injure me," he said.

Morris again counseled silence. "He also mentioned his mother," Morris noted, "but I discouraged that also."[218]

With a guard in place that could at least call for help, if not absolutely prevent an escape or a lynching, Major Preston, Mayor Jordan and Colonel Smith also departed.

"As we left the jail," Smith later testified, "the Mayor expressed great apprehension lest there might be violence on the part of the Cadets. I told him what had passed and gave assurance that no apprehension need be entertained."

With that, the ailing Colonel Smith went home to bed, apparently convinced he'd done all he could do for the night.[219]

While Smith had been busy with the Cadet Corps, the mayor and a murder investigation, Smith's opposite number at Washington College, the Reverend Dr. George Junkin, had been caring for some of the other victims of the evening's sad proceedings.

He stopped by the home of Samuel McDowell Moore immediately after the tragedy, probably after helping Sandy Bruce escort Mary Evelyn Anderson home from the church. While at the Moore house, Junkin reassured the family that everything was going as well as might be expected, and that "Col. Smith has had Christian arrested and his room searched."[220]

Samuel McDowell Moore, no doubt terribly shaken by the events, retired as well, but only after taking time to write Anderson's father a long, detailed and remarkably accurate account of what had happened. Moore closed his letter to Frank Anderson by reassuring his brother-in-law that the situation was well in hand and that he was completely convinced that justice would be done. Christian, already in jail, was clearly a murderer, an "assassin" in Moore's words, and would be punished accordingly.

Moore's first and overriding concern, however, was for the two women who would be most affected by the tragedy: Frank Anderson's daughter, Mary Evelyn, and his own wife, Evalina Moore. His last words to his brother-in-law, and, in all probability, his last on that fateful day, sought to reassure him.

Despite some thoughtless behavior on the part of both Mary Evelyn and her aunt Evalina, Samuel McDowell Moore was convinced that neither could be blamed for Blackburn's death. Public opinion, however, could be cruel, and Moore warned Anderson's father that she, in particular, would soon need his unwavering support and reassurance.

> *Both Mary E. & my wife are deeply disturbed at what has occurred, and seem disposed to think that they may be blamed for what has occurred to some extent...I hope it will suit you to come down immediately, as the expression of your opinion will relieve Mary E., no doubt, from her apprehension that she may be censured as being the cause of what has occurred. I have no hesitation in saying that she is clear of all just blame in this matter. The blame must rest upon the [illegible] assassin.* [221]

Part VI

PREPARATION AND MOURNING

23

A Morning Tour

Justice moved swiftly in Lexington that January. Charles Christian had been arrested within an hour of Tom Blackburn's death. A postmortem examination of Blackburn's body and a formal inquest were set for the next day, Monday, January 16, 1854.

Early on the morning of the sixteenth, Colonel Francis Henney Smith, Major John Thomas Lewis Preston, Dr. George Junkin and James W. Massie (the only member of the group to actually witness the deadly struggle) met beside the Presbyterian Church on Nelson Street to "examine the ground" on which the fight had taken place.[222]

They were not the first, nor would they be the last to do so. The busy street between White's Corner and the Presbyterian Church had not been sealed off and had already attracted a number of sightseers.[223]

Major Preston, a graduate of Washington College and a UVA-trained lawyer, had arrived early. Some time between eight and nine in the morning, he made what he called "a cursory examination" of the crime scene.

Massie, who had studied law under Judge Brockenbrough, came for a very specific purpose. The night of the killing, after he'd looked at Blackburn's body for the last time, Massie had gone into the Presbyterian Church to sit quietly, think and perhaps pray about what had happened. While he was there, he said, it suddenly occurred to him, "as a material point, to ascertain at what time during the progress of the fight, the knife was used." Blood on the ground would be the "best evidence in that regard," he reasoned, and it was important that "it be found before the crime scene was materially disturbed." Emotionally drained and physically exhausted, however, Massie had gone home that night without examining the ground.

On the morning of January 16, he went looking for blood.[224]

The crowds that had gathered the night before had left the crime scene "very much trampled in every direction around," Massie later noted. Worse, the unusually warm January weather meant that the ground had not been frozen on Sunday night. Worse still, when Massie arrived, around 10:00 a.m., he found fifteen or twenty "sightseers" already there ahead of him.

Distressed but undeterred, Massie carried on. His plan was to begin at the engine house and then trace the path of the fight as he remembered it, moving slowly and carefully examining the ground as he walked. He had just reached the "upper corner of the hay-scales," he later testified, "when the crowd seemed to see me, and came up to where I was; as it seemed to be generally known that I had seen the fight the night before."[225]

Massie obliged the assembled multitude with what he later described as "a running description" of the preceding night's struggle, talking as he walked "the general line of the scuffle." At one point, as he led the crowd back and forth over the soft ground on the unpaved street, he reiterated to whomever might have been listening that it was particularly important, "to know whether there was any blood spilt near the place I was then standing...near the upper corner of the hay-scales."[226]

Apparently not finding any, Massie then walked down the street to meet Colonel Smith, Major Preston and Dr. Junkin, followed by most of the crowd of curiosity seekers.[227]

Preston immediately suggested that Massie, the only eyewitness present, repeat his story in as much detail as he could remember for Smith, Junkin and himself before they examined the ground. The four men thus adjourned to John Lyle's bookstore to hear Massie's blow-by-blow account of the struggle. The crowd followed them and, according to Massie, "gathered around the door and in the room to hear my statement."[228]

Massie reviewed what he thought he had seen. When he admitted that, during his examination of the ground that morning, he "could find no blood near where the

John Thomas Lewis Preston (1811–1890) in 1855. *VMI Archives.*

fight commenced," Major Preston suggested that perhaps the four of them should walk the scene of the crime one more time.[229] All agreed, and Massie led the group back to Nelson Street, with the crowd from the bookstore in tow.

When they got there, they encountered yet another group of curious bystanders. In the midst of what was now becoming a considerable crowd, Massie walked his companions along what he remembered as the path of the struggle, once more looking for bloodstains, tracks or other evidence that would support his own memory of the *"rencontre."*[230]

They started again at the engine house. There they found nothing—"not a drop," according to Massie. The group then moved about twenty feet, almost directly across the rutted street, from the engine house toward White's Corner. They walked slowly, three abreast, with Massie in the center, flanked by Preston on the right and Smith on the left. Dr. Junkin and the crowd of curiosity seekers apparently brought up the rear.

Between the Engine House and White's Corner, in the place where Massie had first seen Blackburn and Christian struggling in silence, "the ground was saturated with blood."

"There appeared to be no splashes," Massie later recalled, "but only what remained of a large pool of blood." He described it as "a distinctly defined outline of an elliptical form, eighteen by twelve inches."

Though no one had noticed even a trace of blood on the ground between the engine house and the blood they had just found, the group retraced their steps just to make sure, stalking slowly back to the engine house, then once more to what Massie now believed was the "first pool" of blood.

From the elliptical "first pool," they walked west toward the corner of Main and Nelson, "along a course roughly ten or fifteen feet long." At the place where Massie remembered seeing Blackburn shoved, stagger and fall, a point about twenty-five or thirty feet from the engine house, they found a second pool of blood. Massie described it as "more upon the surface" and "irregular in form."

There was almost as much blood in the second pool as there was in the first, Massie said, but it was different. "The wagons had pressed the earth hard," at that place in the street, and "it had not absorbed the blood; and much was clotted on the surface."

Finding little or nothing else of note at the scene, the crowd dispersed. Massie, Smith, Preston and Junkin departed, ready for the inquest later that day and united in the opinion that there were but two pools of blood to mark the path of the fight on Sunday night.[231]

Much to their surprise, their views would not long remain uncontested.

24

AUTOPSY AND INQUEST

VMI cadets had stood watch over Tom Blackburn's body throughout the night of January 15.

Around noon on January 16, 1854, a Jury of Inquest met in Major J.T.L. Preston's classroom to hear the results of an autopsy conducted earlier that morning, question witnesses and make an official decision about the cause of Thomas Blackburn's death. Most of Lexington appears to have been there.[232]

All agreed the examination of Blackburn's body had to be done quickly. The sooner witnesses could be deposed, the less likely they would be to forget what they had seen or heard. The weather was also unseasonably warm, and it was more than 140 miles down the Shenandoah Valley to Blackburn's home and the family graveyard, just south of Ripon.

Dr. James Jordan, the lead physician for the autopsy, arrived at "Church Harbor" early on the morning of the sixteenth. Waiting for him were three other physicians: Dr. William A. Graham, Dr. Edward Graham and Dr. Henry Gamble Davidson.

The four MDs were soon joined by a doctor of divinity, the Reverend George Junkin, who had, in his own words, "fortified himself with some physiological reading for the purpose."[233]

Dr. Jordan and the other physicians began by removing Blackburn's uniform and washing his body. As they did so, the British-born VMI commissary, John Tracy Gibbs, carefully examined Blackburn's clothing. He found little: only a pocket handkerchief and a pair of gloves.

When the doctors turned Blackburn over, they saw that he had been stabbed in the back on the right side. The wound was at least an inch and a half wide, and the knife had gone deep, "passing rather obliquely under the right shoulder blade" until it was "arrested by a rib." The blade of Christian's borrowed Bowie knife, measured carefully by the examining physicians, was precisely one and one-half inches wide.[234]

Turning Blackburn on his back, the physicians next examined the wound in his throat. Removing the skin and two or three muscles, they "found first a very large and important nerve entirely severed." The nerve, "the *parvagum* or pneumo-gastic nerve," was believed in the mid-nineteenth century to supply "the stomach, lungs, and other organs with 'nervous fluid or influence.'" The physicians present believed that, in time, the severed pneumo-gastic nerve alone would have killed Blackburn by making it impossible for him to breathe.

Probing deeper, slightly behind the severed *parvagum*, they found Blackburn's left carotid artery cut halfway through, his windpipe cut slightly and his esophagus "very badly cut." Bleeding from the wound to his carotid would have also killed Blackburn fairly quickly, depriving his brain of oxygen.

All agreed that the knife had gone in on the left side of Blackburn's throat and that the blade had been driven in until it was stopped by the angled part of the dead cadet's jawbone, on the other side of his face. Careful measurement again revealed that the wound was made by a blade the same size as that of Christian's borrowed Bowie knife.

After washing Blackburn's head, the physicians discovered one more wound, obviously made by the same weapon driven into the bone just above Blackburn's left temple, a little behind his temporal artery. Blackburn had been stabbed there with enough force, they noted, to "sever a small portion of the bone, bend it down and turn it in."

Turning next to Blackburn's blood-soaked uniform, they found a gash in the back where something had passed through both his overcoat and blue furlough coat. The gash matched the position of the wound in Blackburn's back. A second gash, in the collar of his overcoat, matched the wound in his throat.

Upon closer examination of the back of the overcoat, the doctors found several other gashes, including one in the lower end of the cape and one through the middle of the back. Precisely how many times the knife had been driven through Blackburn's overcoat could not be determined, they said, as it was clear that at least some of the gashes were the result of one knife-stroke passing through several folds of cloth.

Given the patterns of blood on Blackburn's clothing, the physicians believed that neither the wound near his temple nor the wound in his back had bled much at all. Most of the blood found in the puddles and pools on Nelson Street, they concluded, had come from the wound in Blackburn's throat.

Reverend Junkin watched closely and was permitted to examine Blackburn's wounds, in Junkin's words, "as they were laid open." The path of the wound in Blackburn's back, Junkin said, gave him pause, and indeed made him suspect the doctors might have erred in their conclusions about when and how Blackburn was mortally wounded. He said

An unidentified VMI cadet from the early 1850s, wearing the distinctive blue furlough coat. *VMI Archives.*

nothing about it at the time, however, deciding instead to revisit the crime scene the next day to test a theory of his own about what had happened.[235]

With the physicians' autopsy complete, witnesses were called for the formal inquest. "None of the town's citizens were to be seen [on the streets] while the inquest was in session," one witness reported, "because most of them had gone to the Institute."

J.W. Massie testified first. He recounted once more the story of the scuffle, dragging the mortally wounded Blackburn to the cap of the cellar door at White's store, the arrival of Dr. Patrick Christian and setting off with Mayor Jordan and his posse to find Charles Christian. The entire episode, from his first becoming aware of the fight until he left Blackburn with Dr. Christian, Massie swore, could not have taken more than eight minutes.

Benton Taylor testified that he had been fifteen or twenty paces ahead of Massie when his "attention was directed to 2 persons on the scales near the church." Though he did not see the scuffle and said he "heard no blows," Taylor did see Christian shove Blackburn, saw Blackburn fall wounded on the scales and watched Christian "run rapidly from the spot." He knew it was Christian, he said, because he "stopped within three feet of me...directly in the light coming from one of the windows of the church."

Mayor William Jordan told the story of the pursuit and arrest of Christian, and the unsuccessful searches for the murder weapon in his room.

Testimony from Cadet G.B. Horner, Henry Hanff, Samuel Henry Conn and Cadet A.G. Strayer took up the rest of the afternoon.

At the end of the day, the Court of Inquiry agreed that Charles Burks Christian had stabbed VMI Cadet Thomas Blackburn to death with a Bowie knife and had delivered the fatal blow while he and Blackburn were standing up, at some point after they had risen from their wrestling match on the ground and just before Christian shoved Blackburn away.

The physicians also agreed that Blackburn's wounds were so devastating that, had he been stabbed in the throat while he and Christian were wrestling on the ground, he could never have stood up, much less walk or stagger several paces before falling to the ground.

Dr. Junkin disagreed but said nothing about his doubts. He would have another chance nine days later at a preliminary court hearing already scheduled for January 25, 1854.[236]

Early Rumors

While Blackburn's body still lay under guard and unexamined in Major J.T.L. Preston's classroom, Colonel Smith began to worry about the rumors already circulating through the VMI barracks, fearing they would, "in a high degree exasperate the feelings of the cadets."

He described one of the most egregious in a report to his Board of Visitors:

> *It was reported that about three or four hours after Mr. Christian had been committed to jail, several persons, masked and otherwise in disguise, some of whom were under the influence of intoxicating liquors, had gone to the jail and demanded admission as the friends of Mr. Christian. It was understood their application was firmly resisted by the jailer. This circumstance occasioned apprehension in the minds of the cadets that an attempt would be made to rescue the prisoner.*[237]

While some in Lexington were hearing that Brockenbrough's law students were on their way to rescue Christian, others were hearing that the VMI cadets were preparing to lynch him.

An "anonymous communication" addressed to a "member of Judge Brockenbrough's Law School" suggested "that if he [Christian] did not leave Lexington in twenty-four hours, more blood would be shed."

An unnamed law student passed the letter on to Judge Brockenbrough. Brockenbrough gave it to Mayor Jordan.[238] Mayor Jordan took it to Colonel Smith and asked him to "intervene."

Smith took the warning seriously. He was especially worried that the local authorities, either out of principle or personal respect for Judge Brockenbrough, might allow Christian to post bail. "Had such an attempt been made and with success," Smith later wrote, "my persuasion was, and is, that violence would have resulted."

The rumors, the anonymous letter and his own "apprehensions" thus led Smith to demand special "vigilance on the part of all the officers of the Institute, by day and by night, to guard against any outbreak or act of violence of any kind." Fortunately, the discipline and rituals of VMI provided Smith with unique tools to address the grief and outrage that had swept the ranks of the young men in his charge.[239]

On the day of the inquest, Colonel Smith issued orders to the Corps, his first official and formal response to Blackburn's death.

> *Head Quarters*
> *V. M. Institute*
> *Jan'y 16th 1854*
> *Order*
> *No. 7*
>
> *It becomes the most painful duty of the Superintendent to announce to the Corps of Cadets the death of their late comrade, Cadet Thomas Blackburn. He died by the hand of violence last night at about 7 o'clock. How mournfully does this sad event impress us with the truth "That in the midst of life we are in death. What shadows we are; what shadows we pursue."*
>
> *The Superintendent has deemed it his duty to dispatch a fellow classmate to bear these sad tidings to the heart stricken parents of the deceased.*
>
> *As appropriate marks of respect to the memory of the deceased, academic duties will be suspended today and the usual badge of mourning will be worn by the officers and Cadets of the Institute for the period of 30 days.*
> *By Order of*
> *Col. Smith*
> *L. W. Allen*
> *Ajt. Va. Mil. In.*[240]

For the next month, the Corps wore its sorrow and anger quite literally on its sleeve. Every morning, every cadet, for every inspection, buttoned the eight gilt buttons neatly "impressed with the arms of the State of Virginia," tugged the jacket of his uniform taut and then adjusted a black band of mourning on the right sleeve, taking care that its borders were parallel to the ground when he stood at attention.

From just the right angle, officers casting a cold eye on the alignment of the ranks would see the pale gray of the double line of cadets marked by a long black slash, a dark wound that ran the length of the Corps. From the hilts of their officer's swords swung the same black emblem of mourning.[241]

Two of Blackburn's friends prepared a formal resolution and a message of condolence from the Corps to Blackburn's parents. One was Cadet First Captain Charles Lightfoot, the Corps' ranking cadet and one of Blackburn's roommates. The other was another roommate, Class President Richard Cornelius Taylor, later class valedictorian and, ironically, the cadet to whom Christian's knife had been surrendered on the night of the murder, the blade still wet with Blackburn's blood.

It took Lightfoot and Taylor nearly a week to finish their work, but on January 21 it was officially and unanimously adopted by an assembly of the Corps and sent to a printer. In their "Preamble and Resolutions," the Corps requested formally that their expressions of sympathy and grief and their unanimous affirmation of Blackburn's superior character be recorded in the Institute's Order Book, sent to Blackburn's family and then dispatched to the newspapers of Lexington, Charles Town, Richmond and Norfolk.

Having been warned, no doubt, not to comment on matters that would soon be before the court, the cadets did their best to explain to Blackburn's parents why they could not say more. Their sad duty, they wrote, was "to remember that the undecided fate of the living impressively demands the charity of our silence."

That said, they wrote what they could in support of their classmate and to the eternal damnation of Charles Burks Christian.

We derive great comfort from the belief that the deceased on that fatal night had left his room to attend divine service, with no feeling of hatred to any human being to disturb the serenity of his thoughts, entertaining no malignant designs within himself and suspecting none in others, that he had even entered the house of God, and was called thence to meet a sudden and awful death under the cover of night and by the hand of violence.

'Tis these comforting reflections, together with a memory of the undaunted firmness with which he met his fate, that now, like moonbeams on a stormy sea, light up our darkened hearts and lend to the surrounding gloom a beauty, soft, sweet, and soothing to the troubled soul, as we call up in long

Richard Cornelius Taylor (1835–1917), VMI Class of 1854. *Courtesy of Sargeant Memorial Collection, Norfolk Public Library.*

review the whole history of our intercourse with the deceased, his numerous acts of kindness and love—his many social virtues, his pure principles and honorable character, as we remember how he shared with us the hardships and pastimes of camp, the duties and anxieties of the school, and then think that his friendly hand can never again be offered with the frankness of a soldier's love, or his voice fall again upon the listening ear of friendship, our sorrow becomes more deep, more bitter, because unheard and unavailing.

From this distress we would not be entirely divorced, for there is a sympathy of heart for heart, a communion of spirit with spirit, in the sad hour of bereavement that softens death and prompts us to cherish a memory for the dearly loved and lost [that] *becomes the earthly shadow of their immortality.*[242]

The words so moved Cadet Thomas Barksdale that he copied the entire resolution in his notebook.[243]

As tempers cooled, Colonel Smith kept up his efforts to reassure and calm his cadets, ever mindful of his promise that he would act *in loco parentis* to see that justice was done. "By personal interview [of] the cadets," Smith wrote to his Board of Visitors, "it was soon manifest that no threat of violence had proceeded [from the Corps], but great concern was expressed by all that the Commonwealth should be [assisted in] the prosecution."[244]

Smith did not arrive at such a conclusion lightly, and his efforts to fulfill his promises to the cadets and to Blackburn's parents would cost him dearly.

HIRING TOM MICHIE

On January 16, 1854, Colonel Smith wrote Thomas Johnson Michie, a "prominent member of the Staunton bar," and a former Commonwealth's attorney for Rockbridge County to ask for help.[245]

Michie was a longtime friend of VMI, would send his son there and would serve on the VMI Board of Visitors during the last two years of the Civil War. Michie had also served in the Virginia House of Delegates alongside James Coles Bruce, the father of Cadet Alexander Broadnax Bruce.[246]

Colonel Smith and VMI Professor Major John Thomas Lewis Preston, however, probably remembered Michie best for starting a mutiny at VMI while trying a murder case in Lexington during Tom Blackburn's freshman year.

In the spring of 1851, Michie had been the chief prosecutor in a murder trial held in the Rockbridge County Circuit Court in Lexington. Colonel Smith was out of town, and Major Preston was standing in as superintendent. Michie was well known for his oratory, and Preston had given the VMI cadets permission to hear his closing arguments.

As Smith later told the story, "Mr. Michie had just reached the height of his argument on Saturday evening when the court adjourned. His speech was one of great power and eloquence, and every one was absorbed in the interest which it excited." The VMI cadets, led by Cadet William Young Conn Humes, asked to be allowed to attend court the next Monday to hear the rest of Michie's summation. Preston refused, whereupon the entire first class, quickly followed by the rest of the Corps, "mutinied."

Colonel Smith, a West Pointer still relatively new in his job at VMI, ordered the entire first class court-martialed and dismissed from the Institute. The Board of Visitors supported his decision, but charitably reduced the punishment to confinement to the grounds until graduation, just enough time, they believed, to allow the mutinous seniors to consider fully the consequences of their actions.[247]

Michie, no doubt remembering the mutiny of '51, responded to Smith's request two days later. He would be willing to help, Michie wrote on January 18, though not without "painful consideration and advisement." When he retired as chief prosecutor in Rockbridge, Michie wrote, he had decided "never [again] to appear for the Commonwealth in a capital case."

There were, however, "considerations" suggested in Smith's letter about the Blackburn affair that, Michie conceded, appeared "to distinguish this case from most other of the like kind."

"I understand from what you say," Michie wrote, "that it will not be expected of me to make any effort in the cause beyond what, as a faithful representative of the Commonwealth, I would feel bound to make, & I further understand that the character of the victim of the unfortunate affair may require to be taken care of."

"Under these circumstances," Michie continued in a shaky hand, "I have concluded to appear for the prosecution..."

He would do so, however, only at a price. Specifically, Michie would appear only "if a fee of five hundred dollars should be considered not too high a compensation." Apparently anticipating a difficult and lengthy trial, followed, no doubt, by an appeal, Michie noted that the $500 fee would cover his services "in both courts, county and superior."

Michie then asked for an answer by return mail. Judge Brockenbrough, he noted, had already sent a letter to a colleague, "Mr. Stuart," telling him Christian's trial had already been scheduled for the following Tuesday. "If I am to go," he wrote to Colonel Smith, "let me know whether this is correct. You state it for Wednesday, the 25th."[248]

With his passing remark about "Mr. Stuart," Michie added significantly to Smith's burdens. "Stuart" was none other than Alexander Hugh Holmes Stuart, recently retired as President Millard Fillmore's Secretary of the Interior, and well-known for both his oratory and his skills as a lawyer. A leading political figure and a possible candidate for the Whig nomination for governor of Virginia, Stuart would represent a significant and perhaps decisive addition to Christian's defense team.[249]

Thus pressed, Colonel Smith quickly agreed to Michie's terms and retained him on his own authority, without consulting either the VMI Board

The Thomas Johnson Michie House, Staunton. *National Register of Historic Places.*

of Visitors or the Blackburn family. Fully aware that his decision to hire Michie would reach the Blackburn family before Tom's body arrived home, Smith worried about how to let Dr. Blackburn know what he had done and just how much money Michie was demanding for his services.[250]

Smith temporized, sending a note to Charles Edward Ambler, an Episcopal priest and the pastor of Zion Church in Charles Town, asking him to tell Dr. Blackburn that he had hired Michie, but not to mention the cost.

"I communicated the contents of your letter to Dr. Blackburn yesterday upon its arrival," Ambler wrote Smith from Charles Town on January 21.

> *He desires me to say in reply that he is very grateful to you for what you have done, both for the preservation of the remains of his son, & for the protection of his reputation by the employment of able counsel.*
>
> *He is exceedingly unwilling, however, to be in the least concerned in the <u>prosecution</u> of the miserable young man who is the author of this calamity. He wishes that Mr. Michie should understand that his only solicitude is in regard to the reputation of his son & he would not have him say one word which is not necessary for that object. He*

desired to say that if such a thing is admissible he would like that Mr. Michie should make on his (Dr. Blackburn's) behalf, a declaration of this to the court & act accordingly. He wants it to be understood that <u>he</u> employs no prosecutor, though he would spare no pains in protecting all that remains of his son, his reputation.[251]

Ambler's letter seemed to say that Dr. Blackburn assumed the Blackburn family would have to bear the cost of retaining Michie. Without intending to do so, however, and in the most complimentary terms, Dr. Blackburn also put Colonel Smith under even more intense pressure to act on his son's behalf.

He desires further to say that he leaves everything to the judgment & good feeling of his friends, Mr. Glasgow, Messrs. J[oseph Reid] & F[rancis Thomas] Anderson & yourself, hoping that his wishes as above expressed will be strictly complied with.[252]

Ambler closed his note with a description of the bereaved Blackburn household, still waiting for their son's body to arrive from Lexington, sustained only, he said, by their intense Christian faith.

I need hardly tell you that the affliction of the bereaved household, especially the parents, surpasses anything ever witnessed by me. Thank God they are not strangers to the only refuge of the weary & heavy laden & while there is nothing else to sustain them they are enabled to bear up under the dispensation as sent by the hand of a God of unchanging pitifulness [sic] & mercy. I hope that it will be the means of calling many to repentance, both here & in your community.[253]

Colonel Smith was being called to repentance, however, by a more pressing if not higher authority: the governing Board of Visitors of the Virginia Military Institute.

Between January 21 and February 6, Smith received no fewer than four letters from the head of that body, Adjutant General of Virginia William Harvie Richardson. Richardson did not have good news for Colonel Smith the first time he wrote, and things did not get any better over time.

From his home in Richmond, Richardson told Smith he had been trying to call the Board together since at least January 17. By the twenty-first, only William Seymour of Hardy County, James Barbour of Culpeper and

William Harvie Richardson (1795–1876) VMI Board of Visitors. *VMI Archives.*

General Douglas B. Layne of Alleghany County had arrived, with General Francis M. Boykin of Isle of Wight expected shortly.

"It is the opinion of the members here," Richardson informed Colonel Smith, "that the authorities of the Institute ought *not* to link themselves with the prosecution of the murderer of young Blackburn." If help were needed, he suggested, "surely the community where the outrage was committed...or...the friends of the murdered youth" could be counted on for help. The governor might also be of assistance, Richardson suggested, but only if he thought it proper.[254]

By January 26, in response to another query by Smith, Richardson reported that the Board's views against institutional involvement in the case were hardening.

"The views of the Board," he wrote, "were, that the authorities of the Institute ought not to mingle <u>at all</u> in the prosecution of the assassin of poor Blackburn, but that if additional counsel was required it should be up to the community which has been outraged & the relatives of the deceased to do it."[255]

MOURNING AND MICHIE'S MONEY

On January 18, 1854, George Washington Turner and a "Mr. Washington" arrived in Lexington at the request of the Blackburn family to bring Tom Blackburn home.

Turner was a well-to-do farmer and 1831 graduate of West Point. His mother, Catherine Blackburn, was Tom's great aunt. His older brother was named Thomas Blackburn Turner.[256]

"Mr. Washington" was George Fayette Washington, the father of Cadet Matthew Burwell Basset Washington, and a great-grandnephew of the first president. The senior Washington was born at Mount Vernon, where Dr. Blackburn's first cousin, Jane Charlotte Blackburn Washington, was still living.

Colonel Smith assigned three cadets to serve as an honor guard to accompany Turner and Washington on their journey north to Ripon. One was George Fayette Washington's son. The second was William Elzey Harrison of Leesburg, a member of Tom Blackburn's class and the son of Burr William Harrison, a former state legislator. The Harrisons were closely tied to both VMI and Judge Brockenbrough's law school. Cadet Harrison's cousin, Charles Tyler Harrison, was living in Lexington, had taken part in VMI Professor Thomas J. Jackson's wedding and was a law school classmate of the man who killed Tom Blackburn.

The third cadet was younger, a member of the class of 1856 and a Blackburn cousin: James Edward Towson of Falmouth, the very same cadet Blackburn had tied to a chair and propped against Major Jackson's door in the VMI barracks a year earlier.[257]

The funeral procession left Lexington very early on Thursday morning, January 19, 1854, moving at a steady pace down the Valley Road toward Blackburn's home at Spring Grove Farm, near Ripon, more than 140 miles away.

The weather was still warm. The coffin was sealed. One of the cadets carried a lock of hair to give to Blackburn's mother. After three full days on the road, with at least one stop in Staunton, the group reached Winchester just after sunset on January 21.

The next morning at 8:00 a.m., they set off for Spring Grove Farm, some seventeen miles away, passing through Berryville, turning left at the crossroads there, then moving north on the road toward Charles Town. Six hours after leaving Winchester, they reached the Blackburn farm, just over the Jefferson County line, about a mile south of the wide place in the road that bore the name of the Blackburn family's ancestral home in England.[258]

The main house at Spring Grove stands on a small rise, now sheltered by great oaks and maples, but in those days, it was surrounded by clearcut fields, fully exposed to the winter wind. A chest-high stone wall with a cast-iron gate surrounded the family cemetery, a respectful distance away from the Blackburn house, but within sight. From the graveside, mourners could see the western slopes of the Blue Ridge, guiding the Shenandoah River down its own sometimes wild path from the highlands near Lexington past Spring Grove to the Potomac and the sea, through a valley, some said, named for a lost daughter of the stars.

George Washington Turner wrote Colonel Smith the day after the funeral.

> *The sad, sad scene of the meeting of Dr. Blackburn's family with the remains of their murdered son, Thomas, took place yesterday at the grave in which it was deposited at about 2 o'clock.*
>
> *They were all but the younger children there & the agony of the family far exceeds all description.*
>
> *But it is over & Time…offers the only relief which can be afforded them. The Dr. desires me to say that they all feel grateful to you for the friendship & sympathy which you have shown.*
>
> *Mrs. B. prizes beyond the expression of words the locket of hair.*
>
> *All the tenderest sensibilities of this most afflicted family have been gratified by the escort of Cadets & the various other marks of forethought and sympathy.*
>
> *I have been pleased more than I can tell you with those young <u>gentlemen.</u>*[259]

The Blackburn House at Spring Grove, now Olive Boy Farm, Rippon, West Virginia. *Author's photograph.*

George Washington Turner had stopped to see Thomas Michie as Blackburn's body passed through Staunton and knew all about his demand for a fee of no less than $500 to protect Blackburn's name and reputation. He had been shocked both by the size of the fee and by Michie's insistence on charging it. And like Colonel Smith, under the circumstances, he was loath to tell Doctor Blackburn about it.

"When Mr. Michie informed me of the contents of his reply to your letter," he wrote Smith, "I stated to him that the circumstances of Dr. Blackburn were not such as to render the amount of the fee for professional services a matter of total indifference to him." In a postscript he wrote, "I have said nothing to anybody here of the amount of the fee which Mr. M. expects, deeming it inadvisable, just now, to do so."[260]

Unfortunately, before Colonel Smith or Turner found the heart to break the news of Michie's financial demands, Dr. Blackburn heard about them from some other source, most likely Colonel Smith's confidant, the rector of Zion Church in Charles Town, Charles Edward Ambler.

On February 1, 1854, Reverend William Spottswood White, pastor of the Lexington Presbyterian Church, wrote Smith from Charles Town about his own visit to the grieving Blackburn family. Someone had told Tom's father about Michie's fee.

"Our afflicted friend, Dr. Blackburn, desires me to write and inform you," White wrote, "that he has just heard that the distinguished Gentleman you were kind enough to employ to aid in the prosecution of young Christian would not appear for less than the sum of $500, and that he is not able to pay such a fee."

"Dr. B's circumstances are but moderate," White continued, "and as he has no vindictive feelings to gratify in the case, he feels unwilling to pay the fee."

Clearly embarrassed, Dr. Blackburn had offered to pay for whatever services Michie had already rendered at the preliminary hearing and, through Reverend White, asked to be informed of the outcome.[261]

White's letter neither lifted the duty of communicating directly with Dr. Blackburn from the shoulders of Francis Henney Smith, nor made it any easier.

Smith again temporized. On February 6, 1854, he wrote again to Reverend White, still in Charles Town, asking him to speak to Dr. Blackburn directly about Michie's demands for money. White did so, and Dr. Blackburn wrote to Smith two days later.

> *The sum of money demanded by Mr. M as a compensation for his service seems to me to be almost cruel, and altho' I never abandoned the intention of having someone appear for the protection of my son's reputation, I had thoughts of employing a lawyer who would be more merciful to one in my deep, deep, affliction. But as the matter stands now so revealed in your letter, referred to, I am now perfectly satisfied & will take no further steps in the matter. My poor boy has left nothing to his friends but his fair fame and they will protect that to the last extremity.*[262]

Colonel Smith answered on February 10 with what may well have been one of the most difficult letters he had ever written.[263]

"I am truly sorry," he began, "the arrangements entered into with Mr. Michie are not satisfactory to you, and can only say in the part which I have borne in the transaction I endeavored to act as I conceived best for your interest, and with the best light before me."

Smith assured Tom's father that he had no idea Michie would appear at all as late as January 18 or 19, when George Washington Turner,

George Fayette Washington and the cadet honor guard left Lexington with Blackburn's body.

"Indeed it was considered very doubtful," Smith wrote, "but the necessity of a proper legal advisor being present at the trial to protect your son's reputation was so apparent to Mr. Turner, that when he left here he designed seeing Mr. Michie when he passed through Staunton."

Turner's original plan, according to Smith, was to talk to Michie and, if Michie had decided to turn down the job, to "send up Mr. Robt. T. Conrad or some lawyer of equal celebrity." (Conrad, forty-four, was indeed a celebrity, a Philadelphia lawyer, orator, publisher, poet, judge and politician who would be elected the first mayor of Greater Philadelphia in 1854.)

Turner reached Staunton on January 19, Smith reported, "at a late hour of the night." Michie, by then, had decided that he would, in this special case, come out of retirement to serve and communicated both his decision and the fee he would demand to Turner.

Smith told Dr. Blackburn that he, as superintendent of VMI, was expecting "to bear, say, one half of the fee of Mr. Michie myself as representing the interests of the cadets." He was thinking at the time, he said, that it would be impossible for Dr. Blackburn "to engage the services of any one down the valley for a less sum than $250" and given the pressure of time "at once closed the engagement with Mr. Michie."

Smith then assured Dr. Blackburn that he thought Michie was a good man charging a fair price for his services.

> *I will only say that I have known Mr. Michie intimately for 15 years. He is a faithful laborious & conscientious man. I am sure he did not desire this duty, and his letter to me, a copy of which I now enclose, will shew this. His duty is a delicate and responsible one, and judging from the fees which he and lawyers of his standing are in the habit of receiving in civil cases, I considered his charge reasonable and just. You may be assured on one thing, that he will fully protect your interest in this cause.* [264]

Having done his best to explain his decision to hire Thomas Johnson Michie, Colonel Francis Henney Smith, forty-two, West Point Class of '33, superintendent of the Virginia Military Institute, father of three girls and one almost four-year-old son, spoke from his heart to a grieving father just three years older than he.

I think I understood fully the character of your son. He was elastic in mind as well as body – Light hearted – joyous – gleesome – hence whatever errors his youthfulness led him into were the result of his great elasticity of spirit, rather than the settled disposition to do what was wrong. Gifted with uncommon talent he did not require the severe mental effort which others less blessed were compelled to use, and this fact, coupled with the disposition above noticed, encouraged him to enjoy the pleasures of life as they passed, satisfied that with a short and severe effort he could recover time thus spent. Age was blending into a happy medium these various elements, and I was looking forward with much interest and confidence to a distinguished career for him in after life.[265]

Speaking directly to his own "difficulties" with Tom Blackburn, Smith wrote:

He was generous and not unforgiving. Altho' he had supposed that in my official relations to him I had been severe with him, it was with great pleasure I heard from a mutual friend, that on the day previous to his death he had expressed to her the kindest sentiments towards myself, adding that altho' persons might complain of me as being too strict, he was satisfied a different course from the one I adopted would be injurious to the cadets & to the Institution.[266]

Just over a week later, Dr. Blackburn wrote back, worried that Colonel Smith had misunderstood him. Recent events, he told Smith, had all but driven him insane.

I endeavored to make myself understood, but such was the troubled state of my mind that I do not wonder that I was not correctly understood. Indeed, when I look back upon the occurrance [sic] which has brought so much woe upon myself and family & friends, I almost wonder why is it that I have escaped a place in the hospitals destined for those who are "diseased in mind." Hail the mercy of God alone which has spared this calamity to my stricken household. My sensibilities are of that acute character that I should have been a great sufferer even under an act which might have proceeded from the hand of the good God who gave life and being to my dear Tom. But coming from the hands of vile men, it was to me a stroke beyond human endurance.[267]

What he meant to say, Dr. Blackburn wrote, "was that you entirely misunderstood me in thinking that I desired to cast the <u>least</u> censure upon you as to the course which you pursued consequent upon the disaster above alluded to. Far from it. You have my heart's deepest gratitude for all that you have done."

Everyone had spoken highly of everything he had done, Blackburn assured Colonel Smith. "And it may be a further source of satisfaction to you to learn that Messrs. Towson[268] & Washington (my relatives and friends) as also the Cadets who accompanied the remains of my dear boy, all concurred in commending you for the fidelity which you acted, standing as you did in my position as the guardian of the reputation of my dear Thos."

"How can I repay your kindness?" Blackburn continued. Tom, it appears, was always in trouble.

> *You know full well from the correspondence which I have had with you from time to time since my son has been an associate of the Institute, with what deep deep solicitude I was regarding his every step. You know the principal interest which I had felt, for fear the tests of character which you so faithfully depict in your letters might lead him into this sorry path. I feared you would not understand me and make proper allowance for this youthful exhibition of feeling which I felt if properly controlled would lead to innocent result.*[269]

Richard Scott Blackburn's heart was broken. "But all is over!" he wrote. "In my darkest hour I never anticipated the dark deed of villainy which has been perpetrated on him. Only to think that he who was the <u>soul of honor</u> should have fallen a victim to an act that would only become man in a savage state, and entirely bereft of those noble qualities which distinguish him from the brutes that perish." Tom, he wrote, was more than a son.

> *It is, my dear sir, a sad, sad thing to have all your hopes and all your bright certainties in regard to your first born child, crushed in a moment of time, & that by the hand of violence. That boy was the idol of my heart, the subject of my prayers & the sweet hope of the future. I loved his noble being, his high soul'd honor and the joyous heart which lights up his bright countenance. But all is gone. The sleep of death is upon his cold cheek and my heart is desolated.*[270]

Dr. Blackburn truly appreciated Smith's good intentions. "You are a parent & the tenor of your letter shows that your [*sic*] have a feeling heart," he wrote. "May God in his mercy spare you and the rest of the human family all the agony which it has been my unhappy fate to endure."

As for Michie's $500 fee, Dr. Blackburn wrote, "Please let what has passed in reference to the fee of Mr. M. be forgotten and studiously kept from his ear. I regret that it ever was stated. My friend, Mr. White, and also another lawyer in our village thought the fee unreasonably high or it would not have been mentioned."[271]

Part VII

PRE-TRIAL RIOTS AND MANEUVERS

PRELIMINARY HEARING: PRELUDE

On Wednesday, January 25, 1854, witnesses were called to the Rockbridge County Courthouse in Lexington to testify in what VMI Commandant Francis Henney Smith termed an "examination before the committing magistrate."

It was, in fact, a preliminary hearing, the equivalent of a modern grand jury hearing, later described by one participant as a "tedious examination and cross-examination of four days" to determine whether or not Charles Burks Christian would be indicted and, if so, on what charges.[272]

On the first day of the hearing, Doctor William Neeley Anderson wrote to his brother Francis, Mary Evelyn Anderson's father.

> *The prevalent opinion of this enlightened community* [Lewisburg, Virginia] *is that our criminal laws may as well be committed to the flames if Christian is not hung. They think it is now high time that our bloodthirsty young man should be made a signal example of, in order to put a stop to these horrible crimes.*[273]

Yet, despite what appeared to be an open-and-shut case, the process of indicting Charles Burks Christian did not begin well for the Commonwealth of Virginia.

One problem was the lead counsel for the prosecution, Commonwealth's Attorney Captain David Evans Moore. Moore was hopelessly conflicted. He was Samuel McDowell Moore's brother, lived in Lexington and was a second cousin to both Mary Evelyn Anderson and Tom Blackburn. One of his sons, John Harvey Moore, would later marry Samuel McDowell Moore's only daughter, Sallie Alexander Moore. Another son, Andy, a key witness, was one of Judge Brockenbrough's law students and a friend to both Christian and Blackburn.

For reasons unknown, Captain Moore was absent for both the coroner's inquest on January 16 and for the "examination before the committing magistrate" which began on January 25.

At the last minute, William Henry Terrill, forty-nine, prosecuting attorney for Bath County, stepped in as a substitute.[274] Terrill was well known in Lexington. He had served a term on the VMI Board of Visitors in 1848–49 and had spent well over twenty years as a prosecutor in Alleghany, Pocahontas and Bath Counties. A former member of the Virginia House of Delegates, he had studied law under Colonel John Brown Baldwin, the law partner of former Secretary of the Interior Alexander H.H. Stuart. Terrill, Stuart and Baldwin had, by all accounts, remained close friends. Unfortunately for the prosecution, Stuart and Baldwin would also soon be part of Charles Burks Christian's defense team.[275]

With the prosecution already in apparent disarray, Charles Christian suddenly found himself the beneficiary of solid moral and legal support from his extended family in Amherst and Bedford Counties and some of the best legal talent in Virginia.

Christian also knew that the testimony of his friend Andrew Moore would both support his case and undermine the morale of Andy's father, the as-yet missing-in-action chief prosecutor.

Though Christian was required to appear at the preliminary hearings, he never took the stand himself. Throughout the four long days of testimony, his widowed mother and four of his uncles stood behind him.[276]

Christian's mother, Frances Ann Burks Christian, had been a widow since Charles was ten. Her husband, Charles M. Christian, had died in 1845, leaving her to raise their only son and three younger sisters. Her faithful devotion to her husband's memory and to the raising of his four children made her an extraordinarily sympathetic figure.

The Christian family, counted among the founders of Amherst County, Lynchburg City, Bedford and communities in Botetourt County, were well known and well respected on both sides of the Blue Ridge.

The Burks were equally well known. Arguably the most prominent member of the Burks family was Judge Edward Callohill Burks of Liberty, the county seat of Bedford County. Judge Burks had graduated

Rosedale, Charles Burks Christian's house, Walker's Ford, Amherst County, Virginia. *Author's photograph.*

from Washington College with highest honors in 1841, then finished a law degree in record time at the University of Virginia under Henry St. George Tucker. He was, however, only the most prominent of the nine sons of Martin Parks Burks, a man described in later years as "one time the senior in commission of the justices of the old Bedford County Court, a tribunal before which the best lawyer of Virginia delighted to practice, and whose judgments were rarely reversed."

As the sole surviving male in his family, Charles Burks Christian inherited at an early age the title, benefits and nominal responsibilities of head of household. Among the benefits were his stay in Lexington and his education in Judge Brockenbrough's law school, all paid for by his share of his father's estate (divided among the Christian heirs according to the terms of his will on January 1, 1852).

Christian's decision to attend law school was, however, quickly and effectively positioned as that of a young man on a holy quest: seeking to learn an honorable profession so that he might fulfill his moral obligation to support his widowed mother and three sisters.

As nominal head of the family, Christian was also tasked with its physical protection and, no less important, the preservation, protection and defense of the sacred honor of the family name.

Christian would also soon discover he was blessed with defense counsel that both recognized and knew how to fully exploit the tremendous social and emotional capital represented by those assets. His fellow law students had begun advising him while Tom Blackburn's blood was still on his hands.

By the time his preliminary hearing opened, Christian and his family (no doubt with the active support of Judge John White Brockenbrough) were well on their way to bringing together an extraordinary defense team comprising no fewer than nine lawyers. Over the next eight months, they would do their best to counter the Commonwealth's "open and shut" murder case and save Christian from the gallows.

PRELIMINARY HEARING: DENOUEMENT

Though the sessions of the preliminary hearing were officially closed to the public, surviving documents and post-hearing leaks to the press allow a fairly accurate reconstruction of what went on during the four-day process.

James Massie testified for the prosecution, describing what he saw in the street outside the Presbyterian Church on the evening of January 15.

Dr. Jordan, the first physician to reach the dying Tom Blackburn; the doctors who participated in the autopsy on January 16; and perhaps even Dr. George Junkin would have also been called to testify about the severity of Blackburn's wounds and which of the wounds caused his death.

Mary Evelyn Anderson was called and questioned closely by one of the most talented members of Christian's defense team, James Baldwin Dorman.

Dorman was only thirty-one, the son of Charles P. Dorman, a well-known lawyer and the founder of the *Lexington Gazette*, who had served in the Virginia State Legislature for some thirteen years. James Baldwin Dorman had grown up in Lexington and had attended both Washington College and VMI. After graduating second in the VMI class of 1843, he read law and was admitted to the bar. During the Mexican War, he served with distinction in Wood's Texas Rangers and then returned to Lexington and the law to follow in his father's footsteps.

Defending Charles Burks Christian could not have been an altogether pleasant task for Dorman. Both he and his father were lifelong friends and supporters of VMI. One of his VMI classmates had been Richard Scott

Defense Counsel James Baldwin Dorman (1823–1893), VMI Class of 1843. *VMI Archives.*

Blackburn Washington, the son of the last mistress of Mount Vernon, and Cadet Tom Blackburn's second cousin.

Young Dorman, however, had already shown himself to be a conscientious and skillful attorney, "a man of unusual ability," described as "a fluent speaker" and "a master of the English language, whether written or spoken."[277]

At the preliminary hearing, his crisp interrogation of Blackburn's cousin, Mary Evelyn Anderson, nearly caused a riot.

In 1903, Cadet J.H. Sharp still remembered Anderson, "young and beautiful" sitting "closely veiled in the witness chair." She was questioned first by Prosecutor David E. Moore's stand-in, William Henry Terrill. She described meeting Christian, her acceptance of his unexpected invitation to walk with him to church and his "disagreeable" behavior the next night at the Episcopal Church Fair.

According to Sharp, Anderson testified under oath that she had decided not to walk out with Christian well before Tom Blackburn spoke to her and admitted that she didn't let Christian know about her decision until just a few hours before they were supposed to meet. She then described Christian's attempt to call on her at her Uncle Samuel McDowell Moore's house, her refusal to see him, her receipt of Christian's note and the incidents leading to its falling into the hands of Tom Blackburn.

Terrill then opened a door for Dorman by asking about Anderson's personal relationships. Although it cannot be determined with complete certainty, it would appear that Terrill implied that she had a "relationship" with Blackburn. According to longhand notes taken by an unnamed witness, Anderson denied it, noting that Blackburn was engaged to someone else.

Of Mr. Blackburn having an engagement of marriage with any young lady—I knew of an understanding between Mr. B. and a young lady of East Virginia—and Mr. B. had her daguerreotype in his possession at the time of his death. Was not a confidante of the lady, but of the gentleman.[278]

Dorman then set off a small riot by asking Anderson about her relationship to Blackburn's friend and roommate, Alexander Broadnax Bruce. According to Cadet Sharp, "Major Dorman asked the witness...if she was engaged to be married to Bruce. Bruce was infuriated & jumped over the rail among the lawyers & the cadets backed him up, so that question was never answered."[279]

Christian's case was also helped, much to the chagrin of Blackburn's friends and family, by the testimony of the chief prosecutor's son, Christian's law school classmate, Andy Moore.

In a letter written just a few days after the close of the hearing, Magdalene Reid, Samuel McDowell Moore's aunt and the wife of Lexington's Andrew Reid described the difficulty.

> To every right-minded person there is not one mitigating circumstance, yet strange to tell he [Christian] has a number of friends, I am told, your friend Andrew Moore the foremost among them. He [Moore] advised him to see Blackburn and if he would not apologize, to take satisfaction in the way he did. This he told as a witness.[280]

Andrew Moore's declaration apparently followed testimony from several other members of Judge Brockenbrough's law school, called by the prosecution to testify about premeditation.

Magdalene Reid wrote, "Several of the law students heard him [Christian] say he was going to attack Blackburn but they thought him too much of a coward to go through with it." Reid, however, was not convinced. From her perspective, "a coward was the very one to do such an act."[281]

Despite the best efforts of young Dorman, Christian was indicted.

The Lexington *Valley Star* summed up the outcome by imposing a long sentence of its own:

> After a tedious examination and cross-examination of four days, the counsel submitted the case to the judgment of the Court without argument, and the Court being unanimously of [the] opinion that he [Christian] should be sent on for further trial, he was remanded to jail, there to await his final trial before the Circuit Court of this county, on the 12th day of April next, when he will be punished according to his crime, or acquitted.[282]

Major Thomas Jonathan Jackson was more direct. In a letter to his uncle, Alfred Neale, written on January 28, 1854, he wrote, "We have in this little town been much shocked by the murder of a cadet last month. The call court has sent the murderer on to further trial, which will take place next April."[283]

CERTAINTIES AND DOUBTS

F or many in Lexington, Christian's preliminary hearing was all the trial they needed to convict him of murder.

On the third day of the four-day marathon, VMI professor Daniel Harvey Hill wrote to his sister-in-law, Mary Anna Morrison,[284] about "the great state of excitement in our quiet little village" brought about by "a most atrocious murder." Christian, he wrote, was "a vulgar law student," a "ruffian," a "coward" and "assassin."

Though Hill still believed "a reliable Negro was the only person who witnessed the whole of the affray," he found Christian's defense laughable or worse, noting that it rested "upon the alleged fact that the dog told B. that he would meet him again and that he meant that as an instruction to B. to arm himself."

If Christian was trying to create the impression that he had invited Blackburn to "a fair fight," Hill wrote, it was a "flimsy" defense at best, given that Blackburn "was totally unarmed and that he went to church with a lady." The lady, Hill noted, "was almost in a state of derangement for several days" and Mary Evelyn Anderson, he wrote, "must have felt still worse."

"So much," he concluded, "for Sunday gallantry."[285]

On January 29, 1854, Philip St. George Cocke responded in writing to press accounts and letters from his son, John Bowdoin Cocke, at one time Tom Blackburn's roommate at VMI.[286] The senior Cocke was a West Pointer and a prominent, well-published agriculturist, the son of one of the founders and builders of the University of Virginia. He knew well Christian's

Richmond nemesis, the Reverend Robert Ryland, having served with him in the Virginia Society for the Promotion of Temperance and the American Colonization Society.[287]

Cocke also hated dueling. In his view, the "attack upon Cadet Blackburn appears to have been premeditated and with murderous intention." As for Christian's contention that he had thought to make the fight against Blackburn "a fair one," Cocke wrote, "an unarmed man was attacked by one armed with deadly weapons to the teeth—and a foul assassination was committed in violation of the laws of God, of man, & of any honorable sentiment."

Cocke was also worried about the effect of the "murder" on his

Philip St. George Cocke (1809–1861) father of VMI Cadet John Bowdoin Cocke, Class of 1856. *VMI Archives.*

son's grades and demerit count. He pointedly warned young John against pre-judging the case "upon mere hearsay" testimony and "before the decision of the rightful legal tribunal."

"I can well imagine though how deeply hurt you and the Corps must have been by this tragical affair," he wrote, "but let me caution you to take no part in any movement on the part of the Jury now tending towards retaliation."

Cocke had also heard the rumors of a possible lynching. "I was," he wrote, "sorry to see that the Cadets and other persons had in the excitement of the moment assembled about the prisoner soon after his capture and threatened to rescue him from the civil officers & to perpetrate some outrage upon his person."

"It is only the ignorant, the low & the animal masses of the North that seek to take the law into their own hands upon any popular excitement," he reminded his son. "As young Virginians! As Southern Young Gentlemen! The Corp of Cadets should react appropriately to this foul assassination of one of your number and leave to the laws of the land to vindicate the outrage upon society & humanity."

Cocke also encouraged his son to try to calm any ill feelings his fellow cadets might feel toward those who supported Christian, and toward

Christian's fellow law students in particular. Do not, he wrote, "join yourself
to any club or other association hostile to the law students."

> *The young men may <u>individually</u> condemn the acts of their fellow students
> and as decidedly as one of your Corps. Yet if they perceive hostile feeling
> on the part of the Corps towards themselves as a body they will naturally
> repel that hostility, and more mischief may arise. Besides, it is unjust to
> visit upon a class of young men the crime of a single one of their number.*[288]

For all their certainty about Christian's guilt, Blackburn's supporters were
nevertheless worried by the legal talent represented on Christian's rapidly
expanding defense team, not to mention their unseemly and aggressive
tactics. Some believed Christian was pleased, if not delighted, with the
outcome of the preliminary hearing. According to Mary Evelyn Anderson's
cousin Magdalene Reid,

> *Mr. Barclay...said he observed Christian, when he was told he would
> have to go to prison & stay until April for trial—that anyone would have
> supposed he was cleared he laughed and talked so cheerfully. He never has
> seemed to think he has done wrong but that it was quite a chivalrous thing
> & has not even pretended derangement.*[289]

Another chronicler noted, "Judge Brockenbrough and his law class did
everything to save Christian."[290]

Brockenbrough had clearly played a key role in bringing the brilliant
young James Baldwin Dorman onto the defense team, and he was believed
to be recruiting a number of other prominent lawyers to help with the
forthcoming murder trial. Libel suits were already being filed against
some of those who had spoken out against Christian in the days since
Blackburn's death.

Many of Christian's heretofore less-than-supportive fellow law students
were now providing advice, counsel and, most important, supportive
courtroom testimony. The thrill of the contest itself, a real murder trial
involving one of their own, no doubt played some role. Guilt for their lack
of earlier support may well have played another.

Many of Judge Brockenbrough's law students were reported to be
singularly distressed, "thinking," according to Magdalene Reid, "they had
made the creature do the dreadful deed by their teasing and nagging." First
among them, Reid thought, had to be young Andrew Moore. Apparently

wracked by guilt about his role in the affair and by the distress he was causing his own family, he had taken to the bottle. As early as February 2, 1854, Reid confided to a friend:

> *Andrew Moore is drinking very hard and although he is a member of the Temperance Society he never has been reformed, you know this better than I can tell you, for you spent too much time with him not to know it. He was offended with his Uncle Sam and Evalina & vented his spite in this way—he has truly succeeded in afflicting them.*[291]

As Andy Moore began to drink, Anderson found herself increasingly under attack for her role in precipitating the tragedy. Her uncle, William Neeley Anderson, described some of it in a note to Samuel McDowell Moore.

> *I wrote to Mr. [David Evans] Moore on the subject of the murder in Lexington, in which letter I stated the lady [who set off the affair] was censured here for conveying to Mr. Christian the information she new [sic] from Mr. Blackburn. Since courent [sic] statements have reached hear [sic], the same jentlemen [sic] say they think it was necessary that the lady should have made the statement she did to Mr. Christian—it is therefour [sic] thought here by the first people the lady acted right.*[292]

The press, Anderson continued, had clearly blamed his niece for setting off the chain of events that killed her cousin. At first, he said, everyone believed the negative stories about her were true. Now, Anderson continued, "everyone who counted" wanted Mary Evelyn's family to know they'd changed their minds.

> *Mr. McElhany, Mr. Withers, and several other jentlemen [sic] who thought from the first rumor the lady whose name was associated with the affair had done wrong—have since talked the whole matter over with me, and from the last statement rec'd hear [sic] they not only applaud the noble & manly conduct of Blackburn, but also compliment the course persued [sic] by the lady as being necessary & proper.*[293]

As soon as the hearings ended, Mary Evelyn's father took his embarrassed and now apparently ill daughter back to Fincastle. As a lawyer, Francis Thomas Anderson surely knew that worse was still to come, and whatever that might be, it would not be good for Mary Evelyn or for the reputation of Tom Blackburn.

Giles Gunn, a Connecticut Yankee teaching school in Lexington, was by this time absolutely certain that Charles Christian would go free. On February 1, 1854, he wrote to his sister, Molly:

> *Two weeks last Sunday was noted in Lexington for a tragedy...It seems that a young man by the name of Christian had engaged the company of a young lady to go to preaching. She was advised not to go with him by a cousin of hers, a cadet at the Virginian Military Institute. Christian (who was a law student) found out who it was and prepared himself with weapons and on Sunday night waited till he saw Blackburn, the cadet, come into the church with a lady, then he stepped up and touched him, requesting to say a word to him. He took him out into the street and by his vale demanded of him to retract what he had said. Upon Blackburn's refusing so to do he let in on him and before any one could interfere had stabbed him in several places and cut his throat from ear to ear with a bowie knife and killed him so dead that he never kicked. Christian then went and delivered himself up to the authorities and it* [is] *now the general opinion that he will get clear as the provocation was so great. You see how nice a sense of honor the southerners have. In law here if one man calls another a liar and he beats him almost to death for it, the law does nothing with him for it is considered sufficient provocation.*[294]

VMI superintendent Francis Henney Smith was also concerned about changing public perceptions of both Charles Christian and Tom Blackburn. Smith found Judge John White Brockenbrough's involvement in these changes particularly distressing. Brockenbrough had been a friend. From 1843 to 1846, he had served on the VMI Board of Visitors. In 1844, he had successfully defended Smith after a Grand Jury indicted him for "selling goods without a license" from a new, VMI-run "Military Store."[295]

Now, it seemed, Smith's erstwhile friend and defender was not only amassing an army of lawyers, but he was also planning to attack the honor, motives and character of Tom Blackburn.

Smith told his Board of Visitors it was, of course, in the best interests of justice for Christian to be tried fairly but warned "that several of the ablest criminal lawyers of the state had been retained by the prisoner and that he would receive the...counsel of his instructor, Judge Brockenbrough."[296]

Blackburn's family shared Smith's concerns. Blackburn's father had already asked Dr. Robert Glasgow, a first cousin by marriage, to attend the preliminary hearings to protect the interests of the family. Glasgow was shocked at Brockenbrough's tactics, telling Smith that an attack on the good name of Blackburn was, by extension, an attack on the good name of the Virginia Military Institute.[297]

In response to Glasgow's pleas on behalf of Blackburn's father, Colonel Smith again sought in earnest the help of the highly competent, though terribly expensive, Thomas Johnson Michie.

THE RETURN OF CAPTAIN MOORE

C aptain David Evans Moore, Commonwealth's attorney for Rockbridge County, had been, the local press noted, "absent from Lexington" during two key hearings: the coroner's inquest and the "examination before the committing magistrate" that followed.

Moore called on Colonel Smith "as soon as he returned" to Lexington and, at some point between January 29 and February 6, "expressed great gratification" that Dr. Glasgow, on behalf of the Blackburns, had "instructed" Colonel Smith to hire Thomas Michie. No doubt fearing that he might be compelled to recuse himself, Moore told Smith he considered it "a matter of great importance that Mr. Michie should appear in the case!"[298]

Colonel Smith and Captain Moore had both feared that Michie might refuse to serve rather than embarrass Captain Moore. To preempt any such "motives of delicacy," Moore dashed off a note to Michie personally requesting his help. Smith, in the meantime, wrote to the VMI Board of Visitors and to Tom Blackburn's father, explaining his decision.[299]

Smith and Moore were correct about Michie's "delicacy." Before Smith heard from either Blackburn's father or the VMI Board of Visitors, Michie had written "stating the embarrassment which [Colonel Smith's] application to him had produced, and the terms upon which alone he was willing to engage in the case."

An absolute deal-breaker for Michie was having to work with William Henry Terrill, who had appeared in Captain Moore's place at both the coroner's inquest and the four-day preliminary hearing.[300] Michie had heard

The David Evans Moore House, Lexington. *Library of Virginia.*

that Terrill had been engaged in double-dipping: serving as both acting Commonwealth's attorney and as counsel for several witnesses Christian had already sued for slander. Appalled, Michie told Smith that under such circumstances, "all the gold of Australia and California would not have purchased my service in the prosecution."[301]

With Captain Moore back in Lexington, the Terrill matter was, of course, moot.

As for the gold of Australia, Moore and Colonel Smith assured Michie that, somehow, his $500 fees would be paid. Smith, for his part, assumed personal responsibility for retaining Michie. "I had to take the responsibility myself," he later testified, "and employ Mr. Michie, as the Superintendent of the Institute, partly at the expense of Dr. Blackburn, and partly at the expense of the Institute."[302]

The motives of all concerned were the highest, he steadfastly maintained. "The friends of young Blackburn wanted only to protect the character of the deceased, and as the representative of the Institute he only wanted to see justice done and the laws enforced."[303]

Christian's supporters, naturally, had an entirely different view of the Colonel's actions and Smith was soon "attacked on the grounds that he had used public funds" to retain private counsel to help "prosecute" Christian.[304]

Smith considered such allegations slanderous. In his report to the VMI Board of Visitors he wrote:

> *Believing...that the Institute to whose care Cadet Blackburn had been committed by his father, and in which he was rendering a service and duty to the state as a member of the "public guard" to the State Arsenal, I was in duty bound to protect the honor and character of its pupil and to protect*

*and guard the honor, character and lives of the cadets—and further, that as
a public officer, bound to use all legal means to maintain the public peace
and to encourage and train the pupils committed to my charge in correct
sentiments of duty towards the law of the land as administered by our
courts of justice, I deemed it proper...to say to [Michie] that...I desired
him to see that the reputation and character of the cadets were cared for, by a
fair and proper trial, that the confidence might be thereby strengthened in the
issue of the trial, whatever that issue might be...I never conceived that I was
authorized to pay Mr. Michie one dollar from the funds of the institute or
from the deposits of the cadets, or to pledge or in any manner to involve these
funds for any services thus rendered by Mr. Michie. I also firmly refused to
permit any cadet to contribute to such an object.*[305]

Smith made it clear that, "It is for the Board of Visitors...to decide whether
any, and if any, what part of the funds of the Institute, or of the deposits of
the cadets, shall be applied to this object. If they decide against assuming
any portion of the expense the friends of Cadet Blackburn will pay it all."[306]
As for the Commonwealth's prosecution of Christian, Colonel Smith
noted that some felt the governor of Virginia should be encouraged to
appoint "other counsel" to assist.

*In a conversation with [former] Gov'r Frank Thomas of Md., who left here
last night, he suggested what I have no doubt has occurred to you, that if Mr.
Moore should feel scruples as to acting as prosecutor for the Commonwealth,
the Gov'r will appoint a substitute for him. I rather hope this may be soon.*[307]

This idea appears to have foundered quickly once it was pointed out
that the governor of Virginia lacked the legal authority to make such an
appointment and, in any case, would be ill advised to exercise it.[308]
Tom Blackburn's Uncle Frank had some ideas of his own about who
was really supporting Christian. At Blackburn's funeral, he told George
Washington Turner that he was convinced that "the Felon's conduct must
have been planned & advised by an older & cooler head than his own."
Thomas also believed, Taylor said, "that the employment of three young
lawyers in addition to Stuart & Mosby, who can not possibly need this...
clearly indicates a purpose to resort to unfair means to enlist advocates of a
bad cause." If the goal of this "cabal" was "to put the blame of the horrible
transaction in the wrong quarter, & to defeat the ends of Law & Order &
Justice," Thomas declared, "it will be most signally disappointed."[309]

The Ryland Scandal

On February 8, 1854, Dr. Blackburn wrote to Colonel Smith that he had heard that Christian's defense team intended "to prove the previous good character of the felon now awaiting his trial."

Tom Blackburn's father had some rather different notions about the character of Charles Burks Christian and, he said, evidence about it important and reliable enough to pass along to the Commonwealth's attorney.

In Charles Town, he wrote, he had met a Baptist minister, the Reverend Robert Ryland, president of Richmond College, who should definitely be called as a witness. According to Ryland, Christian had been "expelled from 'Baptist College'" after threatening his life "with pistols and other weapons."[310]

Ryland was arguably one of the most celebrated members of nineteenth-century Virginia's Baptist clergy and well known even to the devout Episcopalian Francis Henney Smith.[311] The son of Josiah and Catharine Ryland of "Farmington" in King and Queen County, he had elected to give up the farm that was to be his inheritance and instead "have his portion in money so that he might seek an education." After earning two degrees from Columbian College in Washington, Ryland had been ordained.

Ryland's first pastorate was in Lynchburg, where he served from 1827 to 1832, while Charles Christian's parents were setting up housekeeping just across the James River in Amherst County.[312] He left Lynchburg in mid-1832 to become the first president of the Virginia Baptist Seminary in Richmond. When it opened on July 4 of that year he was also its only teacher.

Three years later, the year Charles Burks Christian was born, Ryland had moved to Charlottesville, serving as chaplain of the University of Virginia, the first Baptist ever to hold that position.[313] By 1840, Ryland's Baptist Seminary received a new charter as Richmond College. Ryland became its first president and stayed on the job until 1866.[314]

At first blush, Blackburn's father could not have asked for a more credible witness to the disreputable character of Charles Burks Christian. Unfortunately, Ryland had problems of his own, especially among some of the "best people" of Richmond.

Reverend Robert Ryland (1805–1899). President of Richmond College (the "Baptist College"). *Courtesy of the Virginia Baptist Historical Society.*

Virginia law, at the time, forbade the training and ordination of "Negro pastors." Nat Turner's Rebellion in the 1830s had "led to the enactment of stringent laws in regard to the assembling of Negroes for religious worship or any other purpose…in any numbers…except in the presence and under the supervision of white persons."[315]

Ryland's response was "to put forth new efforts to evangelize the people of color," a duty he believed applied not only to himself, but also to all white clergymen.[316] Thus, from 1841 until 1866, Ryland served as the pastor of Richmond's First African Church, where he personally baptized some 3,832 members.[317] By 1854, First African Baptist was well on its way to tripling in size. For Ryland, as for Major Thomas Jackson, who ran Sunday school classes for free blacks and slaves in Lexington, such work was "a solace to his soul."

As for slavery, Ryland later wrote that it "had long been a burden" to his mind, and he saw his service as pastor of First African Baptist as a chance "to elevate an unfortunate race, and thus to mitigate, in some degree, their servitude."[318] Such attitudes were not calculated to endear Reverend Ryland to either key elements of Richmond society or to some of their country counterparts west of the Blue Ridge.

In 1852, Ryland's convictions had also led him to engage in what many thought was provocative, inappropriate and scandalous behavior on behalf of a black parishioner just a year after Lexington had armed itself in fear of a rumored slave rebellion.

Richmond in early 1852 had been "terrified by a series of murders of white children by their Negro nurses." In one such case, Jane Williams, a slave was accused of murdering her mistress and her infant child while they slept. Williams was quickly arrested, tried, convicted and sentenced to death on the public gallows. Jane Williams was also a member Robert Ryland's First African Baptist Church.[319]

The Williams hanging reportedly attracted a crowd of some six thousand people, mostly white and mostly angry. Ryland rode into that crowd with Williams, standing beside her in the wagon that carried her across Richmond. At the gallows, Ryland implored the crowd gathered to watch her die, "to have mercy for a fellow creature, sinful though she might be," and then offered up "a fervent prayer for her immortal soul." According to one Richmond newspaper, "Never before did religious ceremonies fall upon more unwilling ears."[320]

Whether or not Christian's threats against Ryland were related to his ties to the black communities in Richmond is unknown. Whatever the case, neither Ryland, nor the story of Christian's threats against him, nor the story of Christian's expulsion from Richmond College, were ever introduced into evidence.

Nor was Ryland's story the only evidence that was reportedly "suppressed." Dr. Blackburn told Smith he had written to "Mr. Humes" about Christian's connections to a mysterious "tragedy in Amherst" that never appeared in court. Dr. Blackburn also reported Mary Evelyn Anderson's father had been sent materials indicating that other important witnesses were either being deliberately ignored or hustled out of town by Christian's defense team.[321]

MISSING WITNESSES, MULTIPLE LAWYERS

On February 8, 1854, Mary Evelyn Anderson's uncle in Lewisburg, William Neeley Anderson, closed a long letter to her father with a strange tale about another "missing witness."

> *There was a man came through this place a few days since from Lexington, by the name of Haff—I did not see him myself, but Mr. Frazer told me he had conversation with him—he told Mr. Frazer he was a segar-maker—that he was on his way to the west—that his evidence might be had in the final trial of Christian.*
>
> *Said he saw the fight, and that Blackburn was standing when he rec'd the fatal stab, when he saw him fall dead—that he pursued him (Christian) to his room. For certain reasons I suspect this man may have been induced to get out of the way, to make it appear the murder was done in self defense, and therefore I have mailed you this communication.* [322]

"Mr. Frazer" was, no doubt, one of the Frazers who had run the Star Tavern and ordinary in Lewisburg since 1830. Their guests were typiclly judges and lawyers attending sessions of the Greenbrier County Court, the Virginia Supreme Court of Appeals and other judicial bodies regularly convened in Lewisburg for the convenience of Virginians on the "far side" of the mountains. So important was this clientele that in 1834 the senior Frazer built a library near the Tavern, which he rented for use as a study by the judges and clerks of the Supreme Court.

"Haff" was clearly Henry Hanff, the "segar-maker" who testified in Lexington at the January 16 inquest. Hanff testified he had stumbled onto the fight at the very beginning, while Christian and Blackburn were "exchanging blows" and before they wrestled each other to the ground. He claimed to have been there before Massie arrived and was, he said, close enough to hear the sound of Christian stabbing Blackburn. "The last blow I heard," he said, while both boys were still standing, was "like a knife went into a bladder." Hanff had helped carry the mortally wounded Blackburn to White's cellar door and was one of the last people to see him alive.[323]

W.N. Anderson believed Hanff's testimony critical to proving Christian had not killed Tom Blackburn in self-defense. Two other eyewitnesses who might have supported Hanff would also never testify: the terrified "tall gentleman in citizen's clothes" described by Massie,[324] and the mysterious "reliable negro" described by D.H. Hill as "the only person who witnessed the whole of the affray."[325]

Missing witnesses, however, were not the only things worrying Anderson. He feared that too many people were saying things that ultimately (and sometimes unintentionally) redounded to Christian's benefit.

Anderson himself was desperately trying to atone for awkwardly phrased remarks in a January 25 letter that implied Mary Evelyn Anderson's behavior in the affair was not above reproach.

On February 8, in an attempt to re-ingratiate himself, he delivered even more damning criticism of Evalina Moore:

> *One word more about the murder—Is it not to be regretted that Mary's Aunt (under whose charge she was placed) had not let her return Christian his letter, as (we have been told) he requested it in his last note to her that he might not be sported with—Mary E, I have frequently heard, is blamed by no one, from any quarter.*[326]

Anderson's criticism of Aunt Evalina, of course, did nothing more than further expose a major and ongoing problem with the prosecution's case: There were many people who could be assigned a role in causing the death of Tom Blackburn and one of them was Blackburn himself.

Indeed, it already seemed clear that a key element of Christian's defense would be an attack on the character of Tom Blackburn. Worse, the attack would be delivered by a large and well-trained team of lawyers.

On March 2, 1854, Dr. Richard Scott Blackburn's half brother, Charles Sinclair Taylor, expressed his concerns to Colonel Smith. Taylor

The William Neeley Anderson House, near Lewisburg, Virginia (now West Virginia). *National Register of Historic Places.*

had just finished reading notes taken by Thomas Johnson Michie at Christian's preliminary hearing sent to him by Hugh Nelson Pendleton, the brother of Colonel Smith's favorite episcopal priest, the Reverend William Nelson Pendleton.[327]

Pendleton strongly believed the Commonwealth needed help, especially in view of the increasing number of lawyers joining Christian's defense team. Pendleton and Taylor also knew that Tom Blackburn's father could not afford to pay the $500 or more Thomas Michie was demanding. Pendleton had thus asked Taylor to at least brief himself and attend the trial in support of the family. Despite Colonel Smith's assurances that Captain David Evans Moore could handle the prosecution alone, Taylor agreed with Pendleton and offered his help.

"The object in employing counsel at all upon the part of the friends of poor Thos. is to protect his reputation," Taylor wrote. "The fate of Christian is of comparatively little moment. The hearts that he has torn by his diabolical act cannot be healed by a forfeiture of his miserable life."

Taylor promised to be at the trial on behalf of the family and asked Colonel Smith to "let him know if he changed his mind" about the need for extra help "caused by increased counsel on the prisoner's part."[328]

The trial would start on Thursday, April 13.

Part VIII

THE TRIAL IN LEXINGTON: WITNESSES TESTIFY

PRELUDE AND DAY ONE:

INDICTMENT, JURY AND FIRST WITNESSES

Wednesday and Thursday, April 13–14, 1854[329]

O n Wednesday, April 12, 1854, crowds began to gather at the Rockbridge County Courthouse, a block north of White's Corner and the Lexington Presbyterian Church. Early in the afternoon, Judge Lucas Powell Thompson gaveled to order a grand jury of the Superior Court of Rockbridge County. Its task: to consider the evidence against Charles Burks Christian for the murder of Virginia Military Institute Cadet Thomas Blackburn.[330]

Judge Thompson was a distinguished jurist. He had been a circuit court judge since 1831, and his home and law school in Staunton, "Hill Top," was already a landmark.[331] By all accounts, he ran his courtroom with great efficiency.

On April 12, Thompson's grand jury "examined a number of witnesses," quickly brought in a "true bill" of indictment and, "after some civil business had been disposed of," adjourned for the day. Thompson scheduled Christian's trial to begin the very next day.

THE LAWYERS

When Judge Thompson opened proceedings at 10:00 a.m. on Thursday, April 13, he found his Lexington courtroom crowded, with an unusually large number of women present.[332]

VMI was also present in force. The cadets did "not attend class recitations during the trial," according to John Howard Sharp, a fact not surprising given the "mutiny" of the Corps in 1851 over their right to hear Thomas Johnson Michie argue a case of significantly less importance.[333]

Captain David Evans Moore represented the Commonwealth of Virginia, assisted (with Moore's thanks and approval) by Thomas Johnson Michie. William Henry Terrill, at Michie's insistence, was no longer part of the prosecution team.

Christian's defense team was both large and talented. No fewer than six lawyers stood with Christian and behind them, in spirit if not physically, stood the reputation and resources of both Judge John White Brockenbrough and his law school.

Over the next two weeks, seven days of grueling testimony and four more of lengthy summation, the six would do their best to deploy legal skills, a keen sense of the prejudices and predispositions of their countrymen and their considerable rhetorical talent to save Charles Christian's life.

Young James Baldwin Dorman, thirty-one, remained with the defense team, despite (or maybe because of) having caused a near riot at the preliminary hearings in January.

With Dorman stood the Honorable Alexander Hugh Holmes Stuart, who had just returned to the valley after serving four years as Millard Fillmore's secretary of the interior. A son of one of Virginia's leading families, the forty-seven-year-old Stuart was one of the best-known lawyers in Virginia. His father, Archibald Stuart Sr., had been a close friend of Thomas Jefferson, and Jefferson himself was said to have designed Stuart's red brick house on Church Street in Staunton. A.H.H. Stuart's brother, "Arch," was the father of a West Point cadet, James Ewell Brown Stewart, class of 1854.[334]

A.H.H. Stuart was a first-rate politician and a formidable stump speaker. In the U.S. Congressional elections of 1840, he had defeated Lexington's James McDowell "in a memorable speaking campaign." (For McDowell, the loss led to his appointment as governor of Virginia by the legislature.) In 1854, Stuart was still considered one of the fast-fading Whig party's last best hopes for the governorship of Virginia.[335]

The third member of the defense team, and a formidable courtroom presence, was Charles Lewis Mosby. Mosby was from Lynchburg and presumably well acquainted with the Christian and Burks families. He was a second cousin to John Singleton Mosby, who had just been pardoned for shooting a fellow student at the University of Virginia under circumstances remarkably similar to the Christian case. Mosby's brother William Washington Mosby was a good friend of Colonel Smith and would later play a key role in healing the rift that grew between Smith and Judge Brockenbrough as the trial progressed. Though only forty-seven years old, Mosby was not in good health.[336]

Christian's fourth defender, Lexington native Samuel Houston Letcher, twenty-six, had been in Christian's room when he was arrested and had advised Christian on the spot to flee if he were guilty. Letcher's brother John was a rising star in the Democratic Party. "Honest John" Letcher, a U.S. congressman at the time of the trial, would later serve as one of Virginia's wartime governors.[337]

The fifth and youngest member of Christian's team, Robert Lewis Doyle, thirty, was also from Staunton and had studied at Washington College. A respected lawyer and a man of great physical courage, he would be wounded, captured, bayonetted and shot dead, in that order, in June 1864.[338]

Sixth on the team was John Douglas Sterret, thirty-one, the son of Robert Douglas Sterret, an Ulster Scot who had emigrated from Ireland to Virginia with his father's family.[339]

Behind them all stood Judge John White Brockenbrough and the vast majority of Brockenbrough's law students.

JURY SELECTION AND PLEA

Before the trial could begin, a jury had to be selected from a pool of at least twenty-four "competent jurors": white, male free-holders who were residents of Rockbridge County. At the time, there were approximately 5,800 free white males in Rockbridge County, of which nearly 2,250 were under the age of twenty. Of the remaining adult men, 110 could neither read nor write. In Lexington proper, there were just over 1,100 residents, of which 650 were white males of all ages.[340]

The prominence of the families of the principals in the tragedy, the sheer prurient interest aroused by the case, local gossip, unofficial tours of the crime scene led by key witnesses and widespread press coverage made finding an unbiased jury a particularly difficult task. Happily for Judge Thompson, most of the adult white population of Rockbridge County, male and female, appears to have been present at the courthouse in Lexington for the beginning of the trial.

By "resorting to 'bystanders' for nine of the twenty-four competent jurors," Judge Thompson was able to "promptly" impanel his jury. The Richmond *Dispatch* special correspondent reported that someone in the crowd remarked that "there never was a more upright jury empanelled in a case of the kind in the county."

The same correspondent also recorded the names of all twelve jurors:[341]

1. William L. Ayres, age thirty-four, a Rockbridge farmer and father of three.
2. James Franklin Bell, thirty, who farmed roughly 350 acres near Goshen.
3. Bell's older brother, Joseph George Washington Bell, forty-one. The Bell family was well respected in the valley. Both jurors were sons of Captain Joseph Bell of Rockbridge County and the grandsons of Joseph Bell, senior, scion of the "Stone Church Bells" of the Fort Defiance area of Augusta County, not far from Staunton.
4. John R. Brown, around twenty years old. He had just married Sarah Ann Terrill, a fourth cousin of William Henry Terrill, the lawyer who had stood in for Commonwealth's Attorney David Moore in January.
5. Alfred Douglass was born in Bedford County around 1807. He later moved to the Buffalo Forge area of Rockbridge County near the Anderson family iron furnaces at Glasgow.
6. James F. Hamilton, age thirty-one, was a member of Oxford Presbyterian Church. His mother, Sarah Letcher Hamilton, was the sister of William Houston Letcher. James was thus a first cousin to Samuel Houston Letcher, one of Christian's primary defense lawyers.
7. Joseph Walker Kelso, thirty-nine, lived near Walker's Creek, at Kelso Gap, almost due north of Lexington. His father (also named Joseph Walker) was eighty years old.
8. Moses J. Ludwick, thirty-eight, was a farmer born in Shenandoah County.
9. Zachariah Johnston McChesney, fifty-eight, was the son of Robert McChesney, a Presbyterian immigrant from County Armagh, Ireland.
10. John A. Reynolds, the son of William and Sarah Armentrout Reynolds, appears to have been only seventeen in 1854. He and his family were members of Oxford Presbyterian Church.
11. William Walker Stuart was born near the Kelso home place on Walker's Creek. A distant relative of defense attorney Alexander H.H. Stuart, William lived all his life in the house in which he was born, a colonial-era fort built out of walnut logs. He was thirty-three.
12. David Henry Whitmore was the son of Peter and Mary Whitmore of the Walker's Creek area and, later, Steele's Tavern in Augusta County. He would have been twenty-nine years old at the time of the trial.

With those twelve men duly sworn, "the prisoner was put to the bar."

Ironically, the first words that Brockenbrough law student Charles Burks Christian ever spoke in a court appears to have been his reply to Judge Lucas Powell Thompson's curt query: "Guilty or not guilty?"[342]

Given the six distinguished lawyers defending him, Christian's reply was not surprising. Standing in the crowded courtroom with "an air of seriousness, without apparent agitation," Christian replied, "Not guilty."

Those two words would be the last he would utter under oath in Rockbridge County Circuit Court.

DAY ONE: A MORNING OF OVERCONFIDENCE

After Christian's not-guilty plea, the Honorable David E. Moore, captain of militia and Commonwealth's attorney for Rockbridge County, moved promptly to make the prosecution's first major error of the trial. Whether out of overconfidence or for dramatic effect, Moore made no opening statement to the jury whatsoever. Instead, he immediately called his first and, arguably, most important witness, James Woods Massie.[343]

Massie, who had been leading unofficial guided tours of the crime scene in the days before the trial, described at length what he had seen and heard on the evening of January 15, from the first sounds of the scuffle to his January 16 re-examination of the ground.

At Captain Moore's prompting, Massie immediately made several remarks that would later redound to Christian's benefit, including comment about Christian's voluntary surrender to the authorities and his claim that he "could not help it."

Massie, though a prosecution witness, was also led to make the case that Blackburn was taller and stronger than Christian. "Blackburn was the largest, being 5 feet 11," Massie swore, "and Christian not more than 5 feet 9. The former weighed, he supposed, 160, the latter 140. The former was the strongest, though not a great deal stronger. Blackburn was larger and fatter, but did no[t] seem to have as much action as Christian. He seemed to be physically softer."[344]

Charles Lewis Mosby cross-examined Massie "at much length" for the defense.

Referring to the sounds of the "lash" Massie said he had heard just after the first noises of the scuffle, Mosby asked if "they might not have been made by a stick used rapidly in parrying off an attack by a person advancing?" Or, he asked, "could not the sounds be produced by a stick against the cadet's buttons?"

Massie had to concede that it was possible, that a stick had been found near the scene of the crime and that he really didn't know if a cowhide or lash had been found.

Mosby also led Massie to re-state his belief that Blackburn had been on top of Christian while the two wrestled on the ground.

Finally, and most damaging to the Commonwealth's case, Massie admitted he had not seen any blows struck after the two men stood up. His back had been turned at precisely that critical moment in the fight.[345]

Inexplicably, on redirect, Captain Moore insisted that Massie reaffirm his conviction in something the prosecution's own exhibits would later bring into question. "As to the sounds," Massie testified once more, "they were as a whip or cowhide—a stick striking such a blow could not have made such sounds—and they were too rapid for a stick."

The prosecution, of course, was in possession of the hickory stick that Christian had borrowed for the occasion, after complaining that his own heavy silver-headed cane had been taken by VMI cadets conspiring against him.

After Moore finished with Massie, Judge Thompson called a recess for dinner.

DAY ONE: THE AFTERNOON

After the midday meal, Captain Moore called two witnesses to support Massie's opening testimony. Both claimed to have seen at least part of the fight and Christian's flight from the scene.

The Commonwealth's second witness was twenty-one-year-old Benton Taylor, a member of the Washington College class of 1853–54 who would later study law under Judge Brockenbrough. Taylor confirmed Massie's account of the fight, testified that he knew Blackburn well and recognized him immediately.

Taylor himself would have been recognized immediately by many in the courtroom as the brother of Robert J. Taylor, the man Tom Blackburn's uncle Frank Thomas had accused of having an incestuous relationship with Sally Campbell Preston McDowell and fathering the child he believed she had aborted.[346]

Seventeen-year-old James Lindsay Kirkpatrick testified he was crossing the street, walking north from the Presbyterian Church to White's Corner, when he heard "a noise as of some one striking another with a stick or switch." He recognized Christian as he fled, passing between Kirkpatrick and two ladies waiting on the corner. James Massie, he said, told him someone had been murdered and sent him to fetch a doctor.

Moore next called a small platoon of physicians: Patrick H. Christian, the first doctor to reach Blackburn's side; James R. Jordan, who presided over the postmortem; and doctors Henry Gamble Davidson, Henry Miller Estill, John Welch Paine, Archibald Graham and Robert Marshall. All had examined Blackburn's body. All confirmed that Blackburn had been stabbed several times: once in his back under his right shoulder blade, once in the head and once in the neck, a wound that severed his carotid artery.

Cross-examination by the defense was both careful and clever. Under questioning by Charles Lewis Mosby, Dr. Christian swore that he believed Blackburn's wounds "were inflicted when the parties were down," an apparently minor point that would later prove critical to Christian's defense. "I cannot see how the [fatal] angular incision could have been made if the parties had <u>not</u> been down," Dr. Christian testified. He also said he believed "Blackburn could...have sprung upon his feet after receiving the fatal wound."

Under redirect questioning by Captain Moore, Dr. Christian re-asserted his belief that Blackburn could have risen from the ground after having his carotid cut, noting that he had personally treated someone who, after being stabbed in the heart, "walked from the street into his house, and conversed and lived for some time."

Dr. Christian was referring to recent events in Lexington. On March 29, 1854, William J. Winn (no relation to Christian's law school friend) had killed Colonel Joseph W. Moore in an "affray in the street in front of the Washington Hotel." Winn had stabbed Moore in the heart, and Moore, though mortally wounded, had ended the fight by "exclaiming 'that's enough.'" Colonel Moore then walked into his house, sat down for a few minutes, rose again and, while "trying to cross the room," reeled, fell and died. Doctors Christian, Jordan and Paine, in fact, had all testified, just five days earlier, on April 8, 1854, as witnesses in Winn's trial for the stabbing.[347]

Mosby next grilled Dr. James R. Jordan, deftly leading Jordan to admit that he had changed his mind about when Blackburn's fatal wounds had been inflicted. Then he coaxed Jordan into explaining how each of Blackburn's wounds could have been delivered by Christian while acting defensively. "I think it probable that Christian assailed, or to use a milder term, 'approached' Blackburn for satisfaction," Jordan mused under oath.

"Satisfaction," he speculated, was something Blackburn seemed determined "not to give and being unarmed, immediately seized and pressed his opponent to the ground."

With Christian's borrowed Bowie knife in hand, Dr. Jordan then walked the jury through the fight as he imagined it: "Christian, as soon as he could, drew his knife, struck Blackburn while his [right] arm was under Blackburn's left…inflicted the upward blow under the right shoulder blade…and then his arm becoming more free by a change of position, he struck downward the blow in the head, and finally inflicted the wound in the neck."

"My first impression," Jordan admitted, "was that the wound on Mr. Blackburn's neck was made while the parties were standing on their feet; I have [now] been induced from mature reflection to change my mind."

Under Mosby's careful questioning, Jordan then outlined the physical evidence that led him to his new, "mature" opinions: the amount of blood found at the point where Massie claimed he saw the two men struggling on the ground, the absence of blood at the hay scales where the fight supposedly started and the blood found *inside* Christian's coat sleeve, but not on his cuff.

The blood inside Christian's sleeve, according to Jordan, "could only have run down the sleeve while the arm of Christian was uplifted towards the face, or wound of Blackburn, as he lay upon him."

That view of the struggle was supported, Jordan said, by the mud on the back of Christian's "pantaloons," the absence of any mud on the front and by the position of a knife slash on the collar of Blackburn's uniform.

Captain Moore's redirect for the prosecution, once more, appeared to best serve Christian's defense. When Moore pointed out to Dr. Jordan how little mud there appeared to be on Christian's clothing, Jordan testified that when he had seen "Christian's clothes at the examining court; there was more mud on the back of the pants than now."

Moore also led Jordan to testify that Christian could have inflicted all of Blackburn's wounds while lying down. "A man in a hard place and pressed closely could have made them very rapidly—some men could make them more rapidly than others."

Things got no better for the prosecution when Dr. Henry Gamble Davidson took the stand. Under Mosby's crisp cross-examination, Davidson agreed completely with Dr. Christian's speculation about what had happened during the fight.

Dr. Henry Miller Estill, on the other hand, disagreed. In his opinion, both of Blackburn's serious wounds were probably inflicted while Blackburn and Christian were standing. If the wounds had been inflicted while the two struggled on the ground, Dr. Estill testified, it would have been impossible for Blackburn to stand up, "as from the serious nature of the injuries, almost instantaneous death would have followed."

Mosby countered by asking Estill if he believed that Blackburn's wounds were worse than a knife-wound to the heart. Estill replied he thought Blackburn's wound was more deadly but had to admit that, in light of the Winn/Moore case, he had been wrong in his beliefs about heart wounds.

Of the three remaining physicians called by the prosecution, two more, Doctors Payne and Marshall, were unshakable in their testimony that Blackburn could not have stood up after having his carotid artery cut.

With opinions evenly split, Doctor Graham came down on the side of Jordan, Davidson and Estill, insisting that, even though mortally wounded, Tom Blackburn could have regained his feet.

Mosby had thus succeeded in getting not only the prosecution's lead medical witness, but also a majority of all the medical witnesses, to testify that they agreed with the defense's view of the fight (namely, that Christian had stabbed Blackburn while he was lying on his back with Blackburn on top of him).

Captain Moore brought the State's presentation for the day to a close with testimony from two VMI cadets: Thomas Philip Mathews and Robert Martin McKinney. Both described the encounter between Christian and Blackburn in the Presbyterian Church vestibule.

Mosby's skillful cross-examination got the nineteen-year-old Mathews to admit he "did not recollect anything unusual in Christian's manner" at the time.

McKinney then testified, "There was some constraint in Christian's manner—he looked agitated and pale. He addressed Blackburn politely, but seriously." Indeed, McKinney swore, on the Saturday night before the killing, someone at his mess table had told him the difficulties between Blackburn and Christian "had all passed over."

After McKinney's final remarks, Judge Thompson recessed the court. It had been a better day for Charles Christian than anyone would have expected.

Having provided no opening statement outlining what he sought to prove, Captain Moore had been compelled to push and prod his own witnesses to conform to a story line of which both they and the jury were completely unaware.

Had he been faced with less daunting opponents, Moore (with Tom Michie's help) might have gotten away with it. But Mosby and company, no doubt with Judge Brockenbrough's aid and counsel, had no intention of letting him do so.

Things would not soon improve for Captain Moore, or for anyone else who believed in the prosecution's case.

DAY TWO: OF VICTIMS AND SCOUNDRELS

Friday, April 14, 1854[348]

THE MORNING

Captain Moore's first witness on Friday, April 14, 1854, was Julia Junkin, "a young and interesting person," according to the Richmond *Dispatch*, "who testified that Mr. Blackburn had accompanied her to the Presbyterian Church." No doubt because she had seen little or nothing pertinent to Christian's defense (or perhaps because of the emotional effect of her presence on Blackburn's arm the night he was killed), she was not cross-examined.

Moore then recalled Doctor Edward Graham, apparently to make the point that Graham had not seen Blackburn's wounds himself and had testified only as an expert witness. Unfortunately for Moore, his redirect examination gave Dr. Graham an opportunity to repeat his testimony in support of the defense's contention that Blackburn was stabbed while he was on top of Christian, as the two struggled in the road.

The prosecution next called Cadet George Baylor Horner of Warrenton, Blackburn's roommate in 1851 and one of his best friends. Horner's role was to testify about what he and Cadet Humes had seen and heard on Saturday, January 14, at the ill-fated "interview" at McDowell's Hotel. Moore also used Humes to introduce both Mary Evelyn Anderson's note declining Christian's invitation to church and Christian's oft-mocked epistle to Anderson.

Captain Moore's goal was clearly to establish, in Horner's words, that "the honor of both Blackburn and Christian required that Blackburn should make the communication to Christian that he did," and that "Blackburn could not have acquitted himself honorably by remaining in the dark, after he knew that his name had been demanded."

Putting the Christian/Anderson correspondence in evidence was, no doubt, painful for Captain Moore given the embarrassment it would cause the Moores, Mary Evelyn Anderson, her family and their friends. The Commonwealth's attorney apparently did so believing he had little or no choice.

Christian's lawyers, of course, had a very different view of the implications of Anderson's curt note to Christian, Christian's response and Tom Blackburn's personal intervention.

They were also both skillful and merciless in eliciting reinterpretations of the prosecution's evidence from the mouths of the prosecution's own witnesses. According to the Richmond *Dispatch* correspondent, Christian's defense team followed Moore's questioning of Horner with "a very tedious and searching cross-examination," so long and detailed that it would have made his newspaper account too long for publication had he reported it in full.

The reporter could not resist, however, relating highlights of Charles Lewis Mosby's skillful dissection of Horner's testimony.

Mosby asked Horner if he "did not anticipate a hostile meeting" between Blackburn and Christian when they met for their fateful "interview" on January 14.

Horner swore he had assumed "words of explanation would ensue and the matter end there."

Mosby was having none of it and led Horner to confess that he, Humes and Blackburn may well have been planning to harm Charles Burks Christian. If Christian had not backed down, Mosby asked, "Did you not conclude that it was prudent for Mr. Blackburn to have friends?"

Horner, according to the *Dispatch*, "preferred not to answer."

Mosby skillfully drove his point home by not pressing it.

Was it not Horner's intention "in leaving the Institute, to attend Blackburn in any emergency?" Mosby asked.

Horner admitted he believed, "as soon as Blackburn informed Christian that he was the calumniator, an altercation would ensue." He and Humes were there with Blackburn, he insisted, "to prevent injury to either."

Mosby, with ill-concealed irony, conceded that he had no doubt this was true. He then asked pointedly if the relationship between Horner and Blackburn was not "more intimate than between him and Christian?"

VMI Cadet George Baylor Horner (1834–1892), class of 1854 as a captain in the First Virginia. *VMI Archives.*

Horner, no doubt realizing that he would now be compelled to say that, if push came to shove, he would have come down on Blackburn's side, tried to escape by taking exception to Mosby's question.

When Judge Thompson instructed him to answer the question, Horner grudgingly "answered in the affirmative."

Mosby bored in. Didn't Horner testify before the examining court, in the preliminary hearings, that he had "informed Blackburn, on the way to Lexington, that Christian would fight" and, indeed, "that the only drawback to a fight between Christian and Blackburn...would be the difficulty of convincing Christian that he had been insulted?"

Trapped, Horner said yes.

Mosby continued the attack, asking how "the idea of Christian's courage [or lack of it] could be reconciled with that of the necessity of convincing him that he was insulted?" Was Christian's "intellect so obtuse as not to enable him to discern insults as other gentlemen?" Mosby asked.

Horner, finding himself in deeper and deeper trouble, again replied in the affirmative.

Mosby now read Horner the transcript of his earlier testimony. Before the "interview" at McDowell's Hotel, Horner had sworn, "I knew that if Christian resented the communication made by Blackburn, he, Blackburn, would strike him...I believe that Mr. Blackburn expected that Mr. Christian...would either strike him or challenge him...I believe that Blackburn came to Lexington with the expectation and purpose to put it to Christian...either to act the coward or the man of courage...from all that passed before we got to Lexington...I know that Mr. Blackburn came to Lexington with a hostile purpose."

Mosby read on. After the "interview" had taken place, had not Horner sworn that he knew, from Blackburn's own disdainful description of the words that had passed between himself and Christian, "that Blackburn had expected him to cower before him and show the white feather?"

As for Horner's personal opinion of Christian, Horner's own words were again, damning: "When Blackburn came back and said what he [Christian] had done, I had a sentiment of revulsion towards Christian as of a disgraced man, and that would have been the estimate of all honorable gentlemen about the place, in my opinion."

Mosby then drove Horner to "confess" that he "considered the failure of Christian to resent the insult as degrading to his reputation for courage, and calculated to blast it forever."

In conclusion, almost as an aside, Mosby asked Horner if he'd ever been asked to contribute money to support the prosecution of Charles Christian. Horner denied it and was allowed, at last, to step down.

Mosby had thus not only skillfully turned Horner into a substantive witness for the prosecution, he had used him to raise an embarrassing question for the prosecution's next witness, the superintendent of the Virginia Military Institute, Colonel Francis Henney Smith.

Captain Moore began his examination of Colonel Smith by walking him through his experiences on the night of the killing, with special focus on his success at calming the outraged Corps of Cadets.

Then he asked the colonel directly about his decision to retain Thomas J. Michie to "assist" the Commonwealth's attorney. Smith was forced to admit that he had personally retained Michie before either the VMI Board of Visitors or Blackburn's father had explicitly authorized such an act. He also denied that his cadets had ever been approached for funds.

Moore next called the third member of the Blackburn-Horner-Humes triumvirate, Cadet James White Humes.

After leading Humes through a description of his efforts to get Blackburn to warn Mary Evelyn Anderson to stay away from Christian, Moore asked him about the events of Saturday, January 14, hoping, no doubt, to shore up Cadet Horner's now badly tattered version of the story of the "interview."

When Moore had finished, Charles Lewis Mosby, as he had done with Horner, effectively turned Humes into a defense witness.

Humes admitted he had believed it was his "duty to inform Blackburn of Christian's reputation" before his cousin Mary Evelyn Anderson walked to church with him.

He confessed that, in view of Christian's letter demanding to know his "calumniator," he told Blackburn "that it was not only proper, but incumbent upon him to call on Christian and let him know that he gave the information to Miss Anderson."

Mosby next all but accused Humes of cowardice. "Did it not occur to you, Mr. Humes," Mosby asked, "that it would be more proper that YOU should assume the responsibility of the information on which Mr. Blackburn acted…Would it not have been more proper for YOU to have stepped forward…and declare that YOU were the individual that was responsible?"

Humes spat back: "Not at all. The information was a rumor, for which [I] was no more responsible than others who circulated it, and which [Blackburn] had heard from half a dozen [others]."

If Blackburn had asked him to see Christian, Humes asserted, he would have been glad to do so. But, he insisted, he himself "was no more responsible [for conveying the rumors about Christian to Blackburn and thence to Mary Anderson] than the pipes in the street for the water they conveyed."

"On those grounds," Mosby retorted, "neither was Blackburn any more responsible than those conduit pipes."

Mosby finished by leading Humes to make a few more points certain to appear in the summation for the defense. Humes conceded that Blackburn had "heard of the engagement to walk with Miss Anderson in connection with comments on Christian's character." Humes also swore Blackburn was not a "suitor of Miss Anderson."

Noting that Christian's letter to Mary Evelyn Anderson was written "in confidence," Mosby then asked Humes whether he thought Blackburn was really required to pay any attention to the contents of the letter at all? Having already testified he had told Blackburn that it was "incumbent" upon him to see Christian, Humes simply repeated his earlier assertions for the benefit of the jury.

Mosby, apparently satisfied, let him go.

There was no redirect, and Judge Thompson called a recess until 2:30 p.m. for the midday meal.

THE AFTERNOON

Having scored heavily in the morning, the defense found little or nothing they couldn't handle in Captain Moore's afternoon performance.

Moore called Cadets Edward Alexander Langhorne and Joseph Peterson Gilliam.

Both testified about their discussions with Christian in the hotel bar prior to the "interview" of January 14.

Gilliam swore that, rumors to the contrary, he had returned Christian's heavy silver-headed stick and that Christian still had it in his hands when he came back from his Saturday meeting with Blackburn.

Langhorne recounted his experiences in Christian's hotel room after the stabbing, testifying that Christian at first seemed ready to flee after being advised to do so by some of his friends.

Sandy Bruce concluded by recounting events at the Moore house on the fourteenth: the reading of Christian's letter, his walk back to the barracks with Blackburn, his advice that Blackburn see Christian and what he described as his joking reference on Sunday morning to his willingness to act as Blackburn's "second" if and when he was challenged.

Charles Mosby then began another successful round of cross-examination.

He led Bruce to admit that he referred to Christian's request to see Blackburn as a "challenge" because Christian "had been insulted." Bruce also admitted he had "inferred from what Mr. Horner said and what was known and said in the Corps, that Christian had disgraced himself."

Mosby closed with a slap at both the quality of judgment and the standards of chivalry of those who had sought to "protect" Mary Evelyn Anderson.

He asked Bruce specifically if he was aware of a phrase in Christian's letter to Anderson that had not been read aloud. Bruce admitted he had "heard something about 'confidence,'" perhaps at Mrs. Moore's, perhaps from Miss Anderson "as a reason against producing the letter."

So far, the prosecution had called twenty witnesses and most, if not all, their testimony had been effectively countered by the defense. With his next ten, Captain Moore, with the best of intentions, would continue the irreparable destruction of his own case, this time with little or no help from Christian's defense team required.

36

Day Three: Surprise

Saturday, April 15, 1854

The Morning[349]

Captain Moore's goals for the Commonwealth on Saturday morning appear to have been to continue his efforts to convince the jury that Tom Blackburn was an unsuspecting and unarmed victim on the night he was killed.

Moore first called Hugh Laughlin, the barkeeper at McDowell's who had, he admitted, done his level best to avoid witnessing anything at all. Under Captain Moore's guidance, Laughlin testified that both Christian and Blackburn "looked changed," after they returned from their "interview" and that "both seemed to be in better humor and looked satisfied."

Next, Moore recalled his own son, Andy, to describe Christian's pistols and the lesson he gave him on the proper way to wear a Bowie knife.

He led Benjamin Davenport Chenoweth to recount his unheeded advice to Christian to choose another time and place for a confrontation, and his subsequent refusal to accompany Christian to church on January 15. It was to Chenoweth's room that Christian fled after stabbing Blackburn, and Moore made him describe in detail Christian's arrival, covered with blood, and how he tossed two pistols on Chenoweth's bed.

Having established that Christian had armed himself to the teeth, Moore next had Blackburn's roommate, Cadet Robert Preston Carson, testify that Blackburn neither owned nor carried weapons. Carson also swore that Christian could have seen Blackburn any time he wanted to and that cadets left the Institute grounds freely, with and sometimes without Colonel Smith's permission.

Charles Lewis Mosby's cross-examination of Carson for the defense focused on two key issues. First, Carson admitted that after the "interview" on January 14, he "regarded Christian as a coward." Second, Mosby made him admit that the cadets were not above ganging up on "cowards," especially those who insulted a member of the Corps.

Captain Moore next called John T. Gibbs, the steward of the VMI mess hall who testified he had looked through the clothes Blackburn was wearing the night he was killed "and found no weapons...nothing but a handkerchief and pair of gloves."

Moore then led Christian's law school friends William Morris and Robert E. Seevers to testify that Christian was not only armed to the teeth when he went to meet Blackburn on Sunday evening, but also that he did so with the firm intention of killing the man.

Morris and Seevers's testimony, however, was rife with hearsay and speculation, all of which would soon come back to haunt Captain Moore.

Moore, not Mosby, for example, led Morris to testify that he thought Christian had been "basely slandered."

Morris similarly swore he thought Christian was deathly afraid of Blackburn and even more afraid of a combination of Blackburn and his cadet friends. Indeed, Morris was afraid "Christian was about to back out" of his decision to meet Blackburn.

When Morris swore that he had advised Christian to express regret, Captain Moore led him to concede that he had given Christian that advice before anyone knew Blackburn was dead.

When asked why he had advised Christian to express regrets, Morris replied that he thought "Christian really felt them," he didn't know "what might happen next," and "the friends of Blackburn were about."

Under questioning by the prosecution, law student Robert E. Seevers corroborated both Morris's and Winn's testimony, repeating what they said they had heard from Christian about his conversation with Blackburn in the passageway at McDowell's Hotel.

Captain Moore had thus allowed all three law students to place in evidence pure hearsay about Christian's reasons for arming himself, his fear of Blackburn and his concern that a "combination" of cadets might act against him.

From Captain Moore's point of view, such testimony ostensibly revealed that Christian was a plotter, a coward afraid of a stand-up fight and incapable of issuing an "honorable" challenge.

For Mosby and the defense team, the very same testimony illustrated clearly that Christian, unsupported and unprotected by his friends, had good reason to fear for his life.

Seevers's testimony along those lines continued well into the afternoon.

A SATURDAY SURPRISE

Late on Saturday afternoon, after Seevers at last stepped down, Moore called William N. Bumpass to the stand, a witness who had not appeared at either the coroner's inquest or during the examining trial (the four-day preliminary hearing held in late January).

Bumpass was a "journeyman tailor" who lived with and worked for Samuel Vanderslice, a founding partner of Norgrove & Vanderslice, suppliers of uniforms and tailoring services to the Virginia Military Institute for a decade.

Earlier testimony had indicated that two distinct pools of blood, critical to the prosecution's case, had been discovered on Nelson Street: the first where Blackburn and Christian had been seen wrestling on the ground; the second where Blackburn fell after rising and staggering a few paces toward Main Street after Christian had "shoved" him.

Bumpass disagreed. Under questioning by Captain Moore, he swore that on the night of the murder and again the next morning he had seen a third pool of blood near the hay scales and engine house on Nelson Street where the fight, ostensibly, had begun. This new "third pool" had apparently gone unnoticed by all previous witnesses.

From the prosecution's perspective, it was hoped that Bumpass's "third pool" would substantially undermine Christian's claim that he had drawn his knife in self-defense, while he was on the ground, on his back, underneath Blackburn, fighting for his life.

Bumpass swore he had seen the third pool on the night of the killing, "after church had broken up, and when the moon was shining." He saw it again the next morning, he said, though, by that time, it was "much trampled, and not so large in space as the night before, when he could see no difference between it and the other pools."

The new "third pool" apparently came as a shock to Christian's defense team, which quickly responded, according to the Richmond *Dispatch*, with "a long and rigid cross-examination."

Bumpass admitted that he had not said anything about the third pool of blood until Tuesday night, January 17, two days after Blackburn's death.

Francis Thomas Anderson (1808–1887). Mary Evelyn Anderson's father. *Courtesy of the Frederick S. Fisher Family, Westover Plantation, Charles City County, VA.*

He brought it up, he testified, during an argument about the case "when he mentioned it to controvert the position assumed by some gentleman in opposition to his own opinions."

Asked why he'd waited so long to come forward, he said he thought everyone had seen it. People were milling around the crime scene, looking at the "other" pools of blood, Bumpass swore, and he simply thought his "third pool" had already been noticed. His "servant boy," Bumpass said, pointed it out to him.

Pressed further, Bumpass testified he thought the third pool was "a matter of public notoriety because he heard no one speak of it." Pressed to justify his convictions on that score, Bumpass said he meant that he had heard "no one speak of either of the pools <u>particularly</u>."

The defense, noting that Bumpass had been present at the preliminary hearing, then led him to admit he had "heard Mr. Massie's testimony… and regarded it as certainly erroneous." Because he had not been called as a witness, Bumpass said he "did not feel disposed to thrust his testimony forward to prosecute Christian," although he "felt anxious that justice should be done."

Shocked, Mosby asked Bumpass if he had thought about the consequences of remaining silent.

Bumpass swore he thought at the time that, surely, someone else would point out the "third pool." Indeed, he said, he thought its presence was "so well known" that he was "surprised" to learn that nobody had mentioned it. He had "mentioned the subject to many gentlemen," he said "and there were others who would testify to the existence of the [third] pool."

Under further questioning by the defense, Bumpass admitted he had not been summoned to court until the very day he testified and that he did not know who had caused him to be summoned. Colonel Smith of

VMI had told him that he would be called, he said, and as an employee of Norgrove & Vanderslice he was indirectly an employee of Colonel Smith. Bumpass also testified that he had "never pronounced the murder a *black* assassination." He had called it an "assassination" in the past, he admitted, because "he so considered it."

Having clearly shocked the defense, Captain Moore next called James Lindsay Kirkpatrick to corroborate Bumpass's testimony.

Kirkpatrick's testimony was only marginally helpful. He first testified that on "the morning after the murder" he "saw but two pools of blood." Not until "two or three days after the called Court," he said, "did he change his mind." It was "about the 30th [of] January," he testified under direct examination, that he "saw Mr. [Samuel] Campbell and others standing near the hay scales, and went to them."

"Mr. Campbell asked me if I had noticed this spot of blood, pointing to a spot I had not seen before," Kirkpatrick continued. "I said I had not."

When Kirkpatrick asked Campbell "if he was not mistaken" Campbell said no, "and took up some of the earth," which Kirkpatrick examined, and "was fully satisfied that it was blood."

Charles Lewis Mosby began his cross-examination with a question about the weather. "There had been heavy rains," Kirkpatrick responded, "between the 15th of January and the time I was with Mr. Campbell."

Before Kirkpatrick could say more, an unnamed member of the jury "complained of being unwell and the Court adjourned until Monday morning."

In the hills around Lexington, there was a definite chill in the air.

A SUNDAY CHILL

As Lexington prepared for church on Sunday morning, a "cold, keen, driving wind" began to blow up the valley from the north, dragging in its wake "a great deal of fine rain, mixed with very fine snow." By nightfall, the rain had changed to snow and the temperature continued to drop. By 9:30 p.m., it was so cold the clock in the courthouse tower froze solid.

Captain Moore and Thomas Michie appear to have planned to drive home their Saturday surprise when court reconvened on Monday. Both clearly believed the new "third pool" proved Christian had used his knife early in the fight, well before he claimed he was on his back, underneath Blackburn and fighting for his life.

Christian's defenders, however, were quickly discovering that Moore and Michie might well be handing them an acquittal.

Time and testimony would tell.

On Monday morning, the special reporter for the Richmond *Dispatch* saw an early end to the proceedings. "The evidence in Christian's case is not yet concluded," he wrote, "but there is but little remaining." He would be as surprised by the next two weeks of testimony as he was at the four inches of snow he watched melting on the courthouse square as he wrote.[350]

37

Day Four: Into the "Third Pool"

Monday, April 17, 1854 [351]

The Morning

Captain Moore followed up his Saturday surprise first thing Monday morning, by calling a thirty-six-year-old wheelright, Rutherford Figgat, to the stand.

Figgat claimed to have seen the "third pool" at about 11:00 a.m. on January 16, the morning after the fight, while most of the town was attending the coroner's inquest at VMI. It was smaller than the other two pools of blood, Figgat testified, "five or six inches in diameter, nearly round, and a little spattered."

Mosby responded for the defense by hammering Figgat, asking many of the same questions he had put to Bumpass, the tailor, on Saturday.

When had he been summoned to court?

On Saturday, two days ago, Figgat replied.

Who had suggested that he be called?

Figgat didn't know, but he had talked to Kirkpatrick on Saturday and understood that he had already testified about the third pool.

Why had he not come forward sooner?

Like Bumpass, he had thought "by the time of the trial his notions of the fray would come out."

Did he have any preconceived notions about Christian's guilt or innocence?

He did, admitting that he "frequently remarked that he believed Christian stabbed Blackburn in the neck immediately after the fray commenced." His reason for believing this, he said, "was the third spot of blood which he had seen."

Had he not already referred to the stabbing in public as a "black crime?"

Figgat replied that he had, indeed, said that the "murder" was a horrid one and he might have said it was a "black crime." He swore, however, that he "had no acquaintance with Christian and no prejudice against him."

Captain Moore next called two more of Judge Brockenbrough's law students.

William Brosius described Christian "playfully" exhibiting his borrowed Bowie knife in McDowell's bar. In the process, Moore also allowed Brosius to say he believed that Christian really did not mean to attack anyone with it.

Moore next led Taliaferro Stribling through what he had seen on Saturday and Sunday, January 14 and 15, before and after the stabbing. Stribling's story, much of it hearsay, was also double-edged: in part reinforcing the defense's assertions that Christian felt honor-bound to accost Blackburn, that he felt unsupported by his friends and genuinely feared for his life.

Moore then returned to the new "third pool," calling Sam Campbell, the man who had allegedly brought it to Kirkpatrick's attention, some two weeks after the stabbing. Campbell claimed that he had "discovered" the third pool "about 7 o'clock the morning after the murder," describing it as "smaller than either of the others, and...splashed as though it had been spilled suddenly from a cup."

Next, Moore called Martin Phillips, who had accompanied Major Jordan and Christian on their circuitous route to jail on January 15. Phillips swore that he too had seen a third pool of blood, smaller than the other two, the morning after the murder. He admitted, however, that on the night of the stabbing he had noticed only two pools.

Almost as an afterthought, Captain Moore then recalled Sam Campbell to explain his role in bringing the third pool to the attention of Kirkpatrick. Campbell admitted he had gone over the ground with Kirkpatrick "about the time of the called court" and that the "spots had all materially changed, being blacker." When he showed Kirkpatrick the third pool (which, he claimed, Kirkpatrick had never seen before), Kirkpatrick "dug some of the earth from this pool and one of the others, and...was convinced from the comparison that it was blood."

With snow now melting rapidly on the courthouse lawn, Moore finished the morning session with a lengthy interrogation of Alfred G. Strayer, also a law student, and a friend of both the Moore family and Charles Burks Christian.

The Rutherford Houston Figgat house at 21 West Washington Street, Lexington, Virginia. *Library of Virginia.*

Once again, Moore's direct examination appeared to contribute more to Christian's defense than to the Commonwealth's murder case.

Strayer asserted that on the day of the "interview" at McDowell's Hotel, Christian had given Blackburn fair warning, by saying, "All right for the present, I will see you again."

Next, Strayer recounted Christian's display of his pistols and borrowed Bowie knife in Seevers's room, before setting out to meet Blackburn. Moore, no doubt believing Strayer's testimony reinforced the prosecution's contention that Christian had set out to meet Blackburn well armed and with evil intent, let him go on at length.

Christian's defense team responded just before the midday recess.

Mosby first led Strayer to swear that Christian had told him he wished to marry Mary Evelyn Anderson "if she would have him." He then guided him through the details of his visit to Samuel McDowell Moore's house after Christian's unsuccessful attempt to see Anderson.

In the process, Mosby elicited an embarrassing description of the disparaging tone of the free-wheeling talk about Christian at the Moore house, Anderson's response and Evalina Moore's assertion that, until Blackburn's death, she thought "Christian was a very pleasant and fluent gentleman, and she would be happy for him to continue his visits to her house."

Strayer also confirmed that he had told Christian all about the conversation at the Moore's house, and that he believed Christian wrote his now-famous note to Anderson as a result what he had told him.

At that point, Captain Moore raised the one and only direct objection to hearsay evidence encountered in the entire trial. "If Mrs. or Mr. Moore were there, and they were called on to testify on these matters, that would be quite different," Captain Moore insisted. "Surely it was a great license to introduce in this way the chit chat of the town."

The defense retorted that "the reputation of the prisoner had been assailed, and it was quite legitimate and just to him to find out the opinion entertained of him in respectable society."

Judge Thompson quickly put an end to the discussion, noting that the question had already been posed, answered and heard by the jury, and there was no need for any further debate about it.

He then called a recess.

THE AFTERNOON

In the afternoon, Captain Moore returned once more to the third pool of blood.

He called William Corbin Charlton, twenty-one, who, like Bumpass the tailor, claimed to have seen it on the night of the stabbing and again the morning after.

Charlton admitted that, until the trial, he had told no one about the third pool. No one else had been looking at ANY of the pools while he was looking at them, he testified, either on the night of the stabbing or on the morning after.

"He was summoned," he claimed, "at the instance of Mr. Bumpass," who said he had heard from a third party, someone Charlton didn't know, that Charlton "had seen three pools of blood."

Incredibly, Moore then recalled Christian's twenty-five-year-old law school classmate, Alfred G. Strayer, ostensibly in an attempt to get the precise chronology of Christian's invitations and rejections correct for the record. Moore's decision to recall Strayer of course opened the door for further cross-examination of a witness whose testimony had already badly hurt the prosecution.

Insisting, perhaps with an eye to Cadet Bruce and his riot-prone friends, that he meant no disrespect to Miss Anderson, Charles Mosby asked Strayer if she were not "a lady of great personal charm." Strayer admitted that she was, indeed. Strayer's testimony would not be the last time Anderson's "charm" was mentioned.

With Strayer done for the second time, Captain Moore next called Cadet George Baylor Horner to confirm that Christian had his silver-headed stick with him at the "interview" on January 14.

By this time, Christian's defenders must have realized that no matter how the prosecution approached the two pools versus three pools controversy, Christian came out ahead. The two pools theory was consistent with Christian's claim that he had stabbed Blackburn in self-defense while lying on his back. The three pools theory put the prosecution in the position of either withholding evidence, discrediting the earlier testimony of their own witnesses or both.

Best of all, neither of the two theories was inconsistent with a claim of self-defense. Both clearly undermined the notion that Christian had grievously wounded Blackburn after they had stood up after wrestling around on the ground.

With apparently little or nothing to lose, the defense called the prosecution's lead witness, James Massie. Under close questioning, Massie admitted he had returned to the scene of the stabbing the day after the "murder" because "the idea presented itself to his mind that the main point of the defence [*sic*] might turn on the question as to the time in the progress of the fight at which the knife was drawn."

Worse, from the prosecution's point of view, Massie also admitted that, upon his return to the scene, "A large number of people were present" and that he had described to them "all he knew about the commencement and course of the fight and remarked upon the importance of knowing where the first blood was seen."

Admitting that he "supposed they, or some of them, examined the ground with this view." Massie thus confirmed it was not only possible but probable that he had tainted the opinions of everyone he'd come into contact with on the day of his "tour" of the crime scene and thus had influenced the opinions of everyone they talked to as well.

Worse, Mosby got Massie to swear that, after his initial, very careful and highly visible re-examination of the crime scene, and after his later careful review of the ground with Colonel Smith and Major Preston, he still believed there were only two pools of blood (plus, of course, the blood that was found where Blackburn had been taken after being dragged out of the street).

Massie, in fact, said he was certain "there could not have been a [third] pool of blood in the line of the fight for a width of eight feet wide" noting that he, Colonel Smith and Major Preston had walked the path three abreast on the day after the fight.

Asked by Mosby how it was possible that others had found a third pool, Massie speculated at length, with devastating effect, and apparently without objection from Captain Moore and the prosecution. "Some days after the fight," Massie swore, "[he] saw some clods saturated or stained with blood near the southeast corner of the scales," precisely where others had seen the mysterious third pool. "It was after the heavy rains about that time," he continued, and "they were lying along the wagon track."

Massie concluded that the blood-soaked clods had simply been "taken up by the wheels of a passing wagon" and deposited somewhere else. The blood found near the hay scales, Massie pointed out, was in the ruts of the main wagon track down Nelson Street. The distance from where the new-found blood-soaked dirt clods of the "third pool" were found was precisely a distance from the hay scales "which might be traversed by the fore wheel of a wagon at one revolution: about twelve feet."

Captain Moore tried to recover but only compounded his problems.

Under redirect, Massie admitted he was nearsighted, "but not so much as that with glasses in the day time he could not see any spot of blood, such as that said to have been discovered there."

Asked by Moore if the men who had seen the third pool were reliable, Massie admitted they were. He then "volunteered" that "had he known at the time of his examination, the nature of the wound in the neck, he would not have been so particular, because he would have felt satisfied at once that it could have been given only when the parties were lying down."

The defense then finished their cross-examination of Massie with one more question, compelling him to swear he "had never heard of three pools of blood until Saturday, and not until it was stated in evidence in the trial."

The defense next recalled Major John Thomas Lewis Preston, who duly confirmed Massie's testimony about the third pool, noting that "in the range of his scrutiny—a width of eight feet—from the place of commencement to the pool where the parties fell—there was no blood."

When the prosecution objected that the path of his examination didn't really cover the area where the third pool was found, Preston replied, "he could say that he had examined, though less particularly, the whole ground—and was of the opinion that there were but the two pools or puddles."

Preston concluded by admitting that when he first looked over the ground, he believed that "the fatal wound was given while the parties were standing" and that he was very surprised when he heard that there were "persons who had seen three pools" of blood.

Christian's defenders closed the day by recalling Colonel Smith, whose testimony supported both Preston and Massie. "He had examined the ground," he claimed, "with [an] earnest desire to find out the true state of the case" and "while he had no theory with regard to the attack of his own" he had not been able to discover the slightest trace of blood, he said, "except the two pools and on the scales."

As for all the rumors of a third pool, Smith testified that "he had heard of the other pool from several quarters; but so many rumors had come to his ears, which he was unable to trace, that he was indifferent to them and paid not attention to this about the blood."

Indeed, Smith swore he "never believed in the existence of such a spot until last Saturday, when a gentleman informed him that there were persons who would swear to it."

This led the defense to ask about the relationship between Bumpass, the tailor, VMI and Colonel Smith.

Smith duly described Mr. Vanderslice as "Tailor to the Institute," and Mr. Bumpass as "a journeyman in his employment." In Vanderslice's tailor shop, Smith testified, he "had heard both of them mention the subject of the 3rd pool; but did not suppose either of them knew any thing themselves on the subject."

With that, and no doubt much to the relief of the now seriously embattled prosecution, Judge Thompson adjourned for the day.

38

Day Five: Of Blood and Character

Tuesday, April 18, 1854[352]

The Morning

On Tuesday morning, April 18, Mosby and Christian's defense team returned to their systematic demolition of the prosecution's new "three pools of blood" theory.

James Woods Massie returned to the stand after spending the morning with Sam Campbell, going over the ground of the "rencontre" one more time, carefully measuring distances as they retraced the path of the fight.

Still under oath, Massie told the court that the length of the path, from the engine house where he believed the fight had started, to the pool of blood marking the spot where the two men wrestled on the ground, near Mr. John McClelland's tailor shop, was eleven yards long.

The spot where Samuel Campbell claimed to have seen the third pool, they determined, was at least five and a half feet off that path. Massie testified he "could not see how it was possible for such a pool as that described to have been at the point indicated and to have escaped his attention."[353]

Under cross-examination, Captain Moore got Massie to admit he "could not fix positively the outline of his range of examination along the supposed line of the fight" but he was sure that the path of the struggle came "within a foot and a half of the point indicated by Campbell" as the location of the third pool of blood. He and Campbell, Massie swore, had "looked, with more or less care, over the whole ground."

Christian's defense team then called Dr. George Junkin.[354] At Blackburn's autopsy, Junkin had wondered about the deep wound in Blackburn's back, where Christian's Bowie knife had been driven through the cape of Blackburn's overcoat, through the coat itself, through Blackburn's uniform jacket and through his chest to the rib cage. The wound was in Blackburn's right shoulder. The physicians on hand had concluded that it had been delivered while the men were struggling on the ground, at the same time as Blackburn's left carotid had been severed.

Junkin wondered, no doubt, how a wound in Blackburn's left shoulder could have been delivered by a man on his back, stabbing wildly, with a knife in his right hand. He disagreed, he said, but remained silent. He was, after all, a doctor of divinity in the presence of no fewer than six doctors of medicine.

Though Junkin had noticed only two pools of blood when he went over the ground with Massie, Colonel Smith and Major Preston on the day after the fight, the autopsy made him reconsider. In view of the testimony of the physicians, Junkin had decided the wound in Blackburn's back, if delivered while Blackburn was on top of Christian, must have been made "by an arm which was closely pressed down by an arm of the deceased."

Then, Junkin testified, he went over the ground again "to see if the facts arranged in his own mind, chronologically, could be sustained." He found blood in a place other than the two pools first described by Massie and the other witnesses, Junkin testified, and he had done so after going over the ground "very minutely...up and down and around about, stooping and [looking] closely upon the ground."

He had seen, however, only "a few splotches...not more than a spoonful" in his "third pool" and those in a place where there had occurred "more tracking than elsewhere."

When he'd gone back over the scene again, this time with Samuel Campbell on the morning of April 18 Junkin testified he had discovered that his "splotches" were at least five feet from the point where Campbell and the others claimed they saw a third pool.

Junkin finished by swearing that he did "not think it possible that he could have overlooked Campbell's 'third pool,' [if] as he and others testified, it was as distinctly marked as either of the two large ones."

If that had been the case, Junkin swore, he could have seen it "50 feet distant."

On redirect, Captain Moore tried to keep the third pool theory alive, pointing out that Dr. Junkin had gone to the scene of the crime with a preconceived notion of what he'd find there.

Junkin simply deflected Moore's argument. It was "true," he said, "that most of the remarkable errors in morals and physics have resulted from the formation of theories first, and then suiting the facts to them; but he had certainly, in part, obtained the facts before he formed his theory about the fight."

It had occurred to no one, apparently not even Junkin himself, that his tiny third pool actually lay on the path of the fight or that small amount of blood in it may have come from the wound in Blackburn's back, arguably the first of the wounds he suffered. Dr. Junkin stepped down.

The extraordinary parade of witnesses called by the defense to refute the three pools of blood thesis concluded with testimony by doctors James R. Jordan and Henry Gamble Davidson. Both swore that they saw only two pools, and both insisted that they could not have missed a third pool of the sort described by those who professed to have seen it.

The defense then called Tom Perry, the jailer, and a law student, John James Davis, to testify that Christian was spitting blood as he sat in jail the night of the killing. Perry testified further that bruises on Christian's neck clearly revealed that he had been choked violently.

Four witnesses then testified to Christian's good character.

Colonel William Dillard, age fifty-seven, of Amherst, said that he had known Christian "since birth" and that he was "a young man of warm heart, of integrity and honor, and good standing, generally." Dillard owned land adjacent to the Christians in Amherst County and had married Sallie Christian, one of Charles Christian's "half third cousins."

Colonel Terisha "Terry" Washington Dillard described him as "warm-hearted, generous and high-minded." Dillard, age thirty-seven, had married Mary Elizabeth Dillard, the daughter of Colonel William Dillard and Sallie Christian, i.e. his own cousin and a cousin of Christian's to boot.

Samuel Jennings Walker, forty-five, agreed with the Dillards. Walker was a "Walker's Ford" neighbor of the Christian family and was another of Charles Christian's third cousins.

The two most telling "character" witnesses, however, were VMI Superintendent Francis Henney Smith and the defense's concluding witness, Benjamin Cabell Megginson, personal physician to Charles Burks Christian's mother.

Colonel Smith, no doubt much to the prosecution's surprise, testified that he felt honor bound to "make a statement which he had not done when formerly on the stand as he was then [being] questioned upon particular matters."

Smith, apparently on his own initiative, stated simply that "upon meeting with Christian after the tragedy, in jail, he [Christian] stepped forward and shook him by the hand."

According to Smith, Christian then remarked upon Smith's relationship to Blackburn, telling the Colonel that what had happened was "a bad affair" and adding, "I had rather it had been me that died than Blackburn."

According to the special reporter for the Richmond *Dispatch*, Smith had come forward for no other reason than that he believed, "it was due the prisoner that he should make the statement."

Having thus established Christian's remorse from an almost unimpeachable source, Charles Mosby closed with a witness to Christian's unbounded love for his mother. Doctor Benjamin Cabell Megginson of Amherst County described himself as "the family physician of Mrs. Christian" and told the court that Christian's father had died "many years since."

Megginson had known young Christian, he said, since 1846 and regarded him as "an exceedingly agreeable young man, whose habits, tastes and associations were those of a gentleman."

Megginson swore that he had "never heard his reputation in the neighborhood impeached," and that Christian was "exceedingly kind and affectionate to his mother and three sisters, who compose the family."

"His family connections," Megginson observed before stepping down, "were as good as any in the county."

After noting that other character witnesses "had been summoned from Amherst" but had not arrived, the defense rested its case.

Captain Moore and Thomas Michie, by now clearly on the defensive, renewed their efforts to shore up their new three pools of blood theory of the fight.

The defense objected on the grounds that "the testimony on that subject was 'evidence in chief'" and "should have been all introduced at once."

Dealing a double blow to a prosecuting team that had cleverly managed to introduce evidence undermining that of its own chief witness, Judge Thompson sustained the defense's objection.

Captain Moore had called his last witness.

Judge Thompson announced that summations would begin with opening of the afternoon session.

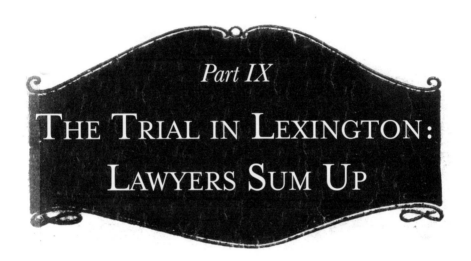

Part IX

THE TRIAL IN LEXINGTON: LAWYERS SUM UP

DAY FIVE: MOORE'S LAW

Tuesday, April 18, 1854[355]

THE AFTERNOON

Instead of closing with a crisp summary of his case against Christian, David Evans Moore chose to lead with a technical discussion of some of the finer points of law relevant to his case, delivered in confusing if not totally abstract terms.

In the words of the special reporter for the Richmond *Dispatch:*

> *After a brief reference to the crime as belonging to that class which could not safely be permitted to go unpunished—to be committed with impunity—he went into a definition of murder and its different degrees under the English Common Law and Statutory Laws of Virginia.*

Rather than simply outlining the facts of his case and drawing a mental picture of what had happened on the night of January 15, Moore delivered a lecture to his jurors on what they could and could not do under Virginia law. What he said was relevant, of course, but arguably more suited to instructing the jury than convincing it.

"The jury were not sitting there as a board of honor to moot points of honor," Moore lectured. "They were not permitted to travel out of those considerations which were to enlighten their verdict under the law of the land."

All killing was "malicious" Moore argued, and all the Commonwealth had to do was prove, beyond a reasonable doubt "that the killing in question had been done by the prisoner at the bar." If there were reasonable doubts (and Moore insisted there were not), then the accused was due "all benefits deriving from them."

Once the fact that Charles Burks Christian had killed Thomas Blackburn was established, however, Moore insisted "the laboring oar was thrown back upon the prisoner" and it was up to Christian to produce "such facts as would amount to a justification" for his actions. For that to happen, Moore insisted, "the evidence must be very strong and conclusive."

Next, Moore raised and then tried to discredit as many of the possible grounds for "justification" as possible, no doubt reminding the jury in the process of each and every possible reason for a verdict of "justifiable homicide."

Moore began with "provocation," arguing that the notion that Blackburn had provoked Christian "would not avail to reduce the offense to murder in the 2nd degree unless it had been so recent and so sudden that the individual had not time to *cool*—had not time for reflection, and his judgment time to parley with itself."

Next he addressed "proportionality," quoting passages at length from works by two British barristers and several legal cases to make the point that for homicide to be justifiable, the "means employed, the weapons used, must not be disproportioned to the provocation."

Turning at last to his own case, Moore once more proceeded to undermine it by conceding how and why Christian might have believed he was both insulted and provoked.

"It appeared that the prisoner was aggrieved by being informed by Blackburn that he gave the information to a lady which induced her to break off her engagement with him," Moore began. Even though the "engagement" was "of no great importance," Moore conceded, "the prisoner was no doubt provoked and conceived that he had cause of offense against Blackburn."

When Blackburn told Christian he was responsible for Mary Evelyn Anderson's decision to spurn him, the admission "was of an offensive character," Moore conceded. "It was a provocation which caused the prisoner to seek revenge but to seek it in a way which the law did not tolerate."

Moore thus defined, indirectly and in terms supportive of the defense, the prosecution's task: to prove that Charles Christian, having been clearly provoked, set out to seek revenge on Tom Blackburn and killed him, "inappropriately" and with malice of forethought.

To win that case, however, the prosecution would have to convince twelve god-fearing Rockbridge County white men that Blackburn's

Mary Evelyn Anderson Bruce (1835–1916). *Courtesy of the Frederick S. Fisher Family, Westover Plantation, Charles City County, Virginia.*

"provocations" were not serious enough for Christian to feel justified in killing the man who had insulted him.

It would not be an easy task.

Moore began by describing Christian's arsenal. "It would be difficult for a man to prepare in a more deadly manner than did the prisoner, to carry out his purpose of revenge," Moore began.

He next cast aspersions on Christian's choice of time and place: "The solemn occasion of religious devotion at Church as a fit one for his purpose."

Then there was motive. "Could it be doubted that he considered the occasion opportune for revenge?" Moore continued. "Could there be any other conclusion than that he repaired thither to perpetrate the deed which he afterwards accomplished?"

Moore clearly believed his contentions were both damning and obvious. Unfortunately, over the past four days, he had painted himself into a corner. To convince the jury that Christian had set out to "perpetrate the deed" on January 15, Moore had to concede that Christian had been "provoked." No doubt much to the glee of Christian's defenders, Captain Moore did an excellent job.

No doubt Christian was taken by surprise when Blackburn called upon him at the Hotel. He may not have been prepared to disclose his course of conduct. He evidently had no idea who had made the communication to Miss Anderson, for his letter to her fishes in the dark. It was entirely certain then, that Christian was taken by surprise and may have been embarrassed, as anybody might have been though having the spirit to resent the insult.

Moore next insisted that Blackburn, unarmed and defenseless, was taken completely by surprise by the well-armed Christian. "Blackburn thought the matter at an end" after his "interview" with Christian, Captain Moore insisted, and even if he were wrong, he was with a woman, at church, on Sunday, when Christian ambushed him.

Moore next described the "deed" itself, more or less reprising James Woods Massie's opening testimony, while he tiptoed around the ever-expanding third pool of blood, a shifting red sea that he could not part.

Moore now conceded that, with regard to the "stains and pools of blood on the ground of the *rencontre*," there was "more discrepancy and conflict than he had ever known in the testimony of any case." These discrepancies, however, were not his problem, but Christian's.

> *The prisoner at the bar selected the opportunity and the weapons. He sought his own occasion when there was no ear to hear and no eye to see. If there was mystery thrown over the affair he was the author of it and he alone was responsible. It was not for the Commonwealth to remove or solve it.*

Moore next addressed Christian's "character." After fleeing the scene of the crime with Blackburn lying "motionless on the ground," Christian must have known that he was "dead or seriously injured," Moore argued. Such behavior was "utterly inconsistent with his declaration at the Hotel that he did not think he had inflicted a serious wound upon him, that he had 'only cut him in the face.'"

At that point, Moore inexplicably returned to the troublesome third pool of blood. Rather than offering an explanation for its existence, however, he simply reiterated his own surprise and confusion about what really happened on Nelson Street. As the special reporter for the Richmond *Dispatch* described it:

> *Commenting upon the character of the struggle as explained by the signs on the ground, the speaker said his own theories had been taken aback by the new testimony introduced on Saturday last as to three pools of blood. His opinion had been that the probabilities were strongly in favor of the idea that the wounds were inflicted when the parties were down. The new testimony, presented by witnesses whose credibility could neither be denied nor doubted, presented new difficulties in the way of previous theories. But these, he would repeat, were not for the Commonwealth to solve.*

Moore then continued to make the defense's case for "reasonable doubt" by bringing up the differences of opinion among his own medical experts.

> *The doctors differed in their theories as doctors had ever done, in nine cases out of ten where half a dozen of them were called upon to decide. If*

criminal cases depended entirely upon their opinions, criminal justice would stop still in every case where they were introduced as witnesses.

Moore's problem, of course, was that Doctors Paine, Estill and Marshall had all testified that Blackburn could not possibly have stood up if his carotid had been severed while he and Christian lay struggling on the ground. The other three doctors were all certain that Blackburn could indeed have risen after having his throat cut, if only to stagger a few steps before lapsing into unconsciousness.

Moore clearly hoped to use the third pool to convince the jury that Blackburn could have been fatally wounded almost at the beginning of the fight, *before* he and Christian fell to the ground locked in each other's arms.

To do that in the face of conflicting testimony from his own medical witnesses, Moore quoted passages at length from British toxicologist Alfred Swaine Taylor's 1844 *Manual of Medical Jurisprudence.*[356]

Thus, despite his insistence that it made no difference at all to his case, Moore proceeded to wade deeper and deeper into the third pool. As the Richmond *Dispatch* correspondent put it, he appeared to have little choice, as the third pool had "an important bearing on the question as to where in the course of the conflict the knife was drawn."

For Christian's defenders, of course, any controversy, no matter how insignificant, introduced some element of doubt about the Commonwealth's case.

Captain Moore pressed on, arguing next the mind-numbingly technical superiority of "positive" testimony over "negative" testimony about the third pool.

The conflict of testimony was great and the jury were the judges. There was no ground to impeach any of the witnesses to that pool. Their testimony was positive while that against them was negative. If one man said, "I saw a thing," and another said, "I didn't see it,"—if one man said, "I heard a thing," and another said, "I didn't hear it,"—the testimony of the men who saw and heard was not disproved by that of those who did not see and hear. The positive testimony of one witness was entitled to more credit than the negative testimony of a dozen witnesses.[357]

"But the jury were the sole judges of the evidence and the credibility of witnesses," Moore argued. His job, as Commonwealth's attorney, was only to "state the case fairly and the law fairly."

In an effort to state the law "fairly," Moore next cited at length passages from Thomas Starkle's *Practical Treatise on the Law of Evidence and Digest in Civil and Criminal Proceedings*. Only then did he return to the testimony in the case at hand, doing his best to make it fit into the technical categories whose definitions he had just read to a jury more likely than not to be incapable of understanding a word of it.

Five witnesses, Moore noted, had testified "positively" (in the just defined legal sense of the word) that they had seen three pools of blood, three had definitely *not* seen a third pool of blood and one had seen a "tiny" third pool in a different place. Massie, Major Preston and Dr. Junkin, Moore argued, were simply prejudiced. Only Colonel Smith, Moore argued, had gone over the ground with no theory in mind as to what he should find.

Having thus cast doubt on the testimony of four of Lexington's leading citizens, including the heads of both VMI and Washington College, Moore pointedly, and inexplicably, reminded the jury that none of his "positive" witnesses had come forward with their discovery of the third pool of blood during either the coroner's inquest or the preliminary hearing. According to Moore, "Their absence from the Examining Court was to be attributed to their reluctance to volunteer their testimony in a case of life and death."

Nor did the social standing of his "positive" witnesses help Moore's case. It was one thing to ask the jury to simply disregard the testimony of Massie, Preston, Junkin and Smith. It was quite another to do so on the basis of testimony by "gentlemen" of lesser social standing, whose stories didn't match and who apparently lacked the moral fiber to step forward in a timely manner in a life-or-death murder trial.

Moore's final ironic volley in the battle of the three pools was his attempt to convince the jury that how many pools of blood there were really didn't matter at all.

"It was proper," Moore noted, "that it should be admitted that in all the evidence at all times, it was never pretended that the parties were down but *once*—the scuffle continued until they were reduced to the prostrate condition."

If Blackburn died from the wound to his carotid, Moore observed, "The same cause that would have ejected blood at one point from a wound given and received while standing, would have strown [*sic*] it over the ground as the scuffle continued."

40

DAY FIVE: MOORE'S CASE

Tuesday, April 18, 1854[358]

Moore concluded the Commonwealth's case with a comparatively crisp, though not entirely flawless, review of Christian's claims of "self defense."

He first made the case that Christian had started the fatal *rencontre*, and that as the "aggressor" he was responsible for the outcome. Moore read the complete definition of justifiable homicide from William Oldnall Russell's *Treatise on Crimes and Misdemeanors* and argued that, under the law, Christian was guilty of no less a crime than first-degree, or at the very least, second-degree murder.

Christian started the fight, Moore insisted.

> *Blackburn was not the aggrieved person. Christian was. Christian went to seek redress. Blackburn had none to ask. It is fair to presume that the person who sought the redress commenced the attack.*

Nor was it logical to believe, Moore continued, that Christian led Blackburn into the dark shadows of Nelson Street because he had nothing more in mind than a "verbal redress of grievances."

> *Why did he go where no human being could witness the redress? If his object was redress, why did he not demand it in [the] presence of others, so that the apology might have been as public and notorious as the injury itself had been? But no, he sought redress in the dark, out of*

the sight and hearing of others, and whatever the apology might have been, it could have been known only to them and to no one else. The difficulty would have remained just where it was at the first interview, of which they alone were the witnesses, and about which there was a total discrepancy between them.

"These circumstances justify a conclusion," Moore continued. "The burden of proof rests on the prisoner; and the presumption is that he commenced the attack."

But what if Christian had not struck the first blow? He was still at fault, according to Moore.

A man has no right to make use of the passions of his adversary. If he offers an insult to a man of spirit whom he knows will attack him, no matter what necessity, what exigency he brings upon himself, he has no right to use his weapons. No man shall take advantage of his own wrong.

But wasn't Christian, at five feet, eight inches tall, at a considerable disadvantage in a stand-up fight against the considerably larger Blackburn? "No doubt," Moore conceded, but Christian put himself in that position and "the preparation made by the prisoner showed that he was fully conscious of the exigency in which he would be placed."

Captain Moore next did his best to depict Christian as a coward. Christian, Moore noted, thought he had been insulted. So, what did he do? Nothing "honorable," Moore contended. "He was advised to challenge Blackburn but he declined [for] reasons not at all satisfactory."

He urged that Blackburn could not leave the Institute to fight him; [that] Blackburn had no right to insult him under circumstances which would not afford him an opportunity for redress; that Blackburn was bound as a man of honor to afford this opportunity, and if he did not, that was his, Blackburn's fault, and upon him would the responsibility rest.

None of that was true, Moore thundered. All Christian had to do was issue a challenge and he would have been "vindicated."

Moore next turned to Christian's arsenal.

He was advised to use his stick. This he declined to rely upon alone. What other resource did he select? He took Blackburn in the dark, to disadvantage,

Special Counsel Thomas Johnson Michie (1795–1873). *"Portraits," William & Mary Quarterly (1930).*

against the advice of friends, insults him, and upon his attacking him, draws his deadly weapon and kills him.

"The case admits of *no* excuse," Captain Moore continued. "Self-defence [*sic*] was brought on himself."

In contrast to Christian's deadly intent, the innocent Blackburn, in Moore's words, "had no expectation of any contact with any human being."

Having thus cast Christian as a petty, plotting, vengeful and cowardly murderer, Moore finished by reminding the jury that he was a liar as well. Recalling Massie's description of Christian, covered in blood, "jumping to the pavement and looking back at Blackburn...seeing him lying motionless on the ground," Moore speculated once more that the young law student's actions "were in conflict with his statement at the Hotel that he thought he only cut Blackburn in the face."

In fact, Moore concluded, "The statement, there too, that he did not intend to kill, was utterly in conflict with what he did, and what he was so thoroughly prepared to do."

Christian had also claimed that his stick had been taken away from him on the day of his first "interview" with Blackburn, Moore noted, "as part of a pre-concerted plan to take him to disadvantage."

Yet, Moore observed, "It was clearly proved that he had his stick when he and Blackburn entered the passage [at the McDowell Hotel] together."

At that point, at the very end of his long combination of opening and closing statements, the Commonwealth's attorney inexplicably launched forth on a series of rambling remarks that further undermined his case and provided gratuitous support for the defense.

He reiterated and validated, for example, Christian's excuse for his behavior at his Saturday "interview" with Blackburn at McDowell's Hotel. To give it a "charitable interpretation," Moore argued, "Christian was no doubt greatly excited, and his memory confused under the influence of wounded honor taken by surprise. Besides, there were Cadets present, which might naturally enough have excited the apprehension of a combination against him."

He next expressed confidence that much of the testimony favorable to Christian was true, pointing out in the process that his own son was one of those who had spoken on Christian's behalf. In the words of the *Dispatch* special correspondent:

Mr. Moore gave to those students of Judge Brockenbrough's Law School (of which Christian was a member) credit for their impartiality in the testimony they had given. They had given testimony that was favorable to the accused, and they had not concealed much that was decidedly unfavorable. He spoke, he said, of all except one, of whom, of course, he could not speak. (This was his son.)

Much to the dismay, no doubt, of Thomas Johnson Michie, the Blackburn family and the VMI Corps of Cadets, Moore next declared, "It was not his duty to cover up Blackburn's faults." That job, Moore said, belonged to Mr. Michie, "who was employed by the friends of Blackburn…to see that his character did not suffer."

Not that Moore minded, of course. He assured the jury that he was "glad" Michie had been employed and "had urged him to accept the proposition to take part in the case." Indeed, Moore continued, Michie's acceptance had "relieved" Moore "from an embarrassing position" since he was, as prosecutor, "sworn as the protector of Christian as well as the Commonwealth."

In that spirit, Moore continued, he would now "express some of his ideas as to the conduct of Tom Blackburn."

"He never thought," he said, that Blackburn's conduct was "justifiable." He didn't think Blackburn should have spoken to Mary Evelyn Anderson, he thought Blackburn was wrong in responding to anything that he'd read in Christian's letter, and finally, as if he hadn't already said enough, Moore shared with the jury his personal opinions about the remark, attributed to Blackburn by others, that "Christian had not the courage to strike a child."

"This was wrong," Captain Moore stated flatly. "A generous man should never have opened his mouth about it."

Having thus raised issues that would exonerate Christian in the eyes of many a twenty-first century jury, Moore closed his case, arguing that, legally, if not morally, Blackburn's faults could not excuse Christian's actions.

In every other respect, the conduct of Blackburn had been highly honorable and creditable. But what avail these exceptions to the prisoner at the bar? Under the law, where there is time for reflection and where the killing is not done on the instant, it is evidence of malice. It makes no difference if the provocation is inflicted with cause, or with great cause, if there is deliberation or even time for it, the law will presume deliberation.

With what was now a full half-day summation at an end, something reminded Captain Moore there was still one more point to be covered, something that would surely be raised by the defense, and something of particular interest to his friends at VMI, namely, "the frequently expressed apprehension of Christian that the Cadets would combine against him, and that they were in the habit of combining."

"In justice to the Institute," Moore insisted, "with rare exceptions, the Cadets were as well behaved and orderly, and indeed more so, than any similar number of young men he ever saw."

As for the "general conclusion, relating to combinations for hostile purposes against individuals," Moore continued, the notion was something he "utterly disbelieved."

That said, Captain Moore closed his summation for the Commonwealth, not with a plea for Christian's conviction, but "by urging the jury to suspend their judgment until the last word of the argument shall be heard."

Judge Thompson gaveled the court into adjournment.

41

Day Six: Dorman for the Defense

Wednesday, April 19, 1854 [359]

W hen Judge Thompson opened the sixth day of what had become one of the most notable trials in Rockbridge County history, Alexander Hugh Holmes Stuart, the defense team's star attorney, was too sick to appear. The large crowd gathered for Stuart's highly anticipated summation for the defense would instead hear young James Baldwin Dorman. [360]

Dorman, twenty-nine, had already started a near riot with his sharp interrogation of Mary Evelyn Anderson during the preliminary hearing. He was well known, competent, fiery and, given the circumstances, an excellent choice as a substitute for Stuart.

Dorman opened by reminding the jury, and, no doubt, the jury members' families and friends crowded into the courtroom, that both he and they had "a deep obligation" to see that justice was done in Christian's case. He then began a systematic and eloquent conversion of Charles Burks Christian from cold-blooded killer to innocent victim.

Dorman began by putting the entire community of Lexington and, by implication, the jurors themselves, on the defensive, noting both "the deep excitement produced in this community" by what he called "the tragic scene" and "the foregone conclusion at once formed against the prisoner before he had a trial."

Dorman then moved deliberately, point by point, to destroy the prosecution's case.

First he conceded and reinforced the prosecution's assertions that "malice" was an "indispensable ingredient" if the Commonwealth hoped to convict Charles Christian of murder. Contrary to Commonwealth's Attorney Moore's view of the law, however, Dorman insisted that not only was "malice not to be presumed" in cases tried in Virginia, "its absence" was to be presumed "unless it must be inferred inevitably from the circumstances proved."

Dorman next announced his complete agreement with Captain Moore's definition of "justifiable or excusable homicide" especially if the accused "was in immediate danger of losing his life or of great bodily harm."

Speaking to Christian's character, Dorman insisted, "he was grievously wronged by Mr. Blackburn" and yet, "despite the insults heaped upon him," he "acted with great forbearance."

He then outlined in sharp detail the defense's version of what had really happened, before, during and after Blackburn's death, something the prosecution had still, inexplicably, failed to do.

Dorman insisted that Christian, from his first days in Lexington as a law student, had "always sustained the character of a gentleman and acted as a gentleman." True, he admitted, his client "had somewhat the frivolities of youth," but he was "temperate in his habits, and was received into the best company."

As for Christian's "frivolities," they were, Dorman noted, singularly benign. One entirely innocent example had been his cultivation of a mustache. Yet, because of it, Christian was "treated with indifference and was in danger of being subject for the scolds and sneers of the community."

That was not the case when it came to Mary Evelyn Anderson, Dorman continued. Mustache or no mustache, there was no doubt in Dorman's mind that Anderson had led his client on, and that Christian had reacted to her charms naturally and honorably.

> *He becomes acquainted with a beautiful and attractive young lady who receives his attentions with appreciation and encouragement, and actually reminding him of his engagement to accompany her to church, showed that she entertained him with high regard. Thus encouraged and smiled upon by the fair one he had even expressed to Mr. Strayer his intention of addressing Miss Anderson.*

The other major villain in the piece, according to Dorman, was Cadet James White Humes, who "struck with Mr. Christian's attentions to Miss Anderson," took it upon himself inform Tom Blackburn, "her distant cousin," that Christian was "not a proper person for her to associate with," and then insisted "that Blackburn should tell Miss Anderson."

Humes, Dorman insisted, was the person responsible for setting off a chain of events that left Christian "slandered, laughed at, and his request to know who did it treated with scorn."

Humes, he charged, led Mary Evelyn Anderson to break her engagement to walk with Christian to church and to refuse to see him when he called on her at the Moore house. Humes's conduct was "offensive" on its face, Dorman charged, and compounded when "it was publicly talked of at Mrs. Moore's house that night."

Nor did Dorman spare Anderson's aunt Evalina Moore. Christian's note to Anderson, he pointed out, was "respectful and complimentary." The words "in confidence" were "written on its face." Yet it was "brought into the room at the request of Mrs. Moore" as "something rich," then given to Blackburn, who read it, "laughing at the end of each sentence, in the presence of Mr. Bruce and Mrs. Moore."

Dorman then read the full text of Christian's note for the jury, translating the Latin passages. The passage that prompted "so much mirth," Dorman noted, could be translated fairly as: "Farewell, farewell, most beautiful maiden, a last farewell."

"Mr. Humes says that he was a gentleman," Dorman growled, but he "told a rumor in the community" about Christian, telling Blackburn, among others, that "because some of the young ladies had slighted him he was not a proper person to accompany Miss Anderson to church."

"Was it right that Christian should be thus treated?" Dorman asked. "Mr. Christian was as much of a gentleman as any of his calumniators."

Neither was Blackburn an innocent, Dorman continued. "Mr. Blackburn, in undertaking to notice anything in that letter was acting ungentlemanly himself." He was, Dorman insisted, "mistaken in his sense of duty" when he took notice of "a note written to Miss Anderson in confidence and which he had no right to see."

Dorman next addressed Blackburn's role in the now infamous January 14 "interview" with Christian at McDowell's Hotel. Blackburn no doubt believed he "should be indignant," Dorman conceded, having been "styled a calumniator in a confidential note." He also no doubt believed that he was being "brave and chivalrous" to seek out Christian.

Yet, Dorman noted, Blackburn "looked for Cadets Humes and Horner, two stalwart fellows, to accompany him to Lexington." As for who was *really* looking for trouble, Dorman reminded the jury that Cadet Horner had admitted that "from the start" the cadets "expected a fight" and had stated openly that their only concern about meeting Christian would be the difficulty of convincing him "that he had been insulted." This, Dorman insisted, clearly demonstrated that Christian was "slow to anger, and would not fight without a good reason."

"Christian," on the other hand, "had every reason to believe that Blackburn was armed," Dorman reminded the jury, noting that Blackburn had gratuitously and dishonorably used the occasion to add insult to the injury already done. According to the Richmond *Dispatch*, Dorman

> insisted that it was a first principle among gentlemen, and also among Christians, to do no one any willful wrong, and that Blackburn had departed from this principle, not only in making [Christian] a mark for the finger of scorn, but in afterwards saying 'that it was just as I expected, he has not courage enough to strike a child,' and that he took pity on him.

Christian, Dorman noted, "embarrassed and taken by surprise at this interview merely told Mr. Blackburn that he would see him again, and in the meantime consulted his friends."

Humes had already admitted, Dorman pointed out, that he and Horner and Blackburn had gone into Lexington specifically to "silence" Christian and prevent him from "making the affair with Miss Anderson a subject of town gossip." But they all knew that "Christian was too much of a gentleman to be talking in that way about a lady, though she had maltreated him, and confidence had been violated."[361]

What, pray tell, was a man of honor to do? Dorman had no doubts in that regard, and he knew full well that the men of the jury he faced had few, if any doubts of their own.

To drive home his point, Dorman chose not to quote from the Virginia state code or the opinions of a British barrister, but from a higher, unwritten code much more familiar to his Rockbridge County jurors.

> Mr. Christian, [had] no remedy at law to stop these slanders against him and the personal insults making him the scorn and contempt of the community. Was he, the only male person of his family, who had not only his own name to uphold, but that of his widowed mother and sisters to do nothing and suffer this thing to go on? He that would not do it has neither the faith of religion nor the dignity of honor.[362]

Christian, with neither family nor friends to speak of in Lexington, turned to "the two oldest and most reliable members of the law class" for advice.[363] After consulting his classmates, Dorman continued, Christian realized that he really didn't know whether Blackburn or someone else was the original source of the things said about him. Indeed, Blackburn could have been only repeating something he had heard elsewhere.

The *only* honorable thing to do, Dorman pointed out, was precisely what Christian did: "demand an explanation." And "given the conditions under which such a necessity had arisen," Dorman insisted, Christian had no choice about how to approach Blackburn.

> *Being immediately responsible to the laws of the country if he sent a challenge, and seeing that it would amount to nothing as it was likely that Blackburn would not leave the Institute, and thinking that Blackburn was armed at the interview, Christian armed himself to meet any contingency that might arise.*

Dorman sneered at the Commonwealth's contention that Christian's weapons implied premeditation of a criminal act.

Citing the American jurist John Bouvier's *Law Dictionary*, Dorman argued that Christian clearly did not premeditate "murder." He carried weapons *not* because he planned to kill Blackburn, but "to be prepared to protect himself from numbers that might combine against him."

All the evidence indicated that Christian had "never breathed the feeling of revenge and malice," Dorman noted, and it was obvious that Christian meant only "to demand of Blackburn a personal explanation, and intended to use the arms only in *extremis.*"

The new "third pool" of blood, Dorman admitted, was a mystery, given "that it seemed not to be known at the preliminary trials." Yet "in the midst of the case" and "without any notice to the prisoner's counsel" the prosecution suddenly sprung a "mine" on poor Christian.

If the third pool really existed, Dorman observed, it was clear "it must have come from some other source, and not from Blackburn."

What were those other sources?

In Dorman's eyes, the "third pool" sprang full blown from the minds of its "discoverers."

After reading aloud his own legal texts about "positive" and "negative" evidence, Dorman pointed out that "every witness who testified to the existence of this third pool was biased and prejudiced against Christian, from the occurrence down to this time."

"Hypotheses," he noted, were "insufficient for conviction." To condemn a man for murder, certainty beyond a reasonable doubt was an absolute necessity. Now there was no certainty. Given the testimony about the fight on Nelson Street, Dorman insisted, "the proof of the third pool throws the whole matter 'at sea' and destroys every theory that has been set up, and throws a doubt at once over the transaction."

Dorman insisted that Massie's account of the fight best explained the physical evidence, especially the blood and mud on Christian's and Blackburn's clothing.

Blackburn, after an initial scuffle, Dorman argued, "must have followed up Christian, across the street where Christian dropped his cane." There, Dorman asserted, Blackburn "downed Christian," and Christian, "being choked until he was unable to cry out drew the knife and struck over him and thus inflicted the wounds on the back, the head, and in the neck."

As for Christian's behavior after the fight, Dorman found that it completely consistent with the actions of someone confident that he had acted in self-defense.

Covered in blood, Christian went straight to his hotel room and made no attempt to conceal himself. Still bloody, he went to another law student's room and from there sent friends to see if Blackburn was badly wounded.

Everything Christian said and did, Dorman insisted, "were consistent throughout" and clearly showed that Christian stabbed Blackburn "in *extremis*—and that he was forced into *extremis* by the misconduct of those with whom he was brought into conflict." Indeed, even though Blackburn had "assumed a spirit and conduct of superiority over Christian, and showed a haughty manner towards him," Dorman insisted, "Christian reasonably expected that Blackburn would make the necessary reparation without any personal violence between the parties."

Just to make sure the jury remembered the defense's version of the tale, Dorman re-told his story, insisting that Blackburn had struck the first blow, attacking immediately after Christian told him he was "no gentleman." His client stabbed Blackburn, Dorman insisted, only after the cadet had choked Christian "until his eyeballs reeled in their sockets."

After the fight, Christian's friends had advised him to flee and had offered to help him do so, Dorman noted. Christian, however, "refused to flee," said he would "stand his ground" and insisted "he had done what he did in self defence [*sic*]." Indeed, Dorman pointed out, his "whole conduct showed that he had no conscientious feelings of having willfully done wrong."

Citing legal authorities on the nature of malice, will and premeditation, Dorman again insisted that Virginia law required the Commonwealth prove the existence of *all three* in a capital case, and prove them beyond a reasonable doubt.

It was obvious to Dorman, of course, that all three were lacking in this case, and that given the absence of any one of them, the jury could not find Christian guilty.

After once more reading from the relevant legal texts, Dorman closed by insisting "if the jury had a doubt of the 'criminal' guilt of the prisoner, they must acquit him."

Dorman's performance, by all accounts, was a legal and emotional *tour de force*. His summation, more than likely prepared at the last minute, had required no fewer than six hours to deliver. The special reporter for the Richmond *Dispatch* pronounced it "a handsome and affecting peroration, drawing tears from a number of person[s] in the large audience assembled to hear this most interesting trial."

The prosecution had, so far, presented nothing like it. For Captain Moore, and Michie, however, their ordeal was just beginning. "The Honorable A.H.H. Stuart," Judge Thompson announced from the bench, "having recovered from his indisposition, will address the jury tomorrow on behalf of the prisoner."

42

DAY SEVEN: STUART'S ATTACK

Thursday, April 20, 1854

THE MORNING[364]

On Thursday morning, April 20, 1854, the crowd around the County Courthouse was larger than ever before, with some looking for seats inside the courtroom and others "disappointed in their search, milling around Courthouse Square," waiting for the Honorable Alexander Hugh Holmes Stuart to "address the jury on behalf of the prisoner." A "host of women," the Richmond *Dispatch* reported, "occupied the bench on both sides of the Judge."

Illness, however, for the second day in a row, threatened to halt or delay the trial. A juror, Alfred Douglas, had "taken ill" and simply did not show up for court. Judge Thompson dispatched a deputy with orders to fetch him.

As soon as Douglas arrived, Thompson's gavel fell, Stuart rose from his seat and the long-awaited performance of the former Secretary of the Interior began.

Upon close examination, Stuart followed, almost exactly, the outline of James Baldwin Dorman's six-hour monologue the preceding day. Given that Dorman had been called upon to appear at the last minute, he may well have worked from Stuart's outline and notes.

"Mr. Stuart…arose," the *Dispatch* reported, "and after alluding to his late indisposition (he complained of still being unwell) spoke of the indisposition of the jurors worn out by this protracted trial."

Following a spontaneous outburst of sympathy from the crowd, Stuart spoke of "the weighty responsibilities resting on all connected with this most important trial."

He spoke of duty: "the duty of the jury in clearing from their minds all pre-conceived ideas, and of their devoting their minds with fixed attention to the real evidence in this cause." He then reminded his fellow citizens they were ultimately answerable to a court higher than the Rockbridge Circuit Court. "Bias and prejudice," Stuart conceded, sometimes produced "a virtuous feeling," but it was also capable of producing "unintended justice." Paraphrasing Saint Paul, Stuart cautioned the jury to "remember that vengeance belongs only to the Most High." The prosecution and its allies knew all about bias, Stuart claimed, and were doing their best to use it to sway the jury. [365]

Perhaps worse, Stuart insisted, "Blackburn's friends and a great Corporation were arrayed to support and sustain the Commonwealth's cause." VMI Superintendent Frances Henney Smith, he charged, was particularly guilty of "improper zeal" in that regard. An unbiased observer could not, Stuart claimed, "see the propriety of bringing the weight of that institution [VMI] against the prisoner."

Nor was Stuart aware, he said, "that the head of that institution could divert funds from their legitimate purpose to the support of a criminal prosecution," especially "when the prisoner was in the hands of the law and there were means provided by law for prosecuting him, and a gentleman recognized and appointed to attend to that duty and to see that the law was executed."

Coating damnation of Blackburn with a thin layer of praise, Stuart insisted:

It was not necessary to employ counsel to defend the reputation of the deceased. He was brave, he was virtuous, he was a young man of noble character and was actuated by good feelings; yet he was arbitrary, he was dictatorial, he was overbearing and haughty in his demeanor.

It was not that Stuart thought less of young Blackburn for those "qualities," he claimed, "but they led to the unfortunate tragedy." Even more unfortunate, he continued, was that Blackburn had been sent to VMI where such qualities, both positive and negative, would be reinforced, and where, as a result, he had been "engaged in several difficulties."

Defense Counsel and former Secretary of the Interior Alexander Hugh Holmes Stuart (1807–1891). *Wikimedia Commons.*

Unlike Blackburn, Stuart observed, Christian was "of excellent character and jovial disposition." He was beloved by his "highly respectable neighbors" and "a kind and affectionate son."

"All his associations," Stuart insisted, "were those of a gentleman." While Blackburn had been admitted to VMI "to learn the arts and sciences of a soldier," Stuart noted, Christian had "come to this community to study law with Judge Brockenbrough, and was received into the best company."

Then, Stuart asserted, poor Christian was seduced and abandoned.

> *A young lady of extraordinary beauty and attractions came here from Botetourt. Christian's young heart was touched by her charms, and he sought her acquaintance, and gave her the most devoted attention. He had even formed in his own mind the determination of seeking her hand and so reveals his secret to one of his companions. He meets with her at the festivals and parties of the winter season, and shows her the most unremitting attachment and devotion. He looked forward with a panting breast to his engagement to go with her to church, and his feelings rise when she reminds him of his engagement to accompany her to church. Thus elated, and his heart buoyant with hope and joy, he receives the cold and chilling note from Miss Anderson, declining to go with him to church, and no reason is given for this singular course.*

What, Stuart asked, was a gentleman to do? He retraced the history of the Christian/Anderson/Blackburn tragedy in the same order, and almost in the same words as Dorman had used the preceding day. When he reached the "interview" at McDowell's Hotel, Stuart spoke once more of duty and honor:

> *Christian was bound to notice the insult in some way or be ostracized from society and from the company of ladies and all gentlemen who highly estimated character, and by every white-livered coward who now condemns him, condemned as a degraded man in their estimation, and he would have felt a sense of degradation.* [Thus] *it was an imperative duty on Christian to his friends, and to himself, to demand of Blackburn an apology or explanation for his conduct.*

As for the fight itself, Stuart summed it up for the jury in simplest terms: "Christian...demanded an apology, and Blackburn refusing to give it, Christian called him a rascal, and Blackburn seized him and had him down, choking him, and...in the last gasp he [Christian] inflicted the fatal wound."

Stuart then turned to the embarrassing contradictions in the Commonwealth's case. At the preliminary hearings in January, Stuart reminded the jurors, the prosecution's witnesses said they believed the fatal wounds were delivered after Blackburn and Christian had risen from the ground, at some point after Massie had seen them struggling there. At that time, Stuart noted, everyone agreed, "If it had been given when they were down, Blackburn could never have arisen."

"Now," Stuart continued, with the new "third pool" of blood theory, "they have changed their front, and are contending that Blackburn was twice down after the fatal stab was given."

No doubt shaking his head, Stuart expressed his personal amazement at the permutations in the prosecution's story, put Captain Moore on trial, questioned his competence and thanked him for helping the defense, all in the same deft stroke.

> *I will acquit the Commonwealth's Attorney of all blame in the matter, as he did not know of the evidence in relation to the alleged third pool of blood until during the progress of this trial…As the Commonwealth has introduced evidence in relation to this third pool of blood, it is incumbent on them to reconcile it with the other facts proved, and to establish their hypothesis beyond a reasonable doubt, and if a reasonable doubt is left, the jury is bound to give the benefit of that doubt to the prisoner.*

Stuart's own opinion (confirmed by the testimonies of Colonel Smith, Major Preston, Dr. Junkin, Mr. Massie and Dr. Davidson), he pointed out, was that the "third pool" simply did not exist. And whatever the number of pools of blood, Stuart insisted, "it was apparent from all the circumstances that Christian had not inflicted the mortal wound until he had been abused, assaulted and choked to suffocation, and then, in *extremis*, he had inflicted the wounds on Blackburn."

Stuart, by that point, had been holding forth for three hours or more, certainly more than poor Alfred Douglas, the sick juror, could bear.

Out of consideration for Douglas, if not for Captain Moore and Mr. Michie, Judge Thompson called a three-hour recess at noon for dinner, rest and recuperation.

Douglas and the other jurors, he made clear, were to be back in the courtroom and ready to hear testimony by three in the afternoon.

43

Day Seven: Stuart vs. Michie

Thursday, April 20, 1854

The Afternoon[366]

After a three-hour dinner recess, Judge Thompson reassembled the jury and ordered Alexander Hugh Holmes Stuart to press on.

Stuart began with a recitation of cases "similar" to that of Christian, in which the accused murderer had been acquitted.

He then reviewed at length the evidence supporting the notion that Christian had been hurt and acted in self-defense: bruises on his throat, spitting blood in the jail, Blackburn's height and weight advantage. Given the desperate situation in which he found himself, Stuart argued, Christian was justified "in the eyes of God, and of man, in killing his adversary."

Indeed, under such conditions men were all too often required to ignore the laws of God and man. "It has been declared by a higher law," Stuart observed "that, 'Thou shalt not kill,' 'Thou shalt love thy neighbor as thyself,' and to 'Do unto others as you would have them do unto you,' and 'When you are struck on one cheek, to turn the other also.'" But, "If these rules were required to be carried out literally," he thundered, "there would be no more Christians." That was why God created both intelligence and juries.

The "spirit" of the law was to be carried out, Stuart argued, "according to the principles of common sense and according to the judgment of the prisoner's peers. If this were not the case, no law could be made practical and carried out in the manner and spirit of the lawmaker."

There is no provision in our Code on the subject of "self defense" because it was of such a nature that the Legislature has never attempted to define what were the rights of "self defense" but left to the juries of the county to settle it according to the circumstances of each particular case, and to give scope to the natural feelings of the jury and their opinion of the case from the circumstances proved.

From Stuart's perspective, it was obvious that Christian was fully justified in killing Blackburn to escape the larger man's stranglehold. He was equally convinced that the jury was honor-bound to acquit Christian because he had not intended to kill Blackburn, but only to wound him badly enough "to escape his deadly embrace."

Stuart begged the jury to put themselves in Christian's shoes. As sinners, "in a few short years they would have to stand as culprits before their God," he preached, and "they should now judge as they wished to be judged."

The special reporter for the Richmond *Dispatch* described Stuart's closing remarks as "a most affecting appeal such as it is in the power of few men to make."

He reminded them of the youth of the prisoner, a friendless and fatherless boy and a stranger among us; that the prisoner trusted to the intelligence, the justice, and the mercy of the jurors in this hour of his deep affliction.

Stuart then reminded the jury, "in a most feeling manner," that none of Christian's friends, associates or fellow law students had deserted him "in his distress and in his wretched condition."

Stuart followed his appeal to the solidarity of men of honor with a call to think of the effect of a conviction on Christian's mother and sisters.

His widowed mother was here, waiting to hear the issue of her son's fate—to know whether her son should be consigned to a felon's doom, or should be set free to join her, and to console her for the short remnant of her days, and be her joy and her hope—or her eternal sorrow. His young sisters just blooming into youthful loveliness and in the springtime of life were here also, waiting to hear a brother's fate and to learn if he was to be consigned to a dark cell and to leave them to mourn his sad fate for the rest of their days.

Stuart concluded with yet another appeal to Scripture which, according to the special reporter for the Richmond *Dispatch*, left many in the courtroom in tears:

> *It was for the jury to say should that son be freed and be delivered back to his friends, and that the joyous message might be carried to that mother and those sisters that her son "was lost, and is found; was bound and is free."*

As Stuart took his seat, Thomas Johnson Michie, counselor extraordinaire, friend of the court and the man retained at great expense to defend Thomas Blackburn's personal reputation, stood up and began to defend his own presence in the courtroom and his fee.

> *After calling the attention of the jury to the serious obligations resting upon them, and that they were bound to acquit the prisoner if he were innocent but that if he was guilty they should execute and enforce the law without fear, favor, or affection* [Michie] *proceeded to* [tell] *the jury how he happened to be engaged to assist the prosecution.*[367]

Michie assured the jury he was in the courtroom "from a high sense of duty, and not for the sake of the fee he was to receive." Both Captain Moore and Colonel Smith, he insisted, "desired his appearance in the case" and that it was because of his "desire to assist *these gentlemen* in the case, and from personal feelings *towards them*, and on the application of *the father* of the deceased, to vindicate the character of the deceased" that he had agreed to "assist the prosecution."

"For the purpose of merely having the law vindicated," Michie continued, "I would never have appeared for this cause for any fee."

Michie concluded his extraordinary opening apologia with a promise that he was not in court "to stretch the law beyond its proper bounds, or seek to inflict vengeance on the prisoner [or] to become the 'persecutor' for the friends of the deceased and the V.M.I."

No doubt having put fear into the hearts of those who had retained him, Michie then proceeded to show why he was worth his fee.

Adopting the tactics of Mosby, Dorman and Stuart, Michie crisply laid out the case for the defense and then proceeded with consummate skill to destroy it.

With withering scorn he reminded the jury that Christian had "induced" Tom Blackburn "to leave the Church of God," and after enticing him "into a dark place, and without one moment's warning," he had killed him. Yet despite those "damning and indisputable facts," he noted, "the defence [*sic*] set up by the guilty party is 'self-defence [*sic*].'"

Even if the jury were to take everything Christian had supposedly said about the affair as the gospel truth, Michie continued, "it is still a case of willful, deliberate, and premeditated murder." And no one knew, of course, what Christian had really said. He had never been called to the stand.

Contrary to the assertions of the Honorable Mr. Stuart, Michie continued, "self defence [*sic*] had been clearly defined in the law."

The accused had to be "reduced into a condition <u>requiring</u> him to kill his adversary" if he wished to claim self-defense. In addition, the accused must not have "caused the emergency to arise" which led him to kill someone. A man who merely feels threatened, Michie observed, "is not justified in killing his adversary."

In Virginia, in 1854, no white man in living memory had been sentenced to death for killing another white man in a "fair" fight.[368] Michie did his best to change that record, by all accounts with extraordinary style and eloquence.

If Christian "brought on the emergency by beginning the affray, and was then reduced to the necessity of killing Blackburn to save his own life," Michie argued, the law is clear: "this is no 'self defence [*sic*].'"

Citing precedent, Michie argued that "'self defence' [*sic*] was intended by the law not to shield the 'guilty' but to protect the 'innocent,'" and there was no way the jury could possibly see Christian's role in the killing of Tom Blackburn as that of an "innocent" man.

Christian, he pointed out, "had made himself a moving magazine before he went into the affray" and "had with him pistols, a bowie knife and a stick."

As for the cases of "justifiable homicide" cited by Stuart, Michie contended they were all irrelevant, not even remotely analogous to the case now before the jury.

Having spoken to the law, Michie now turned, to the matter of Tom Blackburn's good name. Much to the chagrin of Christian's defenders, Michie's defense of Blackburn's character leaned heavily on his taking the offensive against that of Charles Burks Christian.

Michie began by refuting a number of assertions raised explicitly by Christian's defenders, or implied by their comments and questions.

"Mr. Blackburn did not occupy the relation of a lover to Miss Anderson," Michie reminded the jury, "but that of a more disinterested one, of a sister, or an intimate friend, and [one] who felt bound to attend to her reputation and character."

As for the alleged "insults" suffered by Christian, Michie simply dismissed them.

Mary Evelyn Anderson had done nothing more than decline to go to church with him, and had done so with a simple and entirely appropriate note.

Christian had no right to consider her behavior insulting, Michie insisted. "She was merely a casual acquaintance of his and no intimacy had grown up between them."

Christian's missive, on the other hand, Michie described as "a most remarkable letter written to a young lady still in her teens." Christian, Michie pointed out, "addresses her as an old acquaintance," which she surely was not.

Even more ridiculous was Christian's notion that Blackburn, or anyone who advised her not to accompany Christian to church, was "a *slanderer* and a *calumniator.*"

Counsel for the defense, Michie continued, had repeatedly tried to make the jury believe Christian's letter to Mary Evelyn Anderson was written "in confidence" and that Cadet Blackburn was thus honor bound to take no notice of it, even after he had seen it.

Such notions were absurd, Michie argued, and read Christian's letter aloud.

How could Christian have meant for his note to have been concealed "from all the rest of the world," Michie asked, when in it, he accused Anderson's friends of abusing him and then asked her to give up their names?

As for Blackburn telling his cousin about Christian's reputation in the community, Michie reminded the jury that he had warned her "on the recommendation of his intimate friend, Mr. Humes, on whom he could rely."

Once Humes had confided in him, Michie insisted, Blackburn was honor bound to tell his cousin what Humes had said. Blackburn, he contended, was thus "not to blame in the matter."

Michie then did his best to exonerate Anderson's aunt, Evalina Moore. "Mrs. Samuel McDowell Moore," he insisted, "in a spirit of mirth and merriment, advised Miss Anderson to show this ridiculous letter to some persons at her house. It was a letter talking of blood and thunder, and contained sentiments of love and Latin quotations. It was a proper subject for merriment and ridicule."

Blackburn, of course, found himself in a "predicament," a moral dilemma, as soon as he read the letter. And yet, Michie insisted, even though Blackburn "had been overwhelmed with abuse because he had ventured to give advice to his cousin," he continued to behave as "a gentleman."

Blackburn left the Moore house, Michie observed, making "no declarations of vengeance or of retribution, but left smiling, to prevent the ladies from seeing that he felt that he was deeply wronged by the denunciation of Christian, and intended to take no notice of it."

Indeed, it was only after consulting three different friends, Cadets Bruce, Humes and Horner, that Blackburn decided to see Christian at all.

"Mr. Blackburn's motive was a noble and disinterested one," Michie insisted, even though "he had been denounced as a *calumniator* and as a base and envious fellow."

"By the 'code of honor,'" Michie argued, there was more than enough in Christian's letter not only to "justify Blackburn in telling Mr. Christian that he was the person alluded to" but for Blackburn to demand that Christian retract his denunciations. "But this he did not do," Michie continued. By any standard of conduct Blackburn "showed great moderation."

Yet Blackburn had to do *something*. Had Blackburn done nothing, Michie argued, Anderson would have thought he had said something about Christian "he could not sustain" and thus "produce an intimacy between her and Mr. Christian."

Far from threatening or insulting Christian, Michie insisted, Blackburn "*honored* him by going to tell him what he had said of him and that if it was not correct, he could correct it."

Christian apparently agreed, Michie continued, given that he said to Blackburn's face, "If that was your motive, I honor you for your noble principles."

With those words, the seventh day of the trial ended. Michie would return the next morning to finish.

Day Eight: Michie vs. Doyle

Friday, April 21, 1854[369]

By 9:30 on Friday morning, "a crowd of ladies" once more "occupied the bench" of Judge Thompson's courtroom, awaiting Thomas Michie's closing statement for the prosecution and the Honorable Robert Doyle's close for the defense.[370]

Michie remained on the offensive.

"The positions taken by the very able counsel for the defence [*sic*]," he began, "did not mitigate, but increased the guilt of the prisoner."

> *They only showed the existence of malice, or at least such a state of facts from which malice must be inevitably shown, and...they show premeditation from the fact of Christian preparing himself with deadly weapons. No insult or aggravation on the part of Blackburn could justify the course of Christian.*

Though his own role in the case was that of a defender of the good name of Thomas Blackburn, Michie admitted that doing so would "inevitably, and properly" assist in the conviction of Charles Burks Christian. By "acquitting" the conduct of Blackburn, Michie conceded, he could not help but reinforce the clear evidence of Christian's "guilt."

That said, Michie got on with the job.

Christian's letter to Mary Evelyn Anderson, Michie observed, boasted that "he would bring the offender to justice." That phrase, he said, clearly demonstrated Christian's "hostile purpose."

Samuel McDowell Moore's youngest daughter, Sallie Alexander Moore (1840–1920). *Moore, Memories, 16.*

Michie then reviewed the details of the ill-fated Saturday "interview" at McDowell's, contrasting Christian's hostility to Blackburn's "generous disposition and brave spirit."

"Blackburn believed that there was no danger of his interview bringing a difficulty," Michie asserted, "and he boasted not of any vengeance that he was seeking."

In an effort "to do an act of justice and generosity to Christian," Michie continued, Blackburn went to McDowell's and "with a courteous manner and an open demeanor" told Christian "in the mildest terms that he could use" that "although he knew nothing of him personally, he had heard that his standing among the ladies of Lexington was such that he did not think it proper for his cousin to keep his company."

"In making this communication to Christian," Michie observed, Blackburn "did it quietly, gentlemanly and in a more respectful manner than the conduct of Christian deserved."

"It is impossible that Blackburn could have told Christian that his character was infamous," Michie concluded, given the testimony that Christian replied to him, "If that was your motive, I honor you for your noble principles."

Indeed, Michie pointed out, at the end of the "interview," Blackburn gave Christian "a polite 'good morning' and left."

What was surprising, Michie asserted, was that Blackburn had behaved so courteously, even though Christian had "demanded his name from a lady and declared that he would bring him to justice."

Nor did the supposedly outraged Christian "insult Blackburn or demand an apology," even though Blackburn was "there before him unarmed."

After the interview, Michie continued, Blackburn was not at all boastful, even when he told his friends "it resulted just as he expected, and that Christian had not courage to strike a child." Blackburn, Michie said, was simply reporting what had happened and, in Michie's words, "if Christian was injured in the matter he had injured himself."

In contrast to Blackburn's restrained and gentlemanly behavior, Michie pointed out, Christian immediately began "telling tales" in order to gather support from his friends.

> *Did he report to his friends the actual result of that interview? If he had done so his friends would have declined any advice in the matter. But he tells them that he was intimidated, and that Blackburn, he believed, was armed. He was asked why he did not strike Blackburn at the moment; he said that he thought there was a combination among the Cadets to beat him; that one of them had got his stick from him.* [371]

All that was a lie, Michie insisted. "It has been proved here that Blackburn was not armed, and that there was no reason to believe that he was armed. There was a regulation of the V.M.I. against carrying concealed weapons and that it was proved that the Cadets made it a point of honor to observe this regulation."

Christian's lawyers claimed their client was "intimidated" because he had heard stories of the cadets "having combined, and having beat a cow-drover."

That tale was twisted beyond recognition, Michie insisted.

The real story? "A cow drover had abused a young Cadet, a mere boy, who came to the V.M.I. crying." A cadet "had pursued him" and "taken that justice which the heartless drover denied to the boy." The thrashing of the cow-drover, Michie noted scornfully, "was certainly an act of much [greater] aggravation than Mr. Christian had received."

Christian also lied to his friends about the loss of his beloved silver-headed cane. "The Cadet who had taken Christian's stick," Michie observed, had no idea Blackburn was on his way to the hotel, and "merely took it to look at it." At least two witnesses, he pointed out, testified "that the stick had been given back to Christian before Blackburn called him out of the bar-room."[372]

As for Christian's contention that he gave Blackburn fair warning at the end of their "interview," Michie observed, "If Christian had told Blackburn that 'He would see him again' he could not have also said to him, 'If that was your motive I honor you for your noble principles.'" McDowell's barkeeper had also sworn that both Christian and Blackburn "looked satisfied" after the interview, and Blackburn's subsequent conduct clearly showed that he "considered that the matter was at an end."

Christian had put himself in the wrong "from the moment he had made something special out of Miss Anderson's refusal to walk to church with him," Michie argued. "She had a right to refuse and was not bound to give any reasons for her refusal."

Indeed, Michie insisted "Christian's whole cause in the matter was wrong and showed a hostile and revengeful spirit."

> *He had a single-barreled rifle pistol, with which he had been practicing, and boasted that he could "fire five balls in succession into the space of a dollar." This was not sufficient. He went and bought 'this savage revolver' and went out and tried it and found that it shot "tolerable well." He told his companions that the single barreled pistol was a dangerous one, and if he shot at any one with it he would be a "goner." Yet he took this single-barreled pistol, the revolver, and the Bowie knife with him, and "thus armed as a locomotive magazine" he goes to meet Blackburn.*[373]

"And where does he go" to confront Cadet Blackburn, Michie thundered, "despite all advice from his friends and acquaintances?"

"He goes to the house of God—a spot consecrated to holier things and to the affairs of another world." Worse, he went there not once, but twice on the same day, trying, he said, to avoid meeting large numbers of cadets when he confronted Blackburn.

The second time Christian "invaded" the house of God, "with his pockets full of weapons and his arms full of sticks," Michie noted, he saw Blackburn "with a lady." He "must have known" that, if Blackburn were walking a lady to church, "he could not be armed."

Christian's contention that he went heavily armed to church "expecting that the matter would be amicably settled" was simply "nonsense," Michie observed. Christian's friends, Michie pointed out, had advised him to *write* Blackburn to settle the affair. W.M. Morris, Christian's friend and fellow law student, had even drafted a note for him.

But now, Michie argued, Christian's dander was up. He suddenly "remembered" Blackburn "had said that 'he took the responsibility for his and his cousin's acts'" and was "slandering him as a coward over town."

Although Christian himself appeared to be the only witness to this phenomenon, Michie observed, he was now determined that Blackburn would either "retract what he had said on Saturday" or their meeting would be "a hostile one."[374]

Having made his decision, Michie continued, Christian armed himself, went to the church, saw Blackburn and took him outside.

Did Christian at that point still fear a "combination" of the cadets against him?

Michie reminded the jury that two cadets, thinking there might be trouble, followed Christian and Blackburn, "but seeing them go around in the dark, and apprehending no difficulty then returned into the church."

"Was this not enough to have satisfied Christian that there was no combination of the Cadets against him and that his unworthy suspicions against the young gentleman of the noble Institution were unfounded, and to have caused him to refrain from using his deadly weapons?"

Of course not, Michie argued. "They go into a dark corner, and the unarmed one is murdered in a few moments in your streets."

Then Christian "runs briskly to the hotel" and tells his law school friends and companions "he has killed Blackburn in self defence [*sic*]," and that he himself "is not hurt."

"Christian was a lawyer himself, or was here receiving instructions on the laws of his country from the well-stored mind of his able instructor," Michie reminded the jury. "That instructor was also ready to give him advice in any difficulty that he might be in, and stood here [in court] *in loco parentis*." But Christian, Michie insisted, "did not think proper to ask that advice, but misstated the matter to his fellow students and then acted contrary to their advice."

Now, Michie fumed, because he claims Blackburn was choking him, Christian insists that the Commonwealth acquit him on the grounds of self-defense. "The defense continues to insist that it is up to the Commonwealth to prove that Christian did NOT act in self defense but that is simply not so." Once it was proved that someone had killed Tom Blackburn, the case had to be treated as "a crime of the highest degree," Michie argued. The evidence was absolutely clear that Christian killed Blackburn. "To be found innocent," Michie insisted, it is up to Christian "to mitigate it, or to cast a doubt over it" and "if he cannot do that, then the Jury is bound to see that the highest penalty of the law is inflicted."[375]

Though others should suffer with him, though his mother and sisters should have to follow him to a felon's grave, and be ruined by his crime, still the Jury have a sacred duty to perform to their community, to the laws and to the welfare of society.[376]

Michie was apparently just warming up when Judge Thompson broke for the midday meal.

45

Day Eight: Michie Earns His Fee

Friday, April 21, 1854[377]

The Afternoon

Because Charles Christian never testified under oath, critical statements attributed to him were, legally, hearsay. In an effort to help the jury understand what that meant, Thomas Michie began the afternoon portion of his summation with a short lecture on the law.

The defense had insisted, Michie pointed out, that because the prosecution had introduced statements allegedly made by Christian, the court was honor bound to treat them as if they were both accurate and true.

Legally, that simply wasn't true, Michie insisted, citing a number of cases to prove that "if Mr. Christian's declarations are taken as evidence" the jury could "believe or give credit to some parts...and disregard the other parts...or disregard all of it and form their own opinions in relation [to] their truth or falsity."

Indeed, Michie pointed out, if one looked at everything Christian was reputed to have said or done so far, the only real conclusions one could draw were that his "plea of self-defence [*sic*] was swept from under him." Just because Christian *believed* he had acted in self-defense, Michie continued, didn't mean that he was correct.

Turning to the letter of the law, Michie pointed out that, contrary to the defense counsel's earlier statements, Virginia was quite specific on what had to be done by a defendant claiming self-defense.

The party killing his adversary must flee, and in every way try to save his own life, and be in danger of losing his own life or of great bodily harm, before he can rely upon the plea of "self-defence," [sic] and must not, in the same affray, have struck the first blow or begun the rencontre.

Knowing full well that "retreat" was not generally considered a viable option for a Virginia "gentleman," Michie reminded his jurors, "The laws of the land recognize no code of honor, and never authorize the infliction of personal chastisement for personal insults." Christian, a law student himself, must have known as much, Michie asserted, "when he said he killed Blackburn in 'self-defence' [sic] [and] that he was defending his honor and his character."

He certainly began the affray or brought it on designedly. It was his own fault that his honor and character were injured, for he brought it on himself. Whether Blackburn was standing up or bending down over Christian and choking him, or in any other conceivable position, still Christian is not entitled to the plea of "self-defence [sic]."

As for the sterling "character" Christian claimed he was defending, Michie pointed out that Christian had little to defend.

When Christian asked the advice of his friends…brave and straightforward Morris says challenge him.
But Christian said he would not…because "Old Specs" would not let Blackburn fight, and he had no money to go off to fight a duel.
They told him to fight Blackburn [in] a street fight, and he refused.
They told him to fight him with his fist[s]. Christian said Blackburn could whip him.
Mr. Moore told him then to cane him. Christian said they would double on him and that he believed Blackburn was armed and would kill him.
Mr. Moore told him to 'wing him' if he attacked with weapons. Christian made no objection to that course, for he was armed and had determined to use his weapons. He had caps prepared and bullets moulded [sic] and a Bowie knife at hand.

Christian's plan all along, Michie maintained, was to provoke Blackburn into a confrontation that would allow him to use his deadly weapons, ideally with his friends from the law school standing by to help him. Christian did his best to convince those friends to help him in some "outrageous act," Michie continued, and in the process resorted to telling tales about Blackburn that were simply not true.

Turning next to the matter of Christian's infamous "stolen" silver-headed cane, Michie pointed out that Christian had stated openly "a stick would not do in a contest with Blackburn." Instead, Michie insisted, he "intended to use and rely on his other weapons."

> *Then for what purpose did he take Blackburn from the church around into that dark place? He did not take his own stick. He took a lighter one, and said that [it] was enough for his purposes as he had two pistols and that dreadful Bowie knife.*

It was also clear to Michie that Christian's plan was "formed before he went to church." Christian's claim that Blackburn "looked upon him with scorn as he entered the vestibule and he was *then* determined to demand of him an explanation," Michie characterized as a tale no one could believe.

> *He must have gone then to the church to carry out a preconceived purpose, or why did he thus go against all this advice with such weapons about him. He must have, at least, intended to use the pistols and the Bowie knife, if the stick should appear insufficient. They were, at least, intended to be used as a last resort.*

The law was clear, Michie argued. "In such cases the prisoner could not avail himself of the plea of 'self-defence' [*sic*] and that this was a case of murder of the first degree."

As for Christian's alleged remark that he did not "intend" to kill Blackburn, Michie cited both case law and common sense. "If he intended to use the weapons, first or last," Michie insisted, "it is still murder."

> *Every man is supposed, in the eye of the law, to have intended to do whatever is the natural and inevitable consequences of his acts. He uses a frightful Bowie knife, and with it kills Blackburn, and then says he did not intend to do it. Can such an excuse be taken? If it can, then a man may do any act of violence, and afterwards get off with the declaration, "I did not intend to do it."*

Christian's self-serving pleadings came less from his heart, Michie insisted, than from his training as a law student.

Christian had been studying the laws of his country for some twelve months. Christian must have known, when he jumped upon the pavement and looked back and saw Blackburn fall and lie motionless upon the earth that he had killed him. The prisoner, there watching him in the agonies of death, and then running to the hotel, knew full well that Blackburn had received a fatal wound and was dying. Having the deadly weapon in his hand, although it was not his own, he threw it away. Did not Christian, under these circumstances, and with Blackburn's blood on his own face, know that he had killed him? And was not his subsequent declaration of sorrow and anxiety for the recovery of Blackburn dictated for the purposes of his own acquittal?

Michie next showed the jury the bloody clothes worn by Blackburn and Christian, describing as he did so the wounds inflicted by Christian with his borrowed Bowie knife.

Michie then wondered aloud why neither Blackburn nor Christian had called out for help, given that Jim Massie, Benton Taylor and their ladies were within sight and the congregations of both the Presbyterian and Baptist churches only yards away.

If Christian were really afraid he was about to die, Massie pointed out, he could easily have called for help. Tellingly, he remained silent.

Why was Blackburn silent?

With his throat cut, Michie noted, Blackburn "would necessarily lose the power of speech."

The very silence of the struggle, Michie noted, appeared to confirm other evidence that the "fatal wound was inflicted in the early part of the *rencontre.*"

Before yielding the floor to the defense, Michie felt compelled to address once more the attacks launched against him

Cadet Marcellus Newton Moorman (1835–1904), class of 1856. Later Colonel Francis Henney Smith's special courier and liaison. *VMI Archives.*

personally by Christian's lawyers and the difficulties surrounding the "third pool" of blood.

Michie regretted that "Counsel on the other side seemed to think that he was here to seek revenge for others, and to urge a conviction that the law would not sustain."

Michie challenged "those gentlemen" to "meet his argument, and answer logic with logic and law with law, and to confine their arguments to the law and the facts of this case."

As for how many pools of blood were to be found at the scene of the crime, Michie stated simply that it was "enough for him that the two pools of blood were Blackburn's blood, and that Christian had inflicted the mortal wound, and that the circumstances were as stated by Christian himself."

The "third pool" was, to Michie, "a matter of indifference," though it seemed plausible to him that it existed.

> *There were some five witnesses who swore that they saw this third pool of blood, and some five who swore they examined the ground minutely and did not see this third pool. All these were highly creditable witnesses, and deserving of equal credit. Yet those swearing to the fact that they saw it are entitled to more credit than those swearing that they did not see it. The first was positive, and the second was negative. And that positive testimony in such a case is always superior to negative testimony; the first must be true or the witness must have sworn falsely—the second may not be true* simply *by an innocent mistake of the witnesses.*

After a closing argument that lasted the better part of a day and a half, Thomas Michie at last took his seat.

The verdict of the Richmond *Dispatch* on his performance was unambiguous. "Mr. Michie's argument has been pronounced by all persons present as a most masterly effort, and even the greatest that he has ever delivered here. For power and strength no man could have surpassed it."

Judge Thompson ordered the court to reconvene the next morning at the usual hour.

46

DAY NINE: DOYLE FOR THE DEFENSE

Saturday, April 22, 1854[378]

Defense counsel Robert L. Doyle had spoken rarely during the first eight days of Christian's trial, limiting himself to what one observer remembered as "an occasional question," or now and then indicating that he was "looking out for a point in the case that should not be forgotten." He would more than make up for his earlier silence on April 22.[379]

At 9:30 a.m., he began what was described as a "very able and argumentative speech" that would last no less than five and a half hours. Most of Doyle's summation, the fourth on Christian's behalf, was taken up by yet another point-by-point review of the evidence presented in the case, a review that, at least in the eyes of the Richmond *Dispatch* special reporter, was "able" but broke little or no new ground.

Doyle's personal attacks on some of Blackburn's defenders and the "outside forces" behind them, on the other hand, were remarkable, arguably vicious, instructive, logical and highly emotional.

Even Doyle's opening remarks, by all accounts comprising little more than standard warnings against prejudice, appeared to have had a striking effect on those in the courtroom.

"He appealed in a most feeling manner to the Jury," according to one observer, "warning them to exclude from their minds all preconceived notions of the guilt of the prisoner, and to confine their consideration to the legal evidence in the case, and to remember that he was but a youth and a stranger here, without friends."

This poor, friendless stranger, Doyle continued, had already suffered from rumors that had "gone abroad condemning the prisoner before the facts of the case had been heard and before he had had a trial."

"Revenge" was in the air, Doyle insisted, and it was a revenge that "had purchased with base lucre the services of an advocate to pursue the prisoner to his death."

"Gold," he said, "had been given to purchase the blood of the prisoner, and the funds of the friends of the deceased, and the V.M.I. had been appropriated…to purchase this young man's blood."

Thomas Johnson Michie knew better than to engage in such an affair, Doyle proclaimed.

> *Mr. Michie showed from his declarations that he should not have been here, and if he had known the motives of those who employed him, he never would have been here. There had been no attempt made to impeach the character of Blackburn, and he had been imposed upon, under this pretext, to come into this case.*

To the contrary, Doyle insisted, the people who employed Michie were motivated by nothing more than "a fell spirit of revenge." Michie, in Doyle's eyes, was no better than a self-serving gun for hire.

> *Mr. Michie had, like a politician, several times explained his position here. He, although faithful and able, always looked on his own side of a cause, and pursued it to the utmost extent, without seeing anything on the opposite side.*

Doyle, on the other hand, insisted that he "would not be employed to prosecute a prisoner for all the wealth of Golconda's mines." Indeed, "all the diamonds of India" were not worth the "betrayal of the spirit of the law" or, by implication, the dangers to one's immortal soul, inherent in Michie's unethical behavior.

> *The court could appoint counsel to prosecute or to assist the prosecution, but the court would not employ a man to prosecute who had in his pocket a fee from the avenger of blood, or from the next of kin to him who was slain. The courts repudiate the doctrine of private vengeance. This doctrine of private vengeance is also repudiated by the divine law—it is there said that "Vengeance is mine."*

Doyle next reminded his disproportionately Presbyterian audience that, even "under the Mosaic dispensation there were cities of refuge where the murderer remained until he could have a fair trial." In "Christian" Lexington, however, poor Charles Christian was being thrown to the wolves, some of whom were being paid privately. "If Blackburn's parents have, as I learn they have, the proper Christian spirit," Doyle thundered, "they would not wish the prisoner offered up as a sacrifice to the remains of their departed son."

The role of "prosecutor" implied an impartial search for justice, Doyle noted, but Thomas Johnson Michie, "hired by the friends of the deceased could not help but be biased in favor of those who employed him, and he could not occupy that impartial position that the law intended a prosecutor should occupy."

According to Doyle, hiring Michie was improper, probably unethical and, worse, blatantly and repeatedly so.

Michie, he noted, had "several times, during his argument reminded the Jury that if they have a doubt in relation to the guilt of the prisoner, they should acquit him." Hypocrisy, Doyle argued. In reality, Michie "insisted that Christian must be treated as a man of bad character until he shows to the contrary" all the while asserting that it was "a crime for Christian, upon a few days acquaintance, to talk of being in love with Miss Anderson; and that it was a crying sin even to wish to walk with her to church; and that it was indelicate to ask her reasons when she broke her engagement to go with him to church."

Michie's arguments, Doyle asserted, "of course, cannot be sustained."

Doyle then read aloud, once more, Christian's oft-cited note to Miss Anderson.

"His note to her was respectful, and stated that if she had acted from her own whim the matter should end here," Doyle insisted. Far from indicating that Christian had any hostile intent, the note revealed Christian's genuine desire to prove to Miss Anderson that "he could disabuse her mind and [that of] 'the world' of any idea that his character was not good."

Doyle got to the heart of the matter, however, with a blunt appeal to honor and deeply held views on the legitimacy of swift, direct and violent action in its defense.

> *The slanderer is the worst of all enemies, and his venom out-venoms all the worms of the Nile, and in some cases there is no other remedy against him but a Bowie knife or pistol; and although the avenger's course is not to be*

Clyce's "Exchange" Hotel and Tavern. Later the Old Blue Hotel. *Special Collections, Leyburn Library, Washington and Lee University.*

altogether justified by the laws, yet public opinion justifies it, and the juries of the country never inflict punishment on the offender.

"Property of all kinds is protected by the laws," Doyle reminded the jury, yet "character, of greater value than all property…is left without any legal protection that can be made available."

"And if anyone come into a Court of Justice to demand damages for his lost character," Doyle continued, "he is hooted at, and everyone tells him that he should have killed the slanderer."

"Afterwards," of course, "those same persons are found among the crowd demanding that the murderer should be condemned to death, or an infamous punishing, for doing that which they themselves would have done."

For roughly five hours, Doyle led the jury through statement after statement to show that Christian, "a man of mild and gentle disposition and slow to take offence," had been grievously insulted, had killed Blackburn only in self-defense and had, himself, been the victim of a prosecution that couldn't manage its own witnesses, much less prove murder in the first degree beyond any shadow of a doubt.

The heart of Doyle's defense of Christian, however, lay in his unabashed appeal to southern "honor."

He was thus the perfect warm-up for the last member of Christian's defense team to speak, the sharp-tongued Charles Lewis Mosby, scheduled to open the tenth day of testimony on Monday, April 24.

Practically everyone in Rockbridge County was expected to be there to hear him.

They were in for a surprise even more startling and controversial than the mysterious appearance of the "third pool" of blood.

47

Day Ten: Brockenbrough Stands In

Monday, April 24, 1854[380]

W ell before Judge Thompson called the courtroom to order at 9:30 Monday morning, "The Bench was crowded...with ladies who had assembled to hear the argument of Charles L. Mosby, Esq., of Lynchburg" on behalf of the prisoner.

Instead of Mosby, however, the crowds saw former Secretary of the Interior A.H.H. Stuart rise and formally announce that "Mr. Mosby was confined to his bed by sickness." His physician, Stuart said, thought "it would be impossible and dangerous for him to attempt to address the jury."

In Mosby's place, Stuart announced, Judge John White Brockenbrough "would conclude the argument on behalf of the prisoner."

It is not recorded whether Stuart's announcement produced outcries or dead silence in the courtroom. Whatever the case, the impact on those supporting the Commonwealth must have been palpable.

Brockenbrough was Christian's teacher, and in mid-nineteenth century Virginia was under an unquestioned moral obligation to act *in loco parentis* with regard to the students under his purview. He was a professional mentor, a Federal judge and had already been accused of arming Christian with a bag of lawyer's tricks to escape prosecution.

Judge Thompson, who had already demonstrated he was not a man to allow mere illness to delay a trial, had visited Mosby earlier that morning. He confirmed that Mosby was truly ill, "unable from his prostration by sickness to discharge his weighty duty to the prisoner."

Thompson then ruled there "nothing improper or illegal" in having Judge Brockenbrough stand in for Mosby and that "he thought it entirely proper for him to do so."

Judge John White Brockenbrough then took the floor and proceeded to redefine his young student and all those who sought to convict him of murder.

Brockenbrough opened with self-deprecating remarks that the special reporter for the Richmond *Dispatch* described as a "most revealing and affecting statement of his embarrassment in thus appearing before them, and the immense responsibility devolving on him."

> *He quoted a most beautiful and appropriate passage from* Paradise Lost, *where the Poet calls on the Divine Power of Heaven to assist him and empower him to discharge this most weighty duty in a manner consistent with its weighty responsibility.*

Having thus established his credentials as both orator and instrument of heaven, Brockenbrough went on to dissect, sequentially, his fellow officers of the court, beginning with the Commonwealth's most vulnerable target, the venerable Thomas Johnson Michie, and those he considered Michie's evil allies.

Michie "had been employed by the friends of the deceased and the Virginia Military Institute to interpose his great intellect to sustain the cause of the Commonwealth," Brockenbrough began. VMI's role in this, he insisted, was both inappropriate and venomous.

> *The funds appropriated by the Legislature of the State to the purposes of education had been improperly contributed to add additional malignity and venom to this cause. This conduct in perverting these funds was worthy of all denunciation.*

"It has also been said," Brockenbrough continued, "that this fund should be thus misdirected for the purpose of sustaining the character and position of the VMI."

Not so, argued Brockenbrough.

> *Colonel Smith has, through a grave mistake or desire to pander to public prejudice, thus appropriated these funds to seek the blood of the prisoner. This is a singular act of patriotism, to be thus appropriating these funds to a private prosecutor, who has, with great ability, discharged his duty and earned his fee.*

As for the fears of Blackburn's family and friends that Tom Blackburn's good name would be sullied, Brockenbrough pronounced them misplaced. "Who was here to plant a nettle on the grave of that young man? All were willing to extend to him the most irreproachable character."

The Blackburn family's hired gun, on the other hand, sought to minimize "every circumstance and consideration that could weigh in behalf of the prisoner" and "urged his conviction by every argument and every circumstance that could drive the minds of the jury to a conviction of the prisoner of murder in the first degree."

Why?

"Mr. Michie had his clients behind him, urging him on," Brockenbrough argued. Some were there, he claimed, to play a role, "to give a satanic laugh at his jests and jokes, and at the position assumed by the defence [*sic*]."

"Why?" Brockenbrough asked rhetorically.

By taking advantage of "that viper's breath of popular prejudice which has pervaded this community and even entered this sanctuary of Justice, to give weight to the prosecution and to the conviction of the prisoner."

And who was to blame for this perversion of justice?

"This is the course that has been pursued," Brockenbrough told the jury, "by the special and private prosecution of Colonel Smith."

In comparison, Commonwealth's Attorney Moore, in Judge Brockenbrough's estimation, "had…fairly considered the circumstances and evidence in this cause."

Both "Christian and Blackburn," Brockenbrough insisted, "had come here as high-minded respectable young men, and upon a perfect equality, and had been received in the community as gentlemen."

Then, he insisted, Mary Evelyn Anderson had worked her wiles and broke Charles Christian's heart.

> *Christian becomes acquainted with Miss Anderson, a beautiful and accomplished young lady and engages her company to go with him to church, and sometime afterwards she had even thought proper to remind him of his engagement. When his heart was warmed and enlisted for the young lady by her smiles, elicited by his respectful attention, and when he was animated with the purpose of even addressing her and seeking her hand, he receives the chilling note that, "Miss Anderson declines to go with Mr. Christian to church according to engagement."*

Though seduced and abandoned, Christian was no fool. He knew very well, Brockenbrough pointed out, that there "must be some cause for this treatment, and naturally supposing that some one had been slandering him, wrote her a note, asking in the most respectful and flattering manner the name of his 'calumniator,' and if it should not be given, that his note should be returned."

Christian received, of course, neither an answer from Miss Anders nor the return of his note.

Then "some two weeks afterwards, Mr. Christian went to Mr. Moore's to see Miss Anderson, and she refused to see him."

"He bore it all," Brockenbrough said, "believing that he had a secret enemy who was thus secretly injuring him."

In contrast to the noble, silent suffering of his client, Brockenbrough pointed out, Blackburn's friends made jokes at Christian's expense. Christian's note, written in confidence to Anderson, was made "the subject of merriment between Miss Anderson and the unfortunate Blackburn."

With Blackburn's all too public reading of Christian's letter at the Moore house, Brockenbrough argued, the affair had become an affair of honor, both for Blackburn *and* for Christian, a point he was firmly convinced had somehow escaped the jury.

> *It is insisted here that the spirit of honor, as dictated by the code of honor, required Blackburn to notice this letter, as the person who had advised Miss Anderson not to accompany Mr. Christian to church. But this code of honor is denied as applying to Mr. Christian, and from the argument he is not to have the benefit of it.*

Brockenbrough then proceeded, reluctantly of course, to plant at least a small nettle on Blackburn's grave. Blackburn had acted through a mistaken sense of duty and honor, Brockenbrough insisted, and in the process "had violated the fundamental principle of this code, which was to wantonly injure or insult no one."

The tragedy could have been averted, Brockenbrough insisted.

> *If Blackburn had gone to Christian and told him in a proper spirit and courteous manner, the actual state of the case, and that he knew nothing of him personally, and had given him his author, the matter would have been amicably settled, and Mr. Humes, by stating how he got his information of Mr. Christian's character in this community, would also have been honorably acquitted.*

The ruins of the Blackburn family cemetery at Spring Grove. Tom Blackburn's tombstone has disappeared. *Author's photograph.*

Instead, Christian's mentor continued, "Blackburn disregarded this duty to Christian," and sought out "Cadet Humes and Horner, two of the stoutest and most athletic of the corps. He goes with them in a hostile manner—'with a hostile purpose,' as Horner says in his testimony—thinking and intending that Christian should cower before Blackburn."

Indeed, what was poor Christian to think when Blackburn showed up accompanied by two strapping friends? Choosing his words carefully, Brockenbrough asserted that Christian was "challenged" as surely as if Blackburn had slapped him.

> *They call for him at the hotel. Christian and Blackburn were profound strangers to each other; yet Blackburn, without even seeking an introduction to Christian, calls him out and takes him into the passage and says to him, "I am the man who advised Miss Anderson not to accompany you to church," and "I did it because your character is such that I did not think it prudent for her to go with you." Blackburn's purpose, obviously, was to put the alternative before Mr. Christian to cower before him or to fight.*

And to that insult, Brockenbrough asserted, Blackburn added the threat of overwhelming force, throwing young Christian into a hopeless state of confusion.

What happened next?

Christian himself told that story, Brockenbrough noted, in words put into evidence by the prosecution's witnesses, words that were "entirely consistent throughout, and agree precisely with the circumstances proved."

The prosecution, on the other hand, seemed not only confused, but also confused in a way that demanded that Christian be acquitted.

> *In relation to the circumstances in regard to the interview, the two Prosecution Attorneys differ totally, and both of them read the rules on circumstantial evidence showing that if there is a doubt in the minds of the jury, they must acquit. This is of itself enough to throw a doubt over the whole matter, and to justify the jury in acquitting the prisoner.*

If the law required acquittal, Brockenbrough argued, simple justice, and a fundamental sense of honor, cried out for it, especially in view of Blackburn's behavior *after* the ill-fated interview.

> *Christian was then insulted and wronged throughout, and then Blackburn, through a false sense of honor, comes to intimidate him and make him cower before him—Blackburn turns away, having insulted the boy that had never injured him, and tells Humes and Horner that "it was just as he expected. He has not the courage to strike a child."*

Having thus denounced Christian as a coward to friends who would, no doubt, spread the word of it throughout the Cadet Corps, Blackburn then damned Christian in the presence of Mary Evelyn Anderson.

Could anyone then have the slightest doubt, Brockenbrough mused, that Christian "was thus warranted in his conclusion that a combination was forming against him and were bragging that they had put him down, and were resolved to keep him down?"

48

Day Ten: Brockenbrough's Last Stand

Monday, April 24, 1854[381]

O ne of the stickier thorns in the side of Christian's defenders was his choice of the Presbyterian Church, on a Sunday night, for his confrontation with Blackburn.

Brockenbrough addressed the issue by reciting Christian's hearsay rationale, a justification put into evidence by witnesses, he noted, called and examined by the prosecution.

"Christian went to the church," Brockenbrough reminded the jury, because he thought it was "the only place that he could meet with Blackburn."

Once there, "seeing Blackburn pass, and his lip curl with contempt and reproach upon him," Christian "asked him out, and required him to give him an explanation."

Having thus neatly transformed what the prosecution had described as an ambush by Christian into a spontaneous reaction to yet another egregious insult from Blackburn, Brockenbrough conceded that "Christian should not have gone to church at night for the purpose of having an interview with Blackburn. It was an improper time and place, and was the cause of the great public indignation at the time which caused all to style the act which followed from it a 'black assassination.'"

For Brockenbrough, however, Christian's error in his choice of time and place illustrated the undeniable justice of his claim, as a gentleman, to all the defenses due him, both under the law and the unwritten code of honor.

Indeed, Brockenbrough argued, if Christian had only "held his interview with Blackburn in broad daylight, and at a proper place he

VMI cadets in barracks on a Friday night, March 1855. Detail from a sketch. *VMI Archives.*

would have been justified by that very community which has condemned him." In the eyes of the community, "it would have been at least considered a case of excusable homicide."

Christian, however, truly feared a "combination" against him and, in Brockenbrough's paraphrase of Jefferson, "took up arms against his oppressor."

Three persons, Brockenbrough noted, "had come together to the interview at the passage of the Hotel to intimidate him, and cause him to cower before them." As the reporter for the Richmond *Dispatch* noted, "No honorable white male southerner could allow such a thing and continue to hold his head up in society, among his friends, and, indeed, within his own family."

But, Brockenbrough asked again, what was Christian to do?

"It is insisted *by the prosecution*," Brockenbrough observed, that Christian should have "challenged" Blackburn "rather than go into the matter as he did."

The same prosecutors then insist, he continued, "that because Christian did not do what they think he should have done—send a challenge, which itself was a felony—under the circumstances, [he] must be convicted of murder."

What could be more ironic, or unjust, Brockenbrough fumed? "The very persons who now condemn him as a murderer, would have scoffed at him and treated him as a blighted and blasted thing if he had patiently borne his insults." The implications of such an unnatural perversion of justice in the highest sense of the word were, to Brockenbrough, obvious.

> *I then demand his acquittal in the name of that law whose home is in the bosom of his God and whose voice is the universal harmony of nature.*

Approaching the midday recess and now clearly warming to the idea of Christian as victim, Brockenbrough waxed eloquent on the sterling character of his former student, three months a prisoner and now in the dock as his client.

In rapid succession he addressed or re-addressed most of the key elements of Christian's defense.

He praised Christian's neighbors, "who had come here to testify to his excellent character and innocent amiable life," and then planted yet another rhetorical nettle on the grave of Cadet Thomas Blackburn.

> *If Blackburn had been that high-souled chivalrous man that is claimed for him here, and had been actuated by that spirit at the time, he was bound to*

have made an explanation to Christian of his course, and declared to him that his intentions were not to injure him, and that he would try to release him from the imputations which he was forced to hear. Blackburn refused all this, and was determined to rivet this degraded character upon him.

Brockenbrough scoffed at the prosecution's "three pools of blood" theory, reviewing in detail the contradictory accounts of the evidence of the struggle on Nelson Street.

At some point in mid-oration Brockenbrough apparently realized he was doing precisely what he had promised not to do: review old evidence in mind-numbing detail. In the words of the special reporter from the Richmond *Dispatch*:

Judge Brockenbrough then referred to the fact that he had not heard the evidence with the intention of an argument of the cause, yet his great interest in the matter caused him to remember every material circumstance. His love and regard for the unfortunate boy now upon trial for his life (Mr. Christian had been a member of the Judge's law class) had caused him to remember it, and to use every exertion to save his life.

Brockenbrough's last words before the noon recess were reserved for Thomas Michie. Comparing his own motives to those of the prosecution's hired gun, Brockenbrough reminded the jury that Michie had actually gone so far as to suggest that the marks on Christian's neck were self-inflicted in order to support his claim of self-defense.

At that very moment, Judge Thompson adjourned the court for the noon meal. During that two-hour dinner break, Judge Brockenbrough discovered that Michie was not the only lawyer being damned in Lexington. Criticism of Brockenbrough himself was apparently so intense around the courthouse, he felt compelled to open the afternoon session with yet another, only slightly self-contradictory, self-justification.

I hear it suggested on the streets that it is rumored that it was a stratagem between Mr. Mosby and myself for him to pretend to be sick, and to enlist the sympathies of the jury by that means in the prisoner's behalf, and then I would take his place here. This is but the malignity of slander, and I appear here through necessity alone, and to attempt to supply the place of that gentleman, and I did not know that I would be under the necessity of arguing the cause until an hour before I came here. I had a suggestion on last evening that Mr. Mosby would be unable to be here, and that it would be even dangerous for him to come.

Whether or not such rumors were actually circulating (though the notion that they were is more than plausible), Brockenbrough was too good a lawyer to have passed up an opportunity to score Thomas Michie and drive home the notion that Charles Christian was being hounded to the scaffold by outsiders, scoundrels and other parties hopelessly confused about the essence of duty and honor.

Having now positioned himself as equally maligned and insulted, Brockenbrough began his final review of the evidence against Christian or, more precisely, the evidence that damned Christian's "persecutors."

Returning to the story of the fight on Nelson Street, Brockenbrough focused on Blackburn and Christian's departure from the church vestibule. Christian, Brockenbrough reminded the jury, had begun the fateful Sunday night "interview" by simply asking Blackburn for an explanation of his behavior. Blackburn, he insisted, replied with an insult. "Blackburn refused to give it [the explanation Christian demanded]; and thus refusing to do the last act of justice to the prisoner, would make no reparation for the injury he had done."

Under such circumstances, Christian's observation that Blackburn had "acted ungentlemanly" was simply correct. Blackburn, however, responded by telling Christian "not to repeat it," and when Christian replied, "You know it's true," Brockenbrough asserted, Blackburn started the fight that led to his own death.

Under such circumstances, Brockenbrough continued, how was it possible for the community to turn against young Christian, a mere boy? Through lack of judgment or bad decision-making, Brockenbrough answered, the most egregious examples of which were exemplified by VMI's Colonel Smith.

Smith, Brockenbrough charged, had taken personal responsibility for "diverting the funds of the V.M.I. to the prosecution of this 'boy.'" It was "a monstrous error," he argued, for Colonel Smith "to divert those funds to seek the blood of this injured and unfortunate young man."

"With great vehemence," Brockenbrough posited that Smith's behavior "would meet [with] the condemnation all well-thinking thinking men." Smith and his friends at VMI "wanted nothing less than the blood of Christian," Brockenbrough charged, "or they never would have been so eager in diverting those funds to a prosecution."

Turning to the laws related to self-defense, Brockenbrough capped a lengthy review of the literature with the observation that the prosecution seemed to be relying heavily on precedents established in the Selfridge-Austin murder case and the events of "Bloody Sunday," August 4, 1806, on State Street in Boston.

Brockenbrough observed that the "murder" in question occurred in Boston, was tried under Massachusetts law and, despite those original sins, if correctly interpreted, would still require the acquittal of Christian on the grounds that he had struck the fatal blow against Blackburn while in fear of losing his life.

Next, Brockenbrough once more damned the prosecution for its sudden "discovery" of the notorious "third pool" of blood. Brockenbrough clearly believed the Commonwealth and its "hired gun" had been backed into a corner by Christian's defense team and, in desperation, had engaged in what could only be considered grossly unethical behavior.

> *Nearly all the physicians testify that they believe that Blackburn had Christian down and was over him when the fatal wound was given, and the Commonwealth, finding that the testimony would not do, by their outside agents drum up a number of witnesses to prove the second* [sic] *pool of blood.*

Brockenbrough's scorn for the prosecution paled only slightly before his contempt for what he described as the state's "drummed up" witnesses. He assured the jury that even though these witnesses had "seen pools of different sizes and had located them at different places," he had "no doubt but that they believed what they say." That said, (and abstract theories of the relative weight of "positive" and "negative" testimony aside) Brockenbrough insisted the surprise witnesses "belong to a class of persons who, when they hear anything strange, say, 'yes, I knew before,' or 'I expected that it would turn out so.'"

In that regard, Brockenbrough could not resist one more poke at Tom Michie and the people who laughed at his jokes. According to one account, Brockenbrough, "feelingly alluded to an Irish jest of Mr. Michie on the subject of positive and negative proof which had produced a great laugh." It was not funny, Brockenbrough said. Indeed, "it caused the blood to run cold in his veins—that such mirth should be excited at such a jest on the most material part of the evidence in a criminal case of the importance of this… a matter that should be treated with great seriousness."

After one more lengthy review of the evidence, and after insisting, one more time, that "if Christian had not killed Blackburn, that Blackburn would have killed Christian," Brockenbrough concluded his "most able and affecting" five-and-a-half-hour exegesis with "a powerful appeal to the jury urging them to show the greatest mercy to the error of the youthful offender—and if possible, acquit him."

Their duty done, Brockenbrough concluded, the jury could then, with clear conscience, "send him hence admonished to go and commit no wrong hereafter—restore the boy to his weeping mother and heart-broken sisters, and...discharge your duty to the Commonwealth, and to all others, as he has suffered greatly already."

With that, Judge Thompson recessed for the day. The next day, the jury would hear the Commonwealth's closing statement and cast their votes on the fate of Charles Burks Christian.

49

DAY ELEVEN: VERDICT

Tuesday, April 25, 1854[382]

Juror Alfred Douglass was sick again on Tuesday morning, April 25, the day Judge Thompson expected to hear the last of the Commonwealth's closing arguments and send the case to the jury.

Not inclined to prolong a trial that had already consumed an entire session of the Rockbridge County Circuit Court, Judge Thompson had a "couch" brought to the jury box, installed the ailing Douglass and ordered Captain David Evans Moore to proceed with his closing arguments for the prosecution.

Moore was now clearly on the defensive.

After the customary opening exhortation for the jury to put prejudice from their minds and enforce the law as it was written, Captain Moore began his closing summary, not with a review of the case against Christian, but a defense of those who had hired Thomas Michie.

According to Captain Moore, Christian's defense was relying heavily on the contention that "an unwarrantable prejudice had been raised against the prisoner" and the notion that those who believed the unkind things being said about Christian had "employed Mr. Michie to assist the prosecution from a spirit of revenge."

Moore argued that nothing could be further from the truth. "It was right," he insisted, "that additional counsel should be employed to assist the prosecution when a number of counsel were employed on the other side" including "some of the ablest lawyers in the State."

Having defended the decision to hire him, Moore next defended the person of Thomas Johnson Michie.

"Mr. Michie had been the regular prosecutor in this court for a number of years," Moore reminded the jury, "and was a gentleman who would never carry the prosecution farther than he believed it was proper for him to go."

As for Colonel Smith's role in retaining Michie, Moore agued that if Michie "had been employed, and had consented to act under peculiar circumstances [and that] Colonel Smith had acted in the matter from a sense of duty and in order that he might discharge his duty to the young man who had been placed here under his charge and protection."

"But none of these matters," Moore insisted, really had "anything to do with the decision in this case. They were mere efforts to have the whole matter fully investigated."

Moore turned next to law and precedent. He clearly feared the defense had either confused the jury about their legal responsibilities, or worse, had convinced them that they would be justified in ignoring the law if "true justice" were to be served. Murder, Moore noted, is murder, whether in the first or second degree.

"If the intention of killing is conceived before the act is committed, or before the quarrel begins, it is murder of the first degree. If conceived at the time, it is murder in the second degree."

Moore seemed particularly worried that the jury had been convinced that they not only had a right, but a moral obligation, to acquit Christian. His arguments, however, continued to cede points to the defense.

"It is true that Christian had been grievously insulted," Moore admitted, "yet this gives him no right to seek revenge for the redress of his wrongs. This does not change this case from being murder of the first degree."

The law, Moore lectured, required that injured parties resort to the courts for justice, and Christian had "no right to take the matter into his own hands."

If acting under such a grievance of such a nature, he seeks his adversary and commits murder under such circumstances, it is not for you to pardon him for the offence. The pardoning power and the attribute of mercy belong to the Executive alone, and he may exercise it and pardon the prisoner, but you have no power over it.

In theory, Moore was absolutely correct. In practice, however, juries had exercised their power to override the explicit provisions of the law from time immemorial. Moore was of course intimately acquainted with "Golden Rule" appeals to juries and knew full well that juries that regularly delivered such "verdicts contrary to law" in the Commonwealth of Virginia.

As Moore continued, however, Blackburn's family and friends may well have begun to wonder if Moore were not himself in favor of mitigating Christian's sentence. He continued to raise and then concede points critical to Christian's defense.

> *Although the circumstances were suspicious on the part of Blackburn at the interview in the passage, and indicated that Blackburn wished to intimidate Christian and may have been armed, yet Christian had time to reflect and consult his friends. He then went and purchased a revolver, and the circumstance lead to the conviction that he bought it for the conflict. He got possession of Mr. Winn's Bowie knife, and armed himself for the conflict. I did not say, as was alleged by the counsel on the other side, nor did Mr. Michie say that Christian should have challenged Blackburn. We only said that it would have been better for Christian to have done so.*

As for premeditation, Moore again argued that, on the night of the killing, it was patently obvious that Christian planned to confront Blackburn in a way that would require the use of deadly force.

> *Christian, thus armed and hearing the church bell ring, said to his companions, "I must go," and thus he went to the church to look for Blackburn. Can there be a doubt then that the plan was all laid, and Christian had determined to take Blackburn out for the conflict?*

Moore next insisted that Christian's self-serving description of what happened on Nelson Street (or at least the secondhand version of it recounted by his friends and fellow law students) could not be more incriminating.

"They go out into a dark cross street," Moore reminded the jury. "Did he [Christian] think that an explanation made by Blackburn to him alone, there in the dark, would retrieve his reputation in the community, and would be a satisfaction for his wrongs?" If he were really serious about "satisfaction," Moore pointed out, Christian "should have required the explanation to be made in the presence of others."

It made no difference if Blackburn was on top of Christian when he was stabbed, Moore argued, just as it made no difference that Christian was allegedly prepared to back down if Blackburn had offered up an acceptable "explanation."

The secondhand accounts of Christian's description of the fatal encounter left no doubt in the prosecutor's mind that Christian himself had brought on the fight.

> *When Blackburn refused to apologize Christian then insulted him. Expecting Blackburn to strike him, he would then seek his revenge. [But] Blackburn did not strike him at once, but "told him not to repeat it." Christian, according to his own statement, did repeat it, and then Blackburn took hold of him, and Christian used the weapons he had prepared for the purpose.*

Conceding that his opinions about the implications of the Selfridge murder case in Boston differed from both Thomas Michie's *and* Judge Brockenbrough's, the Commonwealth's attorney insisted that if Christian brought on the conflict and Blackburn was killed, Christian was guilty of murder.

Moore scoffed at Christian's claims that he feared for his life.

> *Christian was not in danger of losing his life, or of even great bodily harm, as he alleges, when he inflicted the fatal wound. Few persons are killed by choking in a fight, and it appears from the testimony that Christian was down but a short time and was able to rise immediately, and run briskly away.*

Moore next turned to the "third pool" of blood and its implication for the notion that "the parties must have been on their feet when the fatal blow was given." Moore clearly believed the "third pool" damned Charles Christian by showing that Blackburn had been stabbed early in the fight.

> *The existence of this third pool had been proved by some five respectable witnesses and about the same number has stated that [t]hey had examined the ground of the combat, and could find no blood at that point. The latter seemed to have examined a single line where they supposed the parties to have been, and they seem to have thought that parties fight according to the rules of mathematics, and have accordingly examined only one line, where they supposed the parties were scuffling. The only rational solution is that this third pool had run from Blackburn before the parties fell when seen by Mr. Massie, and that the wound must have been given at the beginning of the fight.*

Despite Christian's self-serving claims to the contrary, Moore continued, he must have known full well that Blackburn was dying before he left the scene of the crime.

> *After the conflict Christian sprang upon the pavement, and stood there to look back and see that Blackburn was lying prostrate on the ground, and dying from his wounds. Christian then must have known, before he went to the hotel, that Blackburn was a dying man. He then threw away the knife and immediately ran.*

Moore then began his final charge to the jury, imploring them to "withdraw from their minds every other consideration except the evidence and the law."

> *If the prisoner is guilty, the jury must discharge their duty by finding him guilty and leave the exercise of mercy to the Executive, who has power to "temper the wind to the shorn lamb."*

"I do not think that Christian intended to flee when he retuned to the hotel," Moore conceded, "and any benefit that he is entitled to on that account, you are at liberty to give him."

That said, Moore launched into a tight summary and rebuttal of each key point offered in Christian's defense.

While conceding that Blackburn bore at least some portion of the blame for the course of events leading to his death, Moore agreed with Judge Brockenbrough "that Christian should do something for his character under these circumstances. But Christian did the worst thing he could have done."

In conclusion, Moore told the jury:

> *You can give whatever weight you think proper to these opinions of mine. If you think that the prisoner is guilty, you must then find him guilty. We have no other way but to act on human testimony in such matters. If you exercise your judgments in fully considering the matter, and then come to the conclusion of guilt, your consciences have no more to do with the matter than those of other persons. The matter is now with you.*

Captain Moore then took his seat, and Judge Thompson sent the jury out to consider its verdict.

Bedford County Courthouse, Liberty (now Bedford), Virginia. *Courtesy of Thomas A. Markham and the Bedford County Museum.*

After fully eleven days of testimony, argument and counter-argument, the jury was out no more than half an hour. They could not agree on a verdict. Judge Thompson "then read to them some instructions that he had prepared defining the law clearly on the distinctions and characteristics of the different degrees of murder and manslaughter and sent them out for a second time."

After about an hour, the jury sent word to Judge Thompson that they were still unable to agree.

Thompson polled them individually. Each and every juror admitted, "there was no likelihood of their agreeing." Thompson, apparently believing he had no other choice, dismissed the jury.

According to the special reporter from the Richmond *Dispatch:*

> *The Judge then suggested that the prisoner had better be removed to another county for his next trial, as it would be impossible to get a jury here without bringing them from an adjoining county, and that owing to the excitement another trial should not be had in this county.*

After considering several counties as alternative venues, "it was at length agreed that the prisoner should be sent to Bedford, to be tried there at the next Circuit Court."

The *New York Times* reported the story on May 8, misidentifying Christian as "a member of the Virginia Military Institute…without family or extensive family influence" and Blackburn as "a gentleman well known in the vicinity." The case "now goes to another county," the *Times* reported, noting that "Both the prosecution and defence [*sic*] were conducted with distinguished legal ability."[383]

Part X

DOUBLE SHOCK

The Agony of Defeat

C aptain Moore's open-and-shut case against Charles Christian had thus come to naught. The *Enquirer* reported that only one juror had voted outright in favor of a capital conviction. Eight others thought Christian guilty of second-degree murder, though "with the express intention of accompanying this verdict with a recommendation to unconditional executive pardon." Of the remaining three, two were for outright acquittal, and one for imprisoning Christian in the county jail. "But the latter," the *Enquirer* reported, "was willing, if necessary, to acquit entirely."[384]

Friends and supporters of Tom Blackburn were outraged, and stories in wild contradiction to the *Enquirer*'s account soon surfaced.

On May 18, "Justice," a Lexington *Gazette* editorialist, reported a much narrower margin of victory for the defense and hinted strongly at jury tampering and corruption.

> *That the jury failed to agree seemed to excite no surprise; the actual result appeared to have been generally anticipated from the moment the jury were impaneled. It was, in fact, curiously rumored, from the time the first witness was examined, and before the facts mainly relied [upon by] the counsel for the accused in his defense had been proved, that a certain named member of the jury would hang it unless the rest would agree to a verdict of acquittal. We shall make no attempt to account for this extraordinary, but notorious fact.*[385]

Cadet John Howard Sharp, writing nearly fifty years after the event, still firmly believed that a single juror had "saved" Christian. "The trial in Lexington ended with eleven members of the jury in favor of conviction," he wrote, "and only one for acquittal." According to Sharp, the "one" was a "watermelon vendor who used to sell watermelons to students and cadets."[386]

Others blamed the Commonwealth's attorney, Captain David Evans Moore and Thomas Johnson Michie.

"Justice" roundly condemned the management of the prosecution's case, noting in particular Captain Moore's failure to make an opening statement, and the easy acceptance of remarks attributed to Charles Christian by third parties, while Christian himself was never put under oath.

By not challenging hearsay testimony attributed to Christian, "Justice" observed, the prosecution had "imposed upon the jury the necessity of receiving his statements as true, unless contradicted by other evidence or shown by circumstance to be unworthy of credit." As the *Gazette* was quick to point out, "any sane man" with sufficient time to reflect would be able "to make up a tale which, if the jury are bound to take it as true, must ensure his acquittal on the ground of self defense."

Christian, of course, had plenty of time to construct just such a story (or stories) and feed them indirectly into the trial through his friends. Protected by his right to avoid testifying against himself, he thus could not be cross-examined and compelled to defend them on the stand.[387]

As for the sheer size of Christian's defense team, "Justice" noted, "no less than six lawyers appeared as the counsel for the defendant." They lengthened Christian's trial unnecessarily and delayed justice, thereby denying it to others.

> *One of the consequences of this, which everyone perceives, was that that whole unusually long term of court was consumed in the trial, not only to the great detriment of all of the suitors in the court, but creating the necessity of another person accused of the same crime* [remaining incarcerated without a trial until the September term of the court].[388]

The other person accused of the "same crime" was, of course, William J. Winn, accused in early April of stabbing Colonel Joseph W. Moore, father of five, in the heart. After a delayed trial and a hung jury in Rockbridge County, it required only five minutes for a jury in Bath County to convict Winn of murder seven months later.

But, in "Justice's" view, Christian's lengthened trial and the delays thus imposed on others were "by no means the only or even the principal evils of allowing persons accused of crimes to engage so many counsel as they have the pecuniary ability to employ."

> *It requires no extraordinary sagacity to enable one to perceive that it multiplies the chance of a wealthy man being able to postpone a trial until the witnesses against him begin to disappear, and thus ensure acquittal.*[389]

Another anonymous editorial, written by an author identified only as "A Voice from the Mountains" concurred. First printed in the *Greenbriar Era*, then reprinted in the Martinsburg *Gazette* under the headline, "Crime in Virginia," the "Voice" railed against easy acquittals and "gentleman's justice" in Virginia and throughout the South.[390]

Tom Blackburn's family was devastated.

Charles Sinclair Taylor had been with Dr. Blackburn and his family at Spring Grove Farm for at least three days when the trial ended. "The trial," Taylor wrote to Francis Henney Smith on May 1, "seems to have opened their wound afresh, & their hearts are bleeding with the same convulsive sorrow as that which characterized the earliest period of their grief."[391]

Dr. Blackburn wrote Colonel Smith on May 5. His hands were still shaking. "Excuse this scrawl," he wrote, "as my nervous system has rec'd such a shock as to almost incapacitate me for any and everything."[392]

Colonel Smith was particularly concerned about some of the things he was reading in the Lexington press. On Thursday, April 20, two days before the Lexington trial ended, the *Valley Star* published its first lengthy account of the proceedings. Headlined "The Christian Trial," the synopsis required nine broadsheet columns to tell the story using snippets of testimony, arranged, in the words of the paper, "chronologically" to "make a connected story of the events of this sad drama."[393]

Dr. Blackburn was not only unhappy with the story, he was convinced the *Valley Star's* version of the tale had been bought and paid for by enemies, political and personal, of both his own family and Colonel Smith.

"Dear Sir," he wrote Colonel Smith on May 5, "I enclose…a slip of republicanism from the Lexington *Star.*"[394]

Smith was, of course, an open, ardent and outspoken Whig, reporting to and dependent for funding on a state legislature and Board of Visitors controlled by equally outspoken and ardent Jefferson/Jackson Democratic Republicans.[395]

Tom's father, an equally ardent Whig, begged the colonel for help. "Is there no other paper in Lexington that has the fairness to chide this attempt to divert public opinion in reference to the <u>merits</u> of this case? All I desire is <u>justice</u>."

Politics aside, there was, of course, no doubt in Dr. Blackburn's mind about who was guilty and who was not, and who was responsible for doing something about it.

> *The wrong has been committed by the felon who murdered my Thos. I <u>appeal</u> to the constituted authorities for justice* [and] *I ask more. The paper above named is evidently in the pay of the felon and his accomplices. If the other paper will report on their attempt to control public sentiment and it is reported by the other paper it will tend to neutralize the influences.*[396]

Finally, Blackburn informed Smith that he would be double-checking the testimony of Tom Blackburn's good friend and senior classmate, VMI Cadet James White Humes. Blackburn was especially concerned about Humes's assertions that Christian had explicitly used the term "seduction" in conjunction with Mary Evelyn Anderson. He asked again for Smith's help.

> *In the mean time I will get the process begun by dutiful enquiry to ascertain whether the felon did not say that "he could seduce any woman." I believe Mr. Humes told me some such thing. I am not <u>sure</u> I rec'd the information through him. This, you are aware, should be sought after with the greatest <u>caution</u>. If not true it would react. Do all in your power my dear sir to procure reliable testimony in the case.*[397]

For Dr. Blackburn, the impact of Christian's escape from justice was exacerbated by an incredibly ill-timed reminder from the Honorable Thomas J. Michie that he would have to pay another $500 if he wanted Michie's help in Christian's trial in Bedford County.

On his way from Lexington to visit the grieving Blackburn family, Charles Sinclair Taylor had stopped off in Staunton at Colonel Smith's request to see Thomas Michie.

He wrote to Colonel Smith about his conversation in a letter from the Blackburn house dated May 1. Michie had told him, he wrote, that "with the end of the trial in Lexington" he considered his "engagement" by Colonel Smith, the Institute and Tom Blackburn's father "at an end." Michie also assured Taylor that John Fletcher Sale, Captain David E.

Moore's designated replacement as prosecutor for the upcoming trial in Bedford, was "a man of very high character, & firm mind & fully competent to take charge of the case."

As for his own role, if any, Michie had his price. He told Taylor in no uncertain terms that "if the friends of poor Thos. (that is, his relations) & yourself considered it important that he should appear and he found it not incompatible with his other engagements, he would do so, charging a fee not exceeding the one already agreed upon."

Michie also expressed concern, as he had in the case of Captain Moore, that the new prosecutor might think employing extra help was insulting. He asked Taylor what he thought Colonel Smith might have to say about the matter. Taylor suggested that, if Mr. Sales were truly insulted, a talk with Captain Moore might convince him to change his mind. Michie told Taylor he thought that was a splendid idea, that he knew Mr. Sale "intimately" and "would write him fully upon that point."

Michie also wanted to know, as soon as possible, what part of his $500 fee for the first trial would be paid by Colonel Smith or VMI or both, and what part would be paid by Dr. Blackburn. Taylor of course had no idea, but he told Colonel Smith that he was "not to pay one cent" of Michie's fee out of his own pocket.

"If the 'Board of Vis[itors]' do not deem it incumbent upon them," Taylor assured the colonel, "I will pay the am't myself." [398]

Who was to pay Michie what, when and on whose authority would all too soon become a major issue for Dr. Blackburn, Colonel Smith, the VMI Board of Visitors and the legislature of the Commonwealth of Virginia.

For Dr. Blackburn, Michie's fee was both a debt of honor and a debt he really could not afford. On May 5, he wrote to Colonel Smith that it was important to him that the role of any "additional" counsel in the Bedford trial be very clearly defined and not appear to be motivated by a personal desire for vengeance. And should such "additional counsel" be retained, Dr. Blackburn made clear, he did not want the Commonwealth's attorney, Francis Henney Smith, VMI or the Commonwealth linked in any way to the decision.

> *In the coming trial I do not wish anyone to participate within the prosecution. If any counsel is employed, I wish to do so without any connection with any other party. I will decide whether it will be judicious & consult with my friends before the day of trial and will apprise you of the course I will pursue.* [399]

Colonel Smith was, in fact, in much the same position as Dr. Blackburn when it came to Michie and his $500 fees. Like Blackburn, Smith felt honor bound to do something to fulfill his promises to act *in loco parentis* for both Tom Blackburn and his entire Corps of Cadets. And for Smith a $500 fee for the first trial and another $500 for the second was a lot of money. If VMI (and thus the taxpayers of Virginia) were to bear all or part of those expenses, Colonel Smith desperately needed after-the-fact approval from his Board of Visitors, the state legislature or both.

Unfortunately, getting money from the state had been a problem since Smith first arrived at VMI. It had not become easier as the Institute expanded under his leadership.

Democrats, who held power in Richmond and thus on the VMI Board, were suspicious of Smith because he was a Whig, fully capable of using the Institute as both a political base and a source of patronage, hiring Whig professors, doing favors for the sons of Whig supporters and educating impressionable young cadets in the evil ways of anti-Democratic-Republican Whiggery.

Smith was also damned as an outspoken and active Episcopalian. He had been personally responsible for the establishment and expansion of the first Episcopal Church in Lexington, a devoutly Presbyterian town with a Presbyterian college run by jealously Presbyterian ministers.

Thus Thomas Michie, though grateful for his $500 contract, was genuinely worried about what retaining him might really cost Colonel Smith, both in Richmond and Lexington.

On May 22, Michie wrote Smith from Charlottesville.

> *I find that the publication of the arguments of counsel in Christian's case has produced a wide spread impression or rather I might say conviction that you took the responsibility of applying the funds of the Va Military Institute to the employment of counsel to aid that prosecution. This belief I fear is producing an impression unfavourable to you & the Institute.*[400]

Noting that "several intelligent gentlemen here and elsewhere" had assumed that Smith had committed state funds without asking permission, Michie told Smith they had "expressed surprise to me that you should have assumed such responsibility."

"Knowing it to be unfounded in truth I thought it my duty to apprise you of its existence," Michie continued, "that you might take such steps in reference to it as you would deem advisable."

"Of course I have given the proper correction & explanation," Michie assured Colonel Smith, "whenever the opportunity was afforded."[401]

William Dabney Stuart, a nephew of Alexander Hugh Holmes Stuart and an 1850 graduate of VMI raised the same issues with his former commandant on May 24.

> *In a review of the evidence and speeches delivered at the trial of Christian I noticed that some remarks were made against you relative to the part you had taken in procuring counsel for the prosecution. Farther than this I have heard nothing & cannot disguise the fact that in this, as well as all other points of a public character, my interest in yourself and all connected with the Institute prompts me to turn Yankee and be impudent enough to ask what was the cause of it.*[402]

Even though his uncle had been one of the most prominent defenders of Christian, young Stuart had no doubts about Christian's guilt or the value of hiring Thomas Michie. "It was a matter of extreme surprise to me how any jury of intelligent honest men could hesitate rendering a verdict against Christian," he wrote, "after hearing Mr. Michie's closing argument."

As for Judge Brockenbrough, Stuart wrote that although he had "never...been one of the ardent admirers of Judge Brockenbrough," he had "taken sufficient interest in him" to make him "regret that he should have taken the part in the trial that he did."[403]

Another of Smith's friends, and one of the most influential, General William Harvie Richardson, was also taken aback by Judge Brockenbrough's participation in the trial and his unkind remarks about Colonel Smith.

Richardson was considered one of the founding fathers of VMI. He had served as both adjutant general of Virginia and a member of the VMI Board of Visitors since 1841. A Whig, he had served as secretary of the Commonwealth of Virginia for twenty years, until 1852, when he was dismissed after a Democratic landslide at the polls.

Though Richardson was worried about both his friend and the Institute, he was disappointed and infuriated by Judge John White Brockenbrough who, in his eyes, had gone over to the "other side" in more ways than one. On April 28, 1854, Richardson wrote Smith from Richmond:

> *Yours of 25 just rec'd conveys information that pains & surprises me. That Brockenbrough should have descended from the dynasty of Mr. Burke to act the more partisan in such a case—forgotten the allegations*

(or lies) of friendship & perverted the truth is unaccountable to me. I regret it most truly.[404]

Richardson remained hopeful, however, that Brockenbrough could, in time, be brought around.

I can only hope that reason & honor may yet resume their sway & prompt him to repair the injury. He cannot believe what he said & must surely have been demented when he assailed you, knowing as he does how often & unjustly you have been attacked & that no man has acquitted himself under all circumstances with more honor, fidelity, integrity & disinterest than have so signally marked your whole course.[405]

The Christian trial had also exacerbated Colonel Smith's already strained relations with Lexington's Presbyterians, including one prominent Presbyterian convert still serving on the VMI faculty. Smith had not been on good terms with Major Thomas J. Jackson for some time. Cadets and their parents complained continuously about Jackson's teaching and odd personal habits. Jackson's 1853 court-martial of Tom Blackburn, quickly overturned by the VMI Board, stood as only one of a series of embarrassing disciplinary problems. Smith had also become suspicious of Jackson's increasingly close ties to the Presbyterian Church in general and Reverend George Junkin, president of Washington College in particular.[406]

When Colonel Smith first hired the West Point graduate and Mexican War hero, Thomas J. Jackson was an Episcopalian. Within a year of his arrival in Lexington, however, Jackson converted, became active in the Lexington Presbyterian Church, and in June 1853 married the Reverend George Junkin's daughter. Once married, Jackson moved out of the VMI barracks and into a newly constructed addition to the Junkin house on the grounds of Washington College.

Dr. Francis Talliaferro Stribling (1810–1874). Member of the VMI Board of Visitors. *Courtesy of Western State Hospital.*

Major Jackson's new father-in-law had long been an outspoken critic of Francis Henney Smith, and Smith had not been reticent about returning the favor.

On May 22, 1854, Dr. Francis T. Stribling warned Colonel Smith about new remarks by Dr. Junkin denouncing "episcopal influences in monopolizing state institutions." Named specifically were VMI and the Staunton Institution for the Deaf, Dumb and Blind. Dr. Stribling, first cousin to one of Christian's best friends and law school classmates, Taliaferro Stribling, served on the board of the latter institution.[407]

Junkin's Presbyterian rage was directed at both Smith's practice of hiring Episcopalians to teach at VMI and the colonel's outspoken criticism of Washington College (and thus Junkin) for preferring Presbyterians. The year of Tom Blackburn's court-martial, for example, Junkin had refused to hire William Nelson Pendleton, a West Point graduate and Episcopal priest, as a professor of mathematics. In justifying his decision, Junkin "explained that each denomination in the state had its own college, including the Episcopalians who had the Virginia Military Institute."[408]

Smith was so angry about the remark that he demanded Junkin meet with the VMI Board of Visitors to explain himself.

Though he never taught at Washington College, Pendleton soon became rector of the Episcopal church Colonel Smith had founded and, as such, hosted the holiday fair at which Charles Burks Christian and Mary Evelyn Anderson first met.

THE TRIAL IN LIBERTY

O n Monday, September 5, 1854, more than four months after an eleven-day trial in Lexington had produced a hung jury, Charles Burks Christian appeared at the Bedford County Courthouse in Liberty, Virginia, to once more face a grand jury and stand trial for murder.[409]

On the bench was Judge George Henry Gilmer, forty-four, a member of one of Virginia's most prominent families, with close ties to VMI. Judge Gilmer's uncle Francis Walker Gilmer had helped Jefferson select the first professors for the University of Virginia. His first cousin Thomas Walker Gilmer had served as governor of Virginia and secretary of the navy. The judge's first wife, Catherine Preston, the daughter of Virginia governor James Patton Preston, had been a first cousin to VMI professor John Thomas Lewis Preston.[410]

Christian's first day in Judge Gilmer's court was anticlimactic. "After having received a lengthy charge" from Judge Gilmer, the members of the grand jury did not move directly to the formal indictment of Christian. Instead, they "retired to inquire into the general state of affairs in Bedford" and did not re-appear until late in the afternoon. Judge Gilmer sent them home with orders to reconvene the next day.[411]

At 10:00 a.m. on Tuesday, September 5, Gilmer again called his court to order. The Bedford County Grand Jury quickly decided to order Charles Christian to once again stand trial for murder.

Christian was "led to the bar" by the Bedford County jailer and once more pled "not guilty."[412]

William Henry Terrill had replaced Captain David E. Moore as chief prosecutor for the Commonwealth.

Thomas Johnson Michie was not in court. Before the trial in Lexington Michie had refused to work with Terrill, whom he believed to be unethical. During that trial, he had been a magnet for criticism: for accepting a role as adjunct prosecutor, charging high fees, getting those fees paid through questionable channels and (ironically) doing a good job.

On the eve of the Bedford trial, however, Michie had praised Terrill, describing him as "a man of very high character & firm mind & fully competent to take charge of this case" to none other than the late Tom Blackburn's father.[413] His absence saved Dr. Blackburn and Francis Henney Smith both the embarrassment of having

Prosecutor in the Liberty trial, William Henry Terrill (1804– 1881). *Courtesy of the Bath County Historical Society.*

to explain his presence and the $500 fee Michie was asking for his help in the second trial.

Christian's defense team had grown even larger. Five lawyers from the Lexington trial were on hand: Charles Lewis Mosby, Alexander Hugh Holmes Stuart, James Baldwin Dorman, Robert Lewis Doyle and Samuel Houston Letcher. Judge John White Brockenbrough appears to have remained behind the scenes but most certainly continued to serve as an advisor. They were joined by three new attorneys: Edward Callohill Burks, James Fullerton Johnson and John Goode.

Burks, thirty-three, was the son of the Bedford County sheriff Martin Parks Burks and a second cousin to Francis Ann Burks, Charles Burks Christian's mother.

Johnson was a respected lawyer, orator and a skilled politician. During the Civil War, he would serve as president pro-tem of the Virginia State Senate. The Johnson family was also closely linked to the Christians.

Goode, twenty-five, had been a practicing lawyer only since April 1851. Years later, after a long career as a lawyer and a legislator in both the Confederate and U.S. Congress, he would still remember the trial in Bedford, one of his first, as "a very exciting one."[414]

Jury selection took less than two hours.[415] During that time, Christian's eight-man defense team struck no fewer than eight jurors from the initial qualified panel of two dozen. From the remaining sixteen, a panel of twelve was chosen by lot.[416]

Like Judge Gilmer, many of the jurors had complex and often close personal and family connections to the principals in the case, including the judge, key witnesses, law enforcement officers, the defendant's family and one another.

Juror Peter Ravenscroft Walker, age forty-one, for example, was related to at least two other jurors and, through a cousin (a Bedford lawyer and politician named William Leftwich Goggin), to Judge Gilmer himself. Walker's cousin Goggin was the administrator of the estate of a recently deceased member of the Christian family.

Walker was also related to fellow juror Samuel Pleasant R. Moorman, the namesake of Goggin's father, Pleasant Moorman Goggin.

Samuel Pleasant Moorman, fifty-six, was a well-to-do, well-connected and politically active local preacher. During the trial in Liberty, one of Moorman's first cousins, VMI Cadet Marcellus Newton Moorman (class of 1856), would serve as a courier between VMI's Francis Henney Smith in Lexington and former VMI cadet and professor of mathematics, James Walkinshaw Allen in Liberty. Allen, a longtime resident of Liberty, was one of Colonel Smith's most trusted observers at the trial.

Bedford County sheriff David W. Quarles was a cousin to both Walker and Moorman, as was Tom Blackburn's classmate, Walter Browne Botts, one of the cadets alleged to have led a lynch mob against Christian. Cadet Botts's father was a member of the VMI Board of Visitors, and his uncle had served in Congress with none other than William Leftwich Goggin.

Also related to Walker, Moorman, Goggin, Quarles and their kin was a juror identified in the press as Samuel T. Gwatkin. Samuel T. was most likely Samuel H. Gwatkin, around twenty-two years old, the son of Samuel Gwatkin and Mary Otey, the aunt of VMI Cadet George Gaston Otey of the class of 1855, just a year behind Tom Blackburn. Four of Otey's brothers would attend VMI. Gwatkin was also related to no fewer than two of the jurors in the Lexington trial: Joseph George Washington Bell and his brother James Franklin Bell.

The remaining jurors were John J. Fariss, around forty-five years old; Jeremiah D. Millner, thirty-one; William H. Elliott, fifty-one; John G. Page, fifty; Josephus Dunnavant (most likely Josephus Dunavant), twenty-four; Stephen P. Smith; James T. Thomas; and Walter Lowrey (most likely Walter K. Lowry), twenty-seven, the son of Milton and Mildred Lowry.

Unfortunately, the names of the twelve jurors would be the last firsthand reporting to emerge from Judge Gilmer's courtroom for the duration of the Bedford County trial.

Before the first witness for the prosecution took the stand, Judge Gilmer ordered the press out of his courtroom. The Lynchburg *Daily Virginian* was not happy.

> *The examination of witness was commenced about noon on Tuesday and as the court refused to allow newspaper reporters a seat for the purpose of reporting the testimony, we are not prepared to give it to our readers. His Honor was convinced of the impropriety of publishing the testimony in any criminal case until the case is finally disposed of.*[417]

Thus, between the absence of press coverage and the later loss or destruction of court documents, little is known of what was actually said or done in Gilmer's courtroom for much of the Liberty trial.

It would appear that most, if not all those who testified in Lexington were called to testify in what turned out to be a lengthy six-day trial in Liberty.

James Lindsay Kirkpatrick, one of the few eyewitnesses to the fight between Christian and Blackburn, was called as a prosecution witness. When he didn't show up, Judge Gilmer ordered "he be summoned to appear before this court forthwith to show cause, if any he can, why he should not be fined for his contempt." Whether he ever testified is unknown.[418]

Hugh Laughlin, the barkeeper and clerk at Christian's Lexington hotel, also failed to appear when he was called. Acting on a motion by prosecutor William Henry Terrill, Judge Gilmer ordered that Laughlin "be summoned to appear here on the first day of the new term to show cause, if any he can, why a writ of *fieri facias* [essentially a claim for damages] should not be issued against him." Whether Laughlin appeared or testified is also unknown.

At the end of the first day of testimony, Judge Gilmer took further steps to ensure that no news of the proceedings would leak to the public. He sequestered the jury. The twelve were, "with the consent of the Prisoner committed to the Custody of the Sheriff."

Sheriff Quarles was directed, in turn, "to keep them together without communication with any other person and to cause them to appear here on tomorrow morning at nine o'clock."[419] As an extra precaution, Judge Gilmer then ordered Deputy Charles A. Andrews sworn in for his special duty.

You shall well and truly to the best of your ability keep this jury and neither speak to them yourself nor suffer any other person to speak to them to [about] *any matter relative to this trial until they return into court tomorrow.*[420]

The trial continued for five more days and appears to have covered most, if not all, the evidence considered in Lexington. Gilmer's courtroom also appears to have remained crowded throughout the trial, with a significant contingent from VMI growing day by day.

On Thursday, September 7, the third day of the trial, Judge Gilmer doubled the guard on the sequestered jury, reinforcing Deputy Andrews with Deputy Thomas A. Kasey, a relative of the wife of juror John Fariss.[421]

Among those crowded into the courtroom were Charles Christian's mother, his sisters and other members of his extended family from Bedford, nearby Campbell and Amherst Counties who stood with him throughout the trial.

On Saturday, September 9, the fifth and last day of testimony, Judge Gilmer halted proceedings entirely to hear two pleadings, *in camera*, both related to members of the Christian family.[422]

The first was the petition filed in Chancery Court against none other than William Leftwich Goggin. Though court records indicated the case was brought by Christian's distant cousin Abner Early Christian, Judge Gilmer's notes clearly indicate the plaintiff was Charles Burks Christian's fourteen-year-old sister, Sarah Elizabeth.

Goggin was not only related to several of the principals in the trial (including the judge), he was, at forty-seven, already a force in Virginia legal circles and Whig party politics. A Bedford County native and a student of Judge Henry St. George Tucker, Goggin had been admitted to the bar at age twenty-one. By 1836, he was a member of the Virginia House of Delegates and by 1838 a member of the U.S. Congress. Though defeated in 1842, he was quickly reelected to replace Judge Gilmer's first cousin, former governor Thomas Walker Gilmer. Goggin had left Congress in 1849 and for the past five years had been running a successful law practice in Liberty.[423]

In the second Chancery case, the defendant was Charles Burks Christian's mother. The petitioner in that case was identified only as a member of the Clemens family. Pleasant Clemens was Samuel Leftwich Goggin's first cousin.

In both Chancery cases, the principals appear to have allowed Judge Gilmer to settle whatever was in dispute, without calling a jury. After short hearings and rulings on both petitions, Judge Gilmer returned to the bench and resumed the Christian murder trial. Enough time remained that day, it would appear, for both the Commonwealth and Christian's defense attorneys to finish their questioning and cross-examination of the last of their witnesses.

Judge Gilmer then ordered both sides to present their closing arguments at the beginning of the next week, giving them Sunday to rest and prepare.[424]

On the sixth day of the trial, Monday, September 11, 1854, Judge Gilmer gaveled his courtroom to order at 8:00 a.m.

Alexander Hugh Holmes Stuart and Charles Lewis Mosby closed for the defense. John Sales summed up for the prosecution.[425]

At that point, according to Judge Gilmer's notes, "Charles B. Christian who stands indicted of murder was again led to the bar in custody of the Jailer of this county and the jury sworn for his trial was brought into court by the sheriff of this county and having fully heard the arguments of counsel retired to consider their verdict."

The jury was out twenty-one minutes. According to Judge Gilmer's notes, the jury "returned into court and upon their oath do say that the said Charles B. Christian is <u>not guilty</u> of the murder of which he stands indicted…and therefore…it is considered by the court that the said Charles B. Christian be acquitted…of the murder aforesaid."[426]

John Goode, half a century later, described the crowd's reaction to the news.

> *When the jury returned a verdict of not guilty, the people in the crowded court-room raised a great shout, rushed upon the prisoner, took him in their arms, carried him across the street and deposited him in the lap of his mother, who was sitting in her room at the hotel waiting for the verdict, with an anxious solicitude which none but a mother could feel. Who can tell the height or depth of a mother's love for her boy?*[427]

Two days later, the Lynchburg *Virginian* reported the verdict in a short story quickly reprinted by the Richmond *Enquirer* under the headline, "Acquittal of Christian."

> *The unfortunate young man gave expression to the deepest feeling on that occasion—threw himself in tears on the neck of a juror, and on leaving the court house was escorted by a large number of sympathizing friends to the room occupied by his anxious mother and sisters.*[428]

Defense Counsel John Goode (1829–1909). *Wikipedia.*

The Richmond *Dispatch* repeated the story almost verbatim in its "Latest Mail News" column on September 14.[429]

It took more than a week for the Charles Town papers to print the story. Under the headline, "Acquittal of Christian," the *Spirit of Jefferson* devoted only four sentences to the trial and verdict.[430]

On September 15, the Richmond *Enquirer* passed on a story that spoke of more than simply happy crowds:

A gentleman from Liberty, the scene of the trial, informs the Petersburg Express, that the jury, after an absence of only 21 minutes rendered a verdict of acquittal and the young man was borne from the courtroom by crowds of his friends. The town was illuminated, music introduced, and bonfires blazed in honor of the event. Colonel Smith of the Military Institute was burnt in effigy, and every demonstration made in the power of the people to give expression of their high gratification at the result of the trial.[431]

Some of the VMI contingent in Liberty for the trial—professors, cadets, alumni, witnesses, native sons and others who managed to steal away for the proceedings—appear to have reacted badly.

It was rumored, for example, that "maltreatment" of some of the new members of the class of 1858 were linked to unseemly events in Bedford.

On September 30, General William Harvie Richardson asked Colonel Smith about Cadet Davidson Bradfute Penn. A member of the VMI Board of Visitors, William Booth Taliaferro, had told Richardson that Penn "had been dismissed on account...of the Blackburn affair."

At the same time, Richardson made his own views on the Liberty verdict quite clear. "The Blackguards who celebrated the triumph of Cowards & murders put you into excellent company," he wrote. Richardson also promised to put Smith's account of his role in the affair and its aftermath "into the papers."[432]

Smith apparently replied to Richardson verbally, or his written answer has been lost. We know, however, that in late September 1854, Cadet Penn was court-martialed and ordered dismissed from the Institute because of an "altercation" with a first-year cadet, one of his second cousins, James Thomas Watt Hairston, of the class of 1858.

Dismissing Penn, like the short-lived 1853 dismissal of Tom Blackburn, was no small thing.

Penn, from Lynchburg, was related to most of Virginia's finest families, including VMI board member William Booth Taliaferro and Charles Lewis Mosby, arguably one of Christian's most effective defenders.

The Hairstons were also forces to be reckoned with. In June 1854, the *New York Times* described Hairston's uncle, Samuel Hairston of Pittsylvania County, as "The Richest Man in Virginia." He owned, the paper wrote, "between 1,600 and 1,700 slaves, with the prospect of picking up another 1,600 or so through inheritance." Though described as "a plain, unassuming gentleman" who had "never made any notice in the world," the *New York*

Times insisted "he could vie with the Bruces, the McDonoughs and Astors." Cadet Hairston's father, Harden Hairston, owned land and some 600 slaves in Lowndes County, Mississippi.[433]

Whether the Penn/Hairston "altercation" stemmed from a disagreement about the verdict in the Christian trial or was a simple case of hazing in the face of new and quite explicit orders forbidding it, both Penn and Hairston survived. Hairston graduated with his class.

MICHIE, MONEY AND RECONCILIATIONS

With the trial in Liberty over and Charles Burks Christian free, Thomas Johnson Michie was still trying to collect the $500 owed him for his legal work in Lexington.

Charles Sinclair Taylor, well aware that Blackburn's father could not afford Michie's fee, had already agreed to split the cost with VMI's Colonel Smith. Taylor could afford it. He was not only a successful farmer, but he was also married to the daughter of William Fowle, one of the richest men in Alexandria.

On October 12, in response to a worried note from Colonel Smith and a verbal reminder from Hugh Nelson Pendleton, Taylor promised to send Smith a personal check for $250, the Blackburn half of Michie's fee, by October 25. "I noticed the high honours you received [from] the demoniacal rowdies at Liberty," Taylor noted in passing, "for your effort to teach the youths under your charge respect for the laws of this State. It is very encouraging to a man who desires to perform his duty."[434]

Smith had good reason to press Taylor for the money. Nearly a month earlier, on or about September 26, Smith had sent Michie the moral equivalent of a post-dated check, with instructions to present it for payment, with interest, in sixty days. Around October 25, Michie noticed that Colonel Smith had, perhaps inadvertently, put an obstacle in the way redeeming it.

"Was it by mistake or design," Michie wrote, "that you made the made the nego[tiable] note for $250 sent me & dated 26th Sept last payable at <u>sixty</u> days at the <u>Valley Bank at Winchester</u> instead of Staunton." Though clearly annoyed, Michie tried to be polite. "I write to inform you that it is payable at Winchester & will have to be provided for at that place, thinking perhaps you had not intended & might therefore be put to some inconvenience by the mistake."[435]

By November 3, Michie still didn't have his money, and he was in trouble with his banker.

From Staunton, he wrote again to Colonel Smith, "I am afraid you will consider me a very great pest about small matters." When Smith's post-dated draft arrived, he noted, the cashier at the Bank of the Valley in Staunton had agreed to advance him the $250, deduct a fee for his troubles and forward Colonel Smith's post-dated note to Winchester to be cashed.

Michie, happy to have cash at last in hand, had then set off for Charlottesville for a three-week engagement.[436]

When he got back to Staunton, his banker sought him out.

Smith's check had, more or less, bounced, and Michie now owed the Bank of the Valley $250.

As Michie described it, the "Mother bank at Winchester," according to the banker in Staunton, "was not an 'office of discount & deficits' & therefore… [Smith's] note was not payable anywhere."

His banker's "objection," Michie noted further, "was stated & insisted on by the Board of Directors."

At a loss, and now himself $250 in debt, Michie enclosed the unpaid note and "a blank note of the same date payable at the same time, but payable at Staunton on which I am apprised I can get this money if you will be good enough to sign it."

Michie had drafted the new note so that it would mature and be fully payable (including the extra interest Michie now owed his bank) around December 1.

Still trying to be both polite and helpful, he told Colonel Smith, "if it will suit you better just add the interest for another month & make it payable in sixty days from this date—only taking care to write it as the printed one is written, as these banks are very particular."[437]

On December 1, 1854, Michie informed Smith that he had returned to Staunton from a trip to Covington the night before and found three letters from the colonel waiting for him, "the first in date inclosing a check for two hundred & fifty dollars, the balance of my fee in the case of Com'th vs. Christian—for which I thank you."[438]

Michie, though paid at last, was not forgotten, especially by Smith's erstwhile friend and legal counsel, Judge John White Brockenbrough. Smith's concern about Brockenbrough's involvement in the case had been a major factor in Smith's decision to hire Michie in the first place. Judge Brockenbrough, in turn, had accused Colonel Smith of inappropriate and "perverse" behavior and either stupidity or a "desire to pander to public prejudice" in hiring Michie to both defame his client and "seek the prisoner's blood."

Smith had replied to Brockenbrough's criticisms, point by point, in an official report to the VMI Board of Visitors on July 4, characterizing Brockenbrough's decision to leave the Federal bench and defend Christian as indicative of the judge's own "one-sided views of duty and propriety."[439]

Ill will and harsh words fouled the air throughout the summer, into the fall and well past the celebrations of Christian's acquittal after the trial in Liberty.

Michie, as late as his December 1, 1854, thank-you note to Smith noted that he was "exceedingly sorry to learn" that in a recent speech Judge Brockenbrough had, once more, complained about Smith's comments about him in his official report to the VMI Board of Visitors. What Brockenbrough should be saying, Michie wrote, was that he "had misunderstood your evidence when he made his speech & was gratified to stand corrected."

Michie's concern was genuine.

He knew and respected both Smith and Brockenbrough and knew they had been friends.

In Michie's view, Brockenbrough simply did not understand why and how Smith had hired him. "This is the whole matter between you," he wrote, "& should not, I think, be allowed to sow the tares of discord between two gentlemen whom I value so highly as yourself & Judge Brockenbrough."

For his part, Michie continued, "I never misunderstood you for a moment. I never was authorized by you, either verbally or in writing, to look to the Institute for my fee or any part of it."

"You, by letter to me," Michie reiterated, "made yourself individually responsible for the whole of it, & that responsibility has been fully sustained by you from first to last."

Michie also recounted a conversation with Smith in which the colonel had explained that Dr. Richard Scott Blackburn's close friend and kinsman Charles S. Taylor "had agreed to relieve you from one half the responsibility & that you had applied to the Visitors of the Institute for relief from the other half—but never intimated that you had any thought of applying the funds of the Institute to its payment unless so authorized by the Board."[440]

By late October or early November, Frances Henney Smith was still trying to correct what he perceived to be Judge Brockenbrough's misunderstanding of both his reasons for hiring of Michie and his feelings toward Brockenbrough himself.

The absence of an official transcript of what Smith had said about Brockenbrough at Christian's trial in Lexington appeared to be part of the problem.

In an effort to help, Michie had approached Alexander Hugh Holmes Stuart on Smith's behalf, asking him to tell Judge Brockenbrough that he had "misunderstood" what Smith had said about him during the trial.

Stuart refused.

As Michie put it in a note to Colonel Smith, "He says he does not wish to become a volunteer in the controversy & therefore declines authorizing me to say to you what you requested—but says he will answer any letter you may address him on the subject."

Michie, still doing his best to forge a reconciliation, then personally assured Stuart that Smith "did not expect or desire a controversy, but merely to put yourself right."

Unfortunately, Michie wrote, his pleas "did not change his [Stuart's] resolve."

Stuart did agree, however, to help indirectly, by sending his notes on Smith's testimony to another member of Christian's defense team, James Baldwin Dorman, with instructions that they should be made available to both Smith and Judge Brockenbrough.

"I certainly do not feel that I am volunteering in any controversy," Stuart told Michie, "but on the contrary...I have given the truth so far as I know it...to be used for the restoration of good feeling than for controversy."[441]

Then, on November 4, 1854, one of Christian's most effective defenders, Charles Lewis Mosby, promised to send Smith "a copy from my notes of your evidence given in the trial of Christian."

Judge Brockenbrough, it seems, had sent Mosby a copy of Smith's July 4 report to the VMI Board of Visitors. Mosby, in turn, sent Judge Brockenbrough a copy of his notes on Smith's testimony and, as a courtesy, told Colonel Smith what he had done.

"I have seen your report which Judge B[rockenbrough] sent me, and [I] sent him a copy of your evidence," Mosby wrote to Colonel Smith. "I am much concerned that you deemed it necessary to make the allusion to the Judge, which is found in it. I think it does him injustice & was not necessary to the placing [of] yourself properly before the Board of Visitors."

"Indeed," Mosby continued, "I feel bound to say that as I understand your report, it is different in an important point from your evidence, as I understood and recorded it, at the trial."[442]

Smith, it seems, had also told Mosby's brother, William Washington Mosby, that he believed Judge Brockenbrough misunderstood what had been said at the trial.

"My Bro. Wm. says you think if you could see & consult with me," Charles Lewis Mosby wrote to Smith, "you could satisfy me that I am myself in error in this belief."

"I am willing to receive any impression which may vindicate you & Judge B both," he continued. "I deplore any serious difficulty between you—but I have great confidence in the correctness of my report of your evidence & as you will remember, took it down with the utmost care."

That said, Mosby tried to be encouraging.

"Learning from my Bro. that you think the matter may be settled between you & Judge B. when you return home, & wishing much to see such a request, I have written a note to him...suggesting that he shall await your return before he makes any reply [to the VMI Board of Visitors]."

Charles Lewis Mosby also regretted that he could not be in Lexington himself to facilitate reconciliation. "As I thought my presence would conduce to an adjustment, I would endeavor to visit Lex," he wrote, "but my condition & engagements here" in Richmond made it almost impossible that "under any circumstance I can leave home in the next six weeks."

Mosby signed his letter, "Most respectfully your friend, C.L. Mosby."[443]

The next day, November 5, 1854, William Washington Mosby wrote Smith, confirming all that his brother Charles had said.[444] "I told C[harles] that you had told me you never designed to injure Judge B. nor had you now any unkind feelings towards him," W.W. Mosby wrote, "that you did not think you had done him any injustice—but that if convinced that you had done him any, would atone for it as a gentleman ought to do— and in short that your views were those of a Christian gentleman and I thought it impossible but that a proper adjustment would be made if time could be had."

W.W. Mosby was so concerned that his brother's letter would not reach Judge Brockenbrough before the Judge addressed the VMI Board of Visitors that he asked N.J. Echols, a friend of Colonel Smith, to deliver it personally, "for there is no reliance on the mail."

"Should it reach Judge B. before he has taken any action, I shall be most happy," W.W. Mosby wrote, "as I presume he will be disposed to do what is

Mary Evelyn Anderson's uncle Joseph Reid Anderson (1813–1892) as a Confederate general. *Wikipedia.*

right & thus the jar which has been produced between two valuable men will be healed, I hope never to be interrupted again."

Mosby concluded with an invitation to Smith to stop by his home in Lynchburg on his trip home from Richmond to Lexington.

"Lastly," he wrote, Smith should feel free "to suggest any way I can serve you in this or any other case. Hoping you may have a pleasant trip and return to your family when you will find all happy, & peace with all men."

He signed his letter, "Most truly your <u>friend</u>, W.W. Mosby."[445]

On December 7, 1854, the Richmond *Whig* published what one chronicler termed "an impersonal reply" by Smith to Judge Brockenbrough's criticisms and "the matter was dropped and the former cordial relations prevailed."[446]

Two days later, Mary Evelyn Anderson's uncle, Joseph Reid Anderson, wrote Smith, "Your cause in this matter meets the approbation of all whose good opinion is valuable if not universal approval when understood."[447]

For some, the healing had begun.

For others, the wounds would never heal.

53

AFTERMATH

THE BLACKBURNS[448]

Thomas Blackburn, who stood second in his class during his third year at VMI, was granted his degree posthumously, on July 4, 1854. The VMI Board of Visitors ordered that he be carried on the rolls as "alumnus, without class standing."[449]

His grave, in the family graveyard at Spring Grove, near Ripon, West Virginia, has remained untended for nearly a century, its stone walls broken, its iron gate cast down by dairy cattle pastured on the land.[450]

Tom was the second child the Blackburns lost. A sister, Mary Grace, born two years before Tom entered VMI, had lived less than a year.

Tom's mother was pregnant while Charles Christian was being tried for the murder of her eldest son. On September 13, 1854, two days after Christian was acquitted, she gave birth to a boy. The Blackburns named him Richard Scott, after Tom's father. The baby lived only two years, until June 30, 1857.

Tom's father, Richard Scott Blackburn, survived the Civil War. He died at age fifty-eight, on September 2, 1867, a broken man. Tom's mother, Sarah Ann Eleanor Thomas Blackburn, outlived her son by forty-four years and her husband by thirty-one. She died at the home of her daughter Jeannie, in Charlottesville, in 1898. She is buried at Spring Grove.

Tom's younger brother, John Sinclair Blackburn, was sixteen when Tom was killed. He served as a cavalry officer and then an ordnance officer

The grave of Richard Scott Blackburn, Tom's father, the last stone standing in the ruins of the family graveyard. *Author's photograph.*

during the war. In 1867 and 1868, he attended the University of Virginia. In 1869, he co-founded the Potomac Academy in Alexandria with his half uncle, none other than Charles Sinclair Taylor.

Tom's little sister Jane "Jeannie" Wormeley Blackburn was twelve when her brother was killed. She became arguably the most famous of the Blackburn children, marrying Francois Elois Berger Moran, a wealthy, horse-loving son of a Belgian-born New York banker: a millionaire, a writer and "one of the principle farmers of Albemarle County, Virginia."

Jeannie became one of the organizing members of the Daughters of the American Revolution and the author of several books, including *Miss Washington of Virginia, What a Man Can do with a Woman's Life, Twin Souls* and other works.

She and her husband were friends of Richard Thomas Walker Duke Jr. ("R.T.W."), a Charlottesville native, prominent jurist and the son of Richard Thomas Walker Duke, VMI 1845, reputedly the last Confederate general to leave the burning city of Richmond in 1865.

In 1899, when she was fifty-seven, R.T.W. Duke described Jeannie Blackburn Moran as:

> *a handsome woman—several years older than Moran—a hospitable, but decidedly curious character & when Moran became rich, she lost her head & made a great fool of herself.*
>
> *I really believe she has been for many years a little "touched in the upper story," but the irony of fate is that poor old Moran lost his mind & died in a Sanatorium some years since.*
>
> *She is still alive—tho' in the eighties* [sic] *& cuts a wide swathe in Washington.*
>
> *Tho' relations had been a little strained between us on account of her tongue—for she was a most reckless talker & "handled the truth rather keerless", we met at the White Sulphur last summer (1923) & she insisted on becoming very friendly & in fact was somewhat "boringly" so.*[451]

For a time, Jeannie and her husband lived in a large house in Charlottesville that had once belonged to the mayor, Samuel McCue.

McCue was hanged in 1905 for murdering his wife.

Ironically, one of the members of McCue's defense team was Jack Lee, who had defeated Charles Burks Christian in an election for Amherst County Commonwealth's attorney and had been challenged to a duel by Christian for his troubles.

Jane Wormely Blackburn Moran (1842–1929). From the frontispiece of her *Miss Washington of Virginia* (1910).

Jeannie died in 1929 at age eighty-seven. She was remembered as one of the grand dames of Washington society. The great bronze entrance doors she contributed to the DAR still grace the front portico of the organization's national headquarters in Washington.

Elizabeth "Eliza" Sinclair Blackburn, eighteen in 1854, married Charles Horace Smith of Berryville, in Clarke County, just south of Ripon. Smith rode with J.E.B. Stuart during the Civil War and later became a successful businessman in Berryville.

Two of Tom's sisters married members of the Washington family, their second cousins, brothers, sons of Thomas Blackburn Washington of nearby Claymont, the largest and arguably the most elegant of the Washington family homes in Jefferson County.

Catherine Thomas Blackburn, who was only fourteen when Tom Blackburn died, married Bushrod Corbin Washington in 1864, while Washington was still serving in the Confederate army. She and her husband had nine children before she died in 1876 at age thirty-five.

Eleanor "Ellen" Thomas Blackburn was ten years old in 1854. In 1874, she married Thomas Blackburn Washington, Jr. He was seven years her junior.

The Washington brothers who married Blackburns both survived the Civil War. Two of their brothers, however, were less lucky. Both George Washington Jr. and James Cunningham Washington served with Confederate cavalry units and were captured during the war. "Jimmy" died of typhoid while a prisoner at Fort McHenry. George Jr. died of wounds while a prisoner at Front Royal.

Mary Watts Blackburn, who was only four in 1854, never married. She was buried in the family plot at Spring Grove in 1919.

The Blackburn family home was sold after the Civil War to Thomas Montague Isbell of nearby Berryville. He had married Frances Thornton Allen, the daughter of David Hume Allen, a neighbor of the Blackburns. Ironically, Montague was a distant cousin of Colonel Terry Dillard, a neighbor and one of the character witnesses for Charles Burks Christian.

Isbell's first cousin Lewis Daniel Isbell lived in Appomattox, just across the river from the Christians. His mother-in-law was Mary Elizabeth Christian, Charles Burks Christian's third cousin.

THE CHRISTIANS[452]

After he was acquitted, Charles Burks Christian became a lawyer in Amherst County.

On April 23, 1861, at Amherst Court House, he enlisted in the Confederate army and was immediately elected captain of the Amherst Rough and Readies, Company B (later Company I) of William "Extra Billy" Smith's famous Forty-ninth Virginia Infantry.[453]

Few if any would dispute the judgment on Christian's military career rendered in 1903 by one of Thomas Blackburn's closest friends and admirers, Cadet John Howard Sharp. "Christian," he wrote, "made a good soldier in the Civil War."

Sharp's opinion was, if anything, an understatement. With the exception of First Manassas, Christian served in every battle fought by the Forty-ninth Infantry until he was captured in the spring of 1864.

On September 17, 1862, at Sharpsburg, the single bloodiest day of the war, he effectively assumed command of the Forty-ninth after both Colonel Smith and Lieutenant Colonel J.C. Gibson were badly wounded.

In January 1863, he was officially promoted to field rank, as a major.

In October 1863, following the bloody battles of Fredericksburg, Chancellorsville and Gettysburg, he was promoted to lieutenant colonel.

In May 1864, at Cold Harbor, Christian was wounded in both shoulders and captured. Later that year, he was one of six hundred captured Confederate officers shipped to Morris Island, off Charleston harbor, where, for forty-five days, they were used as human shields, screening Union siege batteries from Confederate artillery firing from Fort Sumter.

Three of those six hundred officers died of starvation on Morris Island; another thirteen would die of disease soon after they were removed to Fort Pulaski, near Savannah; five more died at Hilton Head; and another twenty-five after their return to the POW facilities at Fort Delaware.

In the South, the officers became known as the "Immortal 600."[454]

Christian remained a prisoner until July 15, 1865, more than three months after the Army of Northern Virginia laid down its arms at Appomattox.[455]

His account of his experiences with the Forty-ninth at Cold Harbor remains a classic.[456]

After the war, Christian lived and practiced law in Amherst County and nearby Lynchburg for more than half a century.

Christian's long-suffering mother died in 1870 when she was only sixty.

Christian's sensitivity to personal insult continued to flare periodically, with all too predictable results.

In May 1887, when he was fifty-three, Christian ran against John L. ("Jack") Lee for the post of Amherst County Commonwealth's attorney.[457] Lee apparently made unkind remarks about Christian. Christian took exception and challenged Lee to a duel. Although Lee refused to accept the challenge, both men were arrested and jailed for their troubles.[458]

Fifteen years later, in 1902, Christian found himself part of a team defending his neighbor, Judge Clarence J. Campbell of the Amherst County Circuit Court, against assault charges.[459] The right Reverend C.H. Crawford, superintendent of the Virginia Anti-Saloon League, had written an article that, in Judge Campbell's view, contained language that was both personally and professionally insulting. Judge Campbell and, by all accounts, most of his friends, including Christian, were drinkers. Amherst County, however, was "dry."

A druggist, reported to be one of Judge Campbell's suppliers, had been accused of selling twenty-five barrels or so of "intoxicants" and brought before Judge Campbell.

According to Reverend Crawford, the judge had instructed the jury hearing the case that, even in a dry county, a licensed pharmacist had every right to sell "medicated whisky."

The jury voted for acquittal.

"Such rulings," Reverend Crawford wrote, "set the people wondering which has been doctored the most, the whiskey or the judge."

Judge Campbell responded by ordering Reverend Crawford to appear in court to defend himself against charges of contempt.

On June 24, 1902, Crawford appeared, with another judge in tow as his attorney.

Judge Campbell dutifully listened to Reverend Campbell's defense and though he quickly dismissed the charges against him, he asked, several times, for a personal apology. When Crawford refused and walked out of the courtroom, Judge Campbell left the bench, chased Crawford down and, according to witnesses, shouted, "I gave you an opportunity to apologize and you would not, now I give you this."

"This" turned out to be eight or nine blows from a horsewhip Judge Campbell had brought to court for the occasion.

In August, Judge Campbell was tried for felonious assault and defended by two friends: Charles Burks Christian and Thomas Payne. Campbell was quickly found not guilty by a jury almost universally considered to be both "wet" and rigged in his favor. Well-oiled celebrations of the verdict reportedly continued late into the night.

Outraged members of the bar from Amherst, Nelson and Campbell Counties, as well as the City of Lynchburg, immediately called for the judge's impeachment by the state legislature. By April 9, 1903, he was out. The Virginia House of Delegates voted sixty-three to eighteen for impeachment. The Senate concurred by a vote of twenty-one to thirteen.[460]

The "wets" and friends of Judge Campbell in Amherst County were, however, undeterred.

In May 1903, Amherst's representative to the House of Delegates, J.B. Ware, announced that he would nominate none other than Charles Burks Christian as a candidate for Campbell's lost judgeship.

A "strongly worded petition" soon reached the legislature calling for the election of one of Christian's opponents. It was reportedly signed by every lawyer in Amherst County, "save two or three" known supporters of former Judge Campbell, by every Amherst County officer, every lawyer in Nelson County and by no fewer than seventeen lawyers from Lynchburg.

On the floor of the House on May 12, a delegate named Whitehead from Norfolk delivered what the Richmond *Times* described as "one of the most vigorous" speeches of the session in opposition to Christian. According the *Times* account, Whitehead declared that, in Christian, Delegate Ware was trying to "thrust upon the people of Amherst as their judge a man wholly unfit for the place."

Whitehead further charged "that Colonel Christian was an habitual drunkard; that he was intoxicated when here as a witness in the Campbell case; and that he had seen him drunk a hundred times."

Christian's nomination was quickly rejected in the Virginia House by a vote of thirty-one to twenty.[461]

In February 1903, while her brother was still in the middle of the Campbell affair, his older sister, Susie, died at seventy-three. She had married twice.

Virginia Lee died unmarried, at seventy, in 1907.

Sarah Elizabeth, the last of Christian's sisters, lived until October 1932, the only female member of the family remaining in Charles Burks Christian's household.

The man who could seduce any woman in Lexington never married.

He was not, however, forgotten.

In 1911, Virginia Military Institute archivist Joseph R. Anderson, a cousin of Mary Evelyn Anderson, carefully filed a fragment of a letter from Christian describing his service with the Forty-ninth Virginia. In the margin he wrote:

> *This is from the man who assassinated Tom Blackburn of the class of 1854 while he* [Christian] *was a student of law in Lexington Va... acquitted of the crime in another county.*[462]

By all accounts, Christian was, in later years, a lonely man, haunted by his past who turned increasingly to alcohol for help. Toward the end of his life, children would lie in wait for him and toss stones at his horse as he rode drunk along the roads near his family home on the north side of the James River.

Christian died in 1916.

The grave of Charles Burks Christian, Walker's Ford, Amherst County, Virginia. *Author's photograph.*

The father of one of the little girls who confessed to tossing stones was at his deathbed.

Christian's last words, he told his daughter, were, "The knife, the knife, hide the knife."[463]

When the Richmond *Times Dispatch* printed Christian's obituary, someone—presumably Blackburn's friend and roommate, Robert Preston Carson, the Institute's oldest living alumnus—clipped and dispatched a copy to the VMI Archives.

Archivist Joseph Anderson carefully placed the Christian obituary in Thomas Blackburn's file, but not before scribbling a note, in red, across the top:

> *Thomas Blackburn*
> *Graduated 1854*
> *His Murderer*
> *Died Jan'y 2, 1916.*[464]

Christian is buried near his family home, Rosedale, near Walker's Ford on the James River in Amherst County. The gravesite, impeccably manicured, is marked by a white marble monument:

> *Charles Burks Christian.*
> *Born Feb. 15, 1834.*
> *Died Jan 3, 1916.*
> *Lieut. Col 49ᵗʰ Va. Regiment*
> *and one of the Immortal 600.*
> *How sleep the brave who sink in rest,*
> *By their country's wishes blest.*

No images of Tom Blackburn appear to have survived.

His tombstone is somewhere under the trampled earth of the Blackburn family cemetery, buried by cattle who pass through its broken stone walls and rest in the shade of trees.

NOTES

Introduction

1. The best published sources for the events recounted in this volume remain the newspapers of the period, particularly the *Lexington Gazette*; the Lexington *Valley Star*; the Richmond-based *Dispatch, Enquirer* and *Whig*; and the Lynchburg *Daily Virginian*. Although mentioned in passing in post-nineteenth-century published works, the case is rarely if ever treated at length. Notable exceptions include Moore, *Memories*, 37–40; Couper, *One Hundred Years*, I, 276–80; and an unpublished dissertation, Wineman, "Francis H. Smith," 365–67. The local press in Lexington also from time to time rediscovered and published the stories and documents related to the events of 1853–54. See Harwood, "Law Student."

Chapter 1

2. The earliest account of Massie's experiences on the evening of Jan. 15, 1854, is found in careful notes taken by an anonymous reporter, perhaps Samuel Houston Letcher, at the inquest held at VMI on Jan. 16, 1854. "Evidence at Inquest." Massie's account is also covered at length in the *Lexington Gazette*; the Lexington *Valley Star*; the Richmond-based *Dispatch, Enquirer* and *Whig*; and the Lynchburg *Daily Virginian*.

3. Though Massie never identified her in his public testimony, it is more than likely that one of the young women was his new wife, Sophonsiba Breckenridge McDowell, daughter of former Virginia governor James McDowell, and at one time the sister-in-law of Cadet Thomas Blackburn's uncle, Francis Thomas, former governor of Maryland. Massie had married Miss McDowell in November 1853. Massie's friend, VMI Professor Thomas J. Jackson, described him to his sister as an "old bachelor friend." See Thomas J. Jackson to Laura

Jackson Arnold, *Stonewall Jackson Papers. 1853.* Nov. 30, 1853. http://www.vmi. edu/archives.aspx?id=8045 (accessed May 16, 2013). Thomas J. Jackson Papers, VMI archives, 1853 11/30

4. Couper, *One Hundred Years*, I, 232, 236–37.
5. VMI Archives, Court Martial Records, Jan. 24, 1853.
6. Francis Thomas, *Statement* (1845).

Chapter 2

7. For the best account of the Thomas divorce in context, see Buckley, *The Great Catastrophe* (2002). For Sally's post-divorce courtship see Buckley, *If You Love That Lady* (2000).

Chapter 3

8. For "famous beauty," see "Genealogy: The Bruce Family," *Virginia Magazine of History and Biography*, XI, 441.
9. "The Testimony of Miss Anderson."
10. Dr. R.S. Blackburn to Francis Henney Smith, Feb. 8, 1854, VMI Archives, Superintendent's Incoming Correspondence Files, 1854, #38.
11. Robert White was a member of Brockenbrough law class of 1853–54, see *Washington and Lee University: Alumni Directory*, 298.
12. "The Testimony of Miss Anderson."
13. Washington and Lee University School of Law (n.d.); Paxton, *A Judge's School* (1971); Crenshaw, *General Lee's College* (1969).

Chapter 4

14. Lee, *Memoirs of William Nelson Pendleton* (1893); Bean, *Stonewall's Man* (1959); Evans, *Confederate Military History*, IV, 649–50.
15. Cadet John Howard Sharp to John Anderson, Dec. 12, 1903. VMI Archives, Alumni Files Collection, Thomas Blackburn, Class of 1854.
16. Though officially the "Lexington Hotel" in 1854, for many it was still known as "Porter's." In late February 1854, cadets were forbidden to loiter there. See VMI Archives, Superintendent's Order Book, General Order No. 16, Feb. 28, 1854.
17. For Christian's physical appearance see *inter alia*, Richmond *Dispatch*, April 22, 1854.
18. Cadet John Howard Sharp to John Anderson, Dec. 12, 1903.
19. One of the debate topics for Washington College's Graham Literary Society in 1854: "Is seduction a greater crime than murder? Is the instigator more to blame than the perpetrator of a crime?" See Bean, *Stonewall's Man*, 9.
20. John Howard Sharp to John Anderson, Dec. 12, 1903.
21. "The Testimony of Miss Anderson."
22. Richmond *Dispatch* (April 20, 1854), *inter alia*.
23. "The Testimony of Miss Anderson."
24. Ibid; Richmond *Dispatch* (April 19, 1854).

Chapter 5

25. "The Testimony of Miss Anderson."
26. The last sentence of Mary Anderson's testimony in the January preliminary hearings reads: "My Aunt did [not] insist on my going into the room." The word, "not," is emphatically crossed out. See "The Testimony of Miss Anderson." Christian's fellow law student, Alfred G. Thayer, testified in court, and in his friend's defense, that Christian intended to ask for Mary Anderson's hand. Richmond *Dispatch* (April 20, 1854).
27. Richmond *Dispatch* (April 20, 1854).
28. Christian's letter is quoted at length by witnesses throughout Christian's trial. It is reprinted in full in Harwood, "Law Student," 37.
29. Thomas, *Statement*, 45–47.
30. "The Testimony of Miss Anderson."
31. See Sally Campbell Preston McDowell to John Miller, June 14, 1855, in Buckley, ed., *"If You Love That Lady Don't Marry Her,"* 265. In a similar vein, Sally wrote to John Miller on June 10, 1856, "Unless you are prepared to court the gossip of I don't know how many different sections of this country I advise you never to tell anything to old Mrs. McClung, or any other Alexander in Virginia. They mean no harm; but they love to talk, & do talk without any restraint imposed upon them by any acute perceptions or principle of delicacy." Ibid., 606.

Chapter 6

32. Lexington *Valley Star* (April 20, 1854)
33. Alexander Broadnax Bruce, Cadet Files, VMI Archives, Preston Library, Lexington, VA; Alexander Broadnax Bruce (1854) in VMI Archives Online Rosters Database, http://www2.vmi.edu/archiverosters/Details.asp?ID=353&rform=search; Lyle and Kennedy, *Architecture, 258-272;* Carrington, *History of Halifax*, 118-133. Bruce ranked thirteenth in his class in "order of merit." See VMI Archives, Superintendent's Order Book, Order No. 46, July 4, 1854.
34. Samuel McDowell Moore to Francis T. Anderson, Jan. 15, 1854. Anderson Family Papers, #001, Leyburn Library, Washington and Lee University, Lexington, VA; "The Testimony of Miss Anderson."
35. Richmond *Dispatch* (April 18, 1854); Lynchburg *Daily Virginian* (April 19, 1854).

Chapter 7

36. *William and Mary College Quarterly Magazine* IV (1895–96), 266.
37. Hageman, *The Heritage of Virginia*, 212; Payne, *Paynes of Virginia*, 246–47.
38. Richmond *Dispatch* (April 18, 1854). "J.B. Horner" is clearly George Baylor Horner of the class of 1854.
39. See, *inter alia, Lynchburg Virginian* (April 18, 1854); Richmond *Dispatch* (April 17, 1854).
40. Richmond *Dispatch* (April 18, 1854).

41. Francis Henney Smith to Richard Scott Blackburn, Dec. 29, 1852, Superintendent's Outgoing Correspondence, VMI Archives, cited in Wineman, "Francis Henney Smith," 324.

42. VMI Court Martial Records, Jan. 26, 1853, VMI Archives. The story of the Blackburn prank was clearly embroidered over time. The best-known variant of the tale claims that Blackburn and Robinson (unnamed in the story) "tied a 'rat' named Towson in a chair and after placing him at the proper angle on the stoop in front of Jackson's door, they knocked on the door and ran. Of course, the tied-up Towson tumbled in." See Couper, *One Hundred Years*, III, 178. While it makes a better story, Couper's account does not square with the court-martial testimony found in VMI Archives, Superintendent's Order Book, Order Number 13, Jan. 29, 1853. The same court martial dismissed Cadet W.W. Page from the Institute for playing cards in the barracks. See also Brown, *Stonewall Jackson: The Christian Soldier*, 7.

43. VMI Court Martial records, Jan. 24, 1853, 301–17, VMI Archives, Lexington, VA. Frank E. Vandiver, the only major biographer of Jackson we have discovered to mention both Tom Blackburn's prank in 1853 and his murder in 1854, fails to connect the two incidents. See Vandiver, *Mighty Stonewall*, 79, 103.

44. VMI Archives, Superintendent's Order Book, Order No. 22, April 2, 1853.

45. Jackson's unpopularity with his students is, of course, legendary. Blackburn's name, and that of his senior-year roommate, Charles Edward Lightfoot, appears on the formal invitation to the July 4, 1853, Military Ball, reproduced in Couper, *One Hundred Years*, I, 258. Katharine L. Brown asserts specifically that "This [the Blackburn court-martial] did not increase Jackson's popularity with the Corps," *Stonewall Jackson: The Christian Soldier*, 7.

46. VMI Archives, Superintendent's Order Book, Order No. 22, April 2, 1853.

47. Virginia Military Institute, *Register of Former Cadets*, 20; Couper, *One Hundred Years*, I, 178.

48. Richard Scott Blackburn to Francis Henney Smith, Feb. 14, 1854, VMI Archives, Superintendent's Incoming Correspondence Files, 1854, #39. Francis Henney Smith to Burr William Harrison, Jan. 23, 1854, Superintendent's Outgoing Letter Book, p. 543, VMI Archives, Lexington, VA.

Chapter 8

49. Samuel McDowell Moore letter to Francis T. Anderson, Mary's father, Jan. 15, 1854, mss in Anderson Family Papers, #001, Leyburn Library, Washington and Lee University, Lexington, VA.

50. Richmond *Dispatch* (April 18, 1854).

51. Charles Edward Lightfoot, VMI Archives Online Rosters Database, www2.vmi. edu/archiverosters.

52. Robert Preston Carson, VMI Archives Online Rosters Database, www2.vmi. edu/archiverosters.

53. Richmond *Dispatch* (April 18, 1854); Lynchburg *Daily Virginian* (April 19, 1854).

54. George Buck, VMI Archives Online Rosters Database, www2.vmi.edu/ archiverosters.

55. Hiram C. Burks, VMI Archives Online Rosters Database, www2.vmi.edu/archiverosters.
56. Richmond *Dispatch* (April 19, 1854).
57. Richmond *Dispatch* (April 18, 1854).
58. Ibid.

Chapter 9

59. Ibid.; John Howard Sharp to John Anderson, Dec. 12, 1903, VMI Archives, Alumni Files Collection, Thomas Blackburn, Class of 1854; Couper, *One Hundred Years,* 277.
60. Lexington *Valley Star* (April 20, 1854).
61. Lynchburg *Daily Virginian* (April 19, 1854).
62. Lexington *Valley Star* (April 20, 1854); Richmond *Dispatch* (April 18, 1854).
63. Ibid.
64. Richmond *Dispatch* (April 19, 1854); Lynchburg *Daily Virginian* (April 20, 1854).
65. Richmond *Dispatch* (April 18, 1854); Lynchburg *Daily Virginian* (April 19, 1854).

Chapter 10

66. Ibid.
67. Richmond *Dispatch* (April 19, 1854).
68. Richard C. Taylor to Walker H. Taylor, Jan. 17, 1854, VMI Archives, Alumni Files Collection, Richard Cornelius Taylor, Class of 1854.
69. Cadet John Howard Sharp to Captain John Anderson, Dec. 12, 1903, VMI Archives, Alumni Files Collection, Thomas Blackburn, Class of 1854.
70. Lynchburg *Daily Virginian* (April 18, 1854).
71. Lexington *Valley Star* (April 20, 1854).
72. Couper, *One Hundred Years,* 277.
73. Richmond *Dispatch* (April 18, 1854).
74. Boley, *Lexington,* 94.
75. Richmond *Dispatch* (April 19, 1854); Lynchburg *Daily Virginian* (April 19, 1854).
76. Ramage, *Gray Ghost,* 20–24.
77. Siepel, *Rebel,* 25–29; Mosby, *Memoirs,* 6–9.
78. Richmond *Dispatch* (April 19, 1854).
79. Richmond *Dispatch* (April 19, 1854). See also Moore, *Memories,* 37–40; Couper, *One Hundred Years,* I, 277; Harwood, "Law Student," 38.

Chapter 11

80. Richmond *Dispatch* (April 19, 1854); Lexington *Valley Star* (April 20, 1854).
81. Lynchburg *Daily Virginian* (April 21, 1854).
82. Ibid.
83. Lexington *Valley Star* (April 20, 1854); Richmond *Dispatch* (April 19, 1854).

Chapter 12

84. Ibid.
85. Ibid.
86. Lynchburg *Daily Virginian* (April 21, 1854).
87. Richmond *Dispatch* (April 20, 1854); Richmond *Dispatch* (April 19, 1854).
88. Lynchburg *Daily Virginian* (April 21, 1854); Richmond *Dispatch* (April 20, 1854).
89. Ibid.
90. Ibid.
91. Harwood, "Law Student," 41–42; "Aunt Magdelen" [Reid] to "Dear Dowell," Feb. 1, 1854, Reid papers, Leyburn Library, Washington and Lee University, Lexington, VA.

Chapter 13

92. Lynchburg *Daily Virginian* (April 20, 1854).
93. Ibid. More informative is the account carried the next day in the Lynchburg *Daily Virginian* (April 21, 1854). It identifies not only the witness ("Mr. Broaches") but also his two companions ("Kahn" and "Curry") and provides details of the encounter, such as Christian's new "hickory stick" and the "fencing" match, not covered in the Richmond *Dispatch* account. Andrew Moore also identified the stick found at the scene as "Lurtee's." See Lynchburg *Daily Virginian* (April 20, 1854).
94. Richmond *Dispatch* (April 20, 1854); Lynchburg *Daily Virginian* (April 21, 1854).
95. Leesburg *Washingtonian* (Jan. 27, 1854); Richmond *Dispatch* (April 20, 1854); Lynchburg *Daily Virginian* (April 21, 1854).
96. Richmond *Dispatch* (April 19, 1854).
97. John Howard Sharp to John Anderson, Dec. 12, 1903, VMI Archives, Alumni Files Collection, Thomas Blackburn, Class of 1854.
98. Lexington *Valley Star* (April 20, 1854).
99. Richmond *Dispatch* (April 19, 1854). See also Samuel McDowell Moore to Francis T. Anderson, Jan. 15, 1854, in Anderson Papers, Leyburn Library, Washington and Lee University, Lexington, VA; Leesburg *Washingtonian* (Jan. 27, 1854).
100. Richmond *Dispatch* (April 18, 1854).
101. Richmond *Dispatch* (April 19, 1854; Lexington *Valley Star* (April 20, 1854).
102. Ibid.

Chapter 14

103. Lexington *Valley Star* (April 20, 1854).
104. Lynchburg *Daily Virginian* (April 20, 1854).
105. Richmond *Dispatch* (April 19, 1854).
106. Ibid.
107. Ibid.
108. Ibid.
109. Ibid.

110. Ibid.

111. Ibid.

112. Richmond *Dispatch* (April 20, 1854).

113. Richmond *Dispatch* (April 18, 1854).

114. John Howard Sharp to John R. Anderson, Oct. 8, 1903, VMI Archives, Alumni Files Collection, John Howard Sharp, Class of 1857. R.T. Carson, writing in 1916, also remembered that Christian had shaved his moustache. See R.T. Carson to Capt. Jos. R. Anderson, Aug. 7, 1916, VMI Archives, Alumni Files Collection, Thomas Blackburn, Class of 1854.

115. Most likely Julia Anne Lewis, the daughter of William C. Lewis and Rebecca Burris.

116. John Howard Sharp to John R. Anderson, Oct. 8, 1903, VMI Archives, Alumni Files Collection, John Howard Sharp, Class of 1857. For mention of the "Bible Recitation," see Richmond *Dispatch* (April 18, 1854).

117. Francis H. Smith to Richard Scott Blackburn, Feb. 10, 1854, Superintendent's Outgoing Letter Book, VMI Archives. (Copy transcribed for the author by Diane B. Jacob, Nov. 1, 2002.)

118. Richmond *Dispatch* (April 18, 1854).

119. John Howard Sharp to John R. Anderson, Oct. 8, 1903, VMI Archives, Alumni Files Collection, John Howard Sharp, Class of 1857, R.T. Carson to Jos. R. Anderson, Aug. 7, 1916, VMI Archives, Alumni Files Collection, Thomas Blackburn, Class of 1854.

120. Moore, *Memories*, 37–40; Couper, *One Hundred Years*, I, 277; Coulling, *Margaret Preston Junkin*, 87.

121. Leesburg *Washingtonian* (Jan. 27, 1854). See also John Bowers, *Stonewall Jackson*, 86.

122. Leesburg *Washingtonian* (Jan. 27, 1854). See also Bowers, *Stonewall Jackson*, 86. Bowers asserts that "Ellie's younger sister, Julia, had been with the Junkin clan and Jackson inside the church when the murder took place." He also asserts that the *Lexington Gazetter* [*sic*] "couldn't cover the story enough," that "day after day the local paper unearthed new facts and theories about the case" and that "the two young men had been rivals for the hand of Julia Junkin." The first two statements do not correspond to the actual coverage in the *Gazette*. Blackburn and Christian were not romantic rivals with regard to either Julia Junkin or Mary Evelyn Anderson.

123. John Howard Sharp to John Anderson, Dec. 12, 1903, in VMI Archives, Alumni Files Collection, Thomas Blackburn, Class of 1854.

124. Richmond *Dispatch* (April 18, 1854).

125. John Howard Sharp to John Anderson, Dec. 12, 1903, VMI Archives, Alumni Files Collection, Thomas Blackburn, Class of 1854. His memory was remarkably correct. See Moore, *Memories*, 37–40; Couper, *One Hundred Years*, I, 277; Samuel McDowell Moore to Francis T. Anderson, Jan. 15, 1854, in Anderson Papers, Leyburn Library, Washington and Lee University, Lexington, VA; Leesburg *Washingtonian* (Jan. 27, 1854). See also Richmond *Dispatch* (April 17, 1854) and Lexington *Valley Star* (April 20, 1854).

126. Richmond *Dispatch* (April 17, 1854).

127. Moore, *Memories*, 37–40; Couper, *One Hundred Years*, I, 277–78; John Howard Sharp to John Anderson, Dec. 12, 1903, VMI Archives, Alumni Files Collection, Thomas Blackburn, Class of 1854; Richmond *Dispatch* (April 18, 1854).
128. Richmond *Dispatch* (April 17, 1854); Lexington *Valley Star* (April 20, 1854).
129. Samuel McDowell Moore letter to Francis T. Anderson, Jan. 15, 1854, in Anderson Papers Leyburn Library, Washington and Lee University, Lexington, VA; Leesburg *Washingtonian* (Jan. 27, 1854); Lexington *Valley Star* (April 20, 1854).
130. John Howard Sharp to John Anderson, Dec. 12, 1903, VMI Archives, Alumni Files Collection, Thomas Blackburn, Class of 1854.

Chapter 15

131. "Deposition of James W. Massie, a Witness," a version of the story Massie told at preliminary hearings shortly after the murder, is reprinted in Harwood, "Law Student," 38. See also Leesburg *Washingtonian* (Jan. 27, 1854). The best and most detailed version of Massie's story, his testimony on day one of Christian's first trial in Lexington, April 13, 1854, is summarized in detail in the Richmond *Dispatch* (April 17, 1854 and ff.). Unless otherwise indicated, the account which follows is taken from Massie's testimony at that trial.
132. Leesburg *Washingtonian* (Jan. 27, 1854).
133. Most likely his wife-to-be, Sophonsiba Preston Breckinridge McDowell, sister of Sally Campbell Preston McDowell, and thus a one-time aunt, by marriage, of Cadet Tom Blackburn.
134. Richmond *Dispatch* (April 17, 1884).
135. John Howard Sharp to John Anderson, Dec. 12, 1903, VMI Archives, Alumni Files Collection, Thomas Blackburn, Class of 1854. In 1903 Sharp thought the other cadet was Thomas Phillip Matthews. It must have been someone else. Matthews later testified that he was sitting in the cadet gallery in the Presbyterian Church when he heard Blackburn was killed, and that he heard the news some ten minutes after Blackburn left with Christian. See Richmond *Dispatch* (April 17, 1854).
136. Lexington *Valley Star* (April 20, 1854).
137. Richmond *Dispatch* (April 17, 1854).
138. Richmond *Dispatch* (April 17, 1854). See also John Howard Sharp to John Anderson, Dec. 12, 1903, VMI Archives, Alumni Files Collection, Thomas Blackburn, Class of 1854.

Chapter 16

139. Lexington *Valley Star* (April 20, 1854).
140. "Evidence at Inquest of Thomas Blackburn" (Jan. 16, 1854) original in the possession of Katie Letcher Lyle, Lexington, VA.
141. "Evidence at Inquest of Thomas Blackburn."
142. Richmond *Dispatch* (April 17, 1854).
143. Lexington *Valley Star* (April 20, 1854).

144. For the musicians, see Couper, *One Hundred Years*, I, 68, 137, 192.
145. Unless otherwise indicated, the following account is based upon the testimony of Doctor Patrick H. Christian on day one of Christian's first trial, April 13, 1854. His testimony is most thoroughly summarized in the Richmond *Dispatch* (April 17, 1854).
146. Richmond *Dispatch* (April 19, 1854).
147. Ibid. See also Richmond *Dispatch* (April 17, 1854); Lynchburg *Daily Virginian* (April 20, 1854).
148. Richmond *Dispatch* (April 19, 1854).

Chapter 17

149. Richard C. Taylor to Walker H. Taylor, Jan. 17, 1854, VMI Archives, Alumni Files Collection, Richard Cornelius Taylor, Class of 1854.
150. Harwood, "Law Student," 38; Leesburg *Washingtonian* (Jan. 27, 1854).
151. Richmond *Dispatch* (April 17, 1854).
152. Lynchburg *Daily Virginian* (April 18, 1854).
153. Ibid.
154. Samuel McDowell Moore to Francis T. Anderson, Jan. 15, 1854, Anderson Family Papers, #001, Leyburn Library, Washington and Lee University, Lexington, VA.
155. "Evidence at Inquest of Thomas Blackburn."
156. Richard C. Taylor to Walker H. Taylor, Jan 17, 1854, VMI Archives, Alumni Files Collection, Richard Cornelius Taylor, Class of 1854. The five who remained, most likely, were Taylor himself, Sharp, Dr. Christian, Dr. Jordan and Bancker, the VMI musician. Massie, by this time, had gone with Mayor Jordan to arrest Charles Christian. Cadet Matthews had returned to church and was sitting in the cadet gallery when he heard Blackburn had been killed.
157. Richard C. Taylor to Walker H. Taylor, Jan. 17, 1854, VMI Archives, Alumni Files Collection, Richard Cornelius Taylor, Class of 1854.
158. Richmond *Dispatch* (April 19, 1854); Lexington *Valley Star* (April 20, 1854).

Chapter 18

159. The following account, unless otherwise noted, is abstracted from the testimony of law student William William R. Winn on day two of Christian's first trial, April 14, 1854, and the testimony of law student B.D. Chenowith on day three of the trial, April 15, 1854, both as reported in the Richmond *Dispatch* (April 19, 1854).
160. Lexington *Valley Star* (April 20, 1854). The account of Winn's testimony published in the Lexington *Valley Star* indicated that Cadet Edward Langhorne was with Morris and Stribling. This was clearly not the case.
161. Richmond *Dispatch* (April 19, 1854). Morris testified he thought this conversation took place "in Strayer's room." Christian didn't go to Strayer's room until urged to do so by Seevers, after Seevers had brought back the news that Blackburn was dead.
162. Lexington *Valley Star* (April 20, 1854).

163. Ibid.

164. Ibid.

165. Richmond *Dispatch* (April 19, 1854).

166. Richmond *Dispatch* (April 20, 1854).

167. Richmond *Dispatch* (April 18, 1854); Lexington *Valley Star* (April 20, 1854).

168. If Langhorne's account is true, he must have left his "lady" at the church early, chatted with the cadets on the porch before Blackburn arrived, left before the commotion on Nelson Street began and dallied along the way back to McDowell's Hotel. Law students began to post themselves on the stairs only after Christian had fled there. No one appears to have ever questioned Langhorne's account in court.

169. Richmond *Dispatch* (April 18, 1854); Lexington *Valley Star* (April 20, 1854).

170. Ibid.

171. Lexington *Valley Star* (April 20, 1854).

Chapter 19

172. Richmond *Dispatch* (April 18, 1854).

173. Lexington *Valley Star* (April 20, 1854).

174. Richmond *Dispatch* (April 19, 1854).

175. Lynchburg *Daily Virginian* (April 20, 1854).

176. Richmond *Dispatch* (April 19, 1854).

177. Ibid.

178. Ibid.

179. Ibid.

180. The "Negro" was no doubt the "reliable negro" later described as the only person who had seen the entire fight. He was never called to testify.

181. Richmond *Dispatch* (April 19, 1854).

182. Ibid.

183. Ibid.

Chapter 20

184. Ibid.; Lynchburg *Daily Virginian* (April 19, 1854).

185. Richard C. Taylor to Walker H. Taylor, Jan. 17, 1854, VMI Archives, Alumni Files Collection, Richard Cornelius Taylor, Class of 1854. See also John Howard Sharp to John Anderson, Dec. 12, 1903, VMI Archives, Alumni Files Collection, Thomas Blackburn, Class of 1854.

186. Richmond *Dispatch* (April 19, 1854).

187. Lexington *Valley Star* (April 20, 1854).

188. Unless otherwise noted, the following account is derived from the testimonies of James W. Massie, Richmond *Dispatch* (April 17, 1854) and Mayor William Jordan, Richmond *Dispatch* (April 19, 1854) and the expanded version of Massie's testimony provided by the Lexington *Valley Star* (April 20, 1854).

189. Lynchburg *Daily Virginian* (April 20, 1854).

Chapter 21

190. Richard C. Taylor to Walker H. Taylor, Jan. 17, 1854, VMI Archives, Alumni Files Collection, Richard Cornelius Taylor, Class of 1854.
191. Francis H. Smith, "Death of Cadet Thomas Blackburn," in Minutes of the Board of Visitors, Volume 3 (1853–64), 49, VMI Archives; VMI Semi-Annual Report, July 4, 1854.
192. Richard C. Taylor to Walker H. Taylor, Jan. 17, 1854, VMI Archives, Alumni Files Collection, Richard Cornelius Taylor, Class of 1854.
193. Wineman, "Francis H. Smith," 365–66.
194. John Howard Sharp to John Anderson, Dec. 12, 1903, VMI Archives, Alumni Files Collection, Thomas Blackburn, Class of 1854; Couper, *One Hundred Years*, 258; Virginia Military Institute, *Register of Former Cadets*, 19.
195. Francis H. Smith, "Death of Cadet Thomas Blackburn," in Minutes of the Board of Visitors, Volume 3 (1853–64), 49, VMI Archives; Testimony of Colonel Smith, Richmond *Dispatch* (April 18, 1854).
196. Wineman, "Francis H. Smith," 365–66.
197. John Howard Sharp to John Anderson, Dec. 12, 1903, VMI Archives, Alumni Files Collection, Thomas Blackburn, Class of 1854. The author has found no other account that supports Sharp's contention that Jackson, rather than Colonel Smith, stopped the Corps from lynching Christian. Jackson is never mentioned in either Smith's court testimony, or, so far as can be determined, in any of his written remarks on the incident, or any of his published works. Tom Blackburn's death is rarely mentioned in the literature on the life and times of "Stonewall Jackson." It is mentioned briefly in Vandiver, *Mighty Stonewall*, 103, and in Bowers, *Stonewall Jackson*, 86. Jackson's role in the affair is not mentioned directly in Couper, *One Hundred Years* or Moore, *Memories*. It is not mentioned at all in Robertson, *Stonewall Jackson;* Farwell, *Stonewall;* Henderson, *Stonewall Jackson;* Chambers, *Stonewall Jackson;* Dabney, *Life and Campaigns;* Jackson, *Memoirs;* Schildt, *Jackson and the Preachers;* Chase, *Story of Stonewall;* Addey, *Stonewall Jackson;* Randolph, *The Life;* Cook, *The Family.*
198. Lynchburg *Daily Virginian* (April 20, 1854).
199. Richmond *Dispatch* (April 18, 1854); Francis H. Smith, "Death of Cadet Thomas Blackburn," Minutes of the Board of Visitors, Volume 3 (1853–64), 49. See also Moore, *Memories*, 37–40; Couper, *One Hundred Years*, I, 278.
200. Richard C. Taylor to Walker H. Taylor, Jan. 17, 1854, VMI Archives, Alumni Files Collection, Richard Cornelius Taylor, Class of 1854.
201. Richmond *Dispatch* (April 18, 1854); Francis H. Smith, "Death of Cadet Thomas Blackburn," in Minutes of the Board of Visitors, Volume 3 (1853–64), 49.
202. Ibid.
203. John Howard Sharp to John Anderson, Dec. 12, 1903, VMI Archives, Alumni Files Collection, Thomas Blackburn, Class of 1854.
204. Richmond *Dispatch* (April 18, 1854). See also Francis H. Smith, "Death of Cadet Thomas Blackburn," in Minutes of the Board of Visitors, Volume 3 (1853–64), 49, VMI Archives.

205. Ibid.
206. Richard C. Taylor to Walker H. Taylor, Jan. 17, 1854, VMI Archives, Alumni Files Collection, Richard Cornelius Taylor, Class of 1854.
207. Richmond *Dispatch* (April 18, 1854).
208. Ibid.
209. Richmond *Dispatch* (April 19, 1854).
210. Lynchburg *Daily Virginian* (April 20, 1854).

Chapter 22

211. Ibid.
212. Richmond *Dispatch* (April 19, 1854).
213. Richmond *Dispatch* (April 18, 1854); Lynchburg *Daily Virginian* (April 20, 1854).
214. Ibid.
215. Richmond *Dispatch* (April 21, 1854).
216. Ibid.
217. Richmond *Dispatch* (April 19, 1854).
218. Lynchburg *Daily Virginian* (April 20, 1854).
219. Richmond *Dispatch* (April 18, 1854).
220. Samuel McDowell Moore to Francis T. Anderson, Jan. 15, 1854, Anderson Family Papers, #001, Leyburn Library, Washington and Lee University, Lexington, VA.
221. Ibid.

Chapter 23

222. Richmond *Dispatch* (April 17, 20 and 21, 1854).
223. Richmond *Dispatch* (April 20, 1854).
224. Ibid.; Lynchburg *Daily Virginian* (April 21, 1854).
225. Ibid.
226. Ibid.
227. Ibid.
228. Ibid.
229. Ibid.
230. Ibid.
231. Ibid.

Chapter 24

232. Richmond *Dispatch* (April 20, 1854).
233. "Evidence at Inquest of Thomas Blackburn"; Richmond *Dispatch* (April 21, 1854).
234. Richmond *Dispatch* (April 17, 1854).
235. After the discovery of the wound to Blackburn's carotid artery, little attention appears to have been paid to the wound in his back, nor to how it could have been delivered by the smaller, right-handed Christian, lying on his back (as he would

later testify) underneath Blackburn. "Evidence at Inquest of Thomas Blackburn"; Richmond *Dispatch* (April 21, 1854); Richmond *Dispatch* (April 17, 1854).

236. "Evidence at Inquest of Thomas Blackburn"; Richmond *Dispatch* (April 21, 1854); Richmond *Dispatch* (April 17, 1854).

Chapter 25

237. Francis H. Smith, "Death of Cadet Thomas Blackburn," in Minutes of the Board of Visitors, Volume 3 (1853–64), 49, VMI Archives.

238. Ibid.

239. Ibid.

240. VMI Archives, Superintendent's Order Book, Order Number 7, Jan. 16, 1854.

241. For VMI uniforms of the period, see the photographs reproduced on the VMI website, http://www.vmi.edu/~archtml/cwsource.html. See also Thomas C. Hathaway, Jr., "One Hundred and Fifty Years of Virginia Military Institute Uniforms," in Davis, ed., *A Crowd of Honorable Youths*, 89–91.

242. Lexington *Valley Star* (Jan. 26, 1854).

243. "On the death of Cadet Thomas Blackburn," in Thomas F. Barksdale notebook, VMI Archives.

244. Francis H. Smith, "Death of Cadet Thomas Blackburn" in Minutes of the Board of Visitors, Volume 3 (1853–64), 49, VMI Archives.

Chapter 26

245. Couper, *One Hundred Years*, I, 48, 278. See also Francis H. Smith, "Death of Cadet Thomas Blackburn," in Minutes of the Board of Visitors, Volume 3 (1853–64), 50.

246. Couper, *One Hundred Years*, I, 48, 278.

247. Ibid, 238–39.

248. Thos. J. Michie to Francis Henney Smith, Jan. 19, 1854, VMI Archives, Superintendent's Incoming Correspondence Files, 1854, #236.

249. Robertson, *Alexander Hugh Holmes Stuart*. See also Bladek, "Virginia is Middle Ground," 47; Holt, *The Rise and Fall*, 528, 927.

250. Smith's decision in this regard is clearly revealed in G.W. Turner to Francis Henney Smith, Jan. 23, 1854, VMI Archives, Superintendent's Incoming Correspondence Files, 1854, #383. Turner knew about the demands, but he too thought the time was not right to tell Dr. Blackburn.

251. C.E. Ambler to Francis Henney Smith, Jan. 21, 1854, VMI Archives, Superintendent's Incoming Correspondence Files, 1854, # 1.

252. Ibid.

253. Ibid.

254. General William Harvie Richardson to Francis Henney Smith, Jan. 21, 1854, VMI Archives, Superintendent's Incoming Correspondence Files, 1854, #311.

255. General William Harvie Richardson to Francis Henney Smith, Jan. 26, 1854, VMI Archives, Superintendent's Incoming Correspondence Files, 1854, #312.

Chapter 27

256. George Washington Turner would be killed by John Brown's raiders on the first day of the great raid on Harper's Ferry.

257. R.S. Blackburn to Francis Henney Smith, Feb. 14, 1854, VMI Archives, Superintendent's Incoming Correspondence Files, 1854, #39. Francis Henney Smith to Burr William Harrison, Jan. 23, 1854, Superintendent's Outgoing Letter Book, p. 543, VMI Archives, Lexington, VA.

258. G.W. Turner to Francis Henney Smith, Jan. 23, 1854, VMI Archives, Superintendent's Incoming Correspondence Files, 1854, #383.

259. Ibid.

260. Ibid.

261. William Spottswood White to Francis Henney Smith, Feb. 1, 1854, VMI Archives, Superintendent's Incoming Correspondence Files, 1854.

262. R.S. Blackburn to Francis Henney Smith, Feb. 8, 1854, VMI Archives, Superintendent's Incoming Correspondence Files, 1854, #38.

263. Francis Henney Smith to R.S. Blackburn, Feb. 10, 1854, Superintendent's Outgoing Letter Book, VMI Archives. (Transcribed by Diane B. Jacob Nov. 1, 2002.)

264. Ibid.

265. Ibid.

266. Ibid.

267. R.S. Blackburn to Francis Henney Smith, Feb. 14, 1854, VMI Archives, Superintendent's Incoming Correspondence Files, 1854, #39.

268. Cadet James Edward Towson of the class of 1856, the cadet Tom Blackburn tied to a chair in the notorious prank that led to his court-martial in Jan. 1853.

269. R.S. Blackburn to Francis Henney Smith, Feb. 14, 1854, VMI Archives, Superintendent's Incoming Correspondence Files, 1854, #39.

270. Ibid.

271. Ibid.

Chapter 28

272. Lexington *Valley Star* (Feb. 2, 1854); Harwood, "Law Student," 41–42; "Aunt Magdelen" [Reid] to "Dear Dowell." Feb. 1, 1854, Reid papers, Leyburn Library, Washington and Lee University, Lexington, VA; "The Testimony of Miss Anderson."

273. W.N. Anderson to F.T. Anderson, Jan. 25, 1854, Anderson Family Papers, Leyburn Library, Washington & Lee University, Lexington, VA.

274. Richmond *Dispatch* (April 18, 1854); Couper, *One Hundred Years*, I, 278. See also Francis H. Smith, "Death of Cadet Thomas Blackburn," in Minutes of the Board of Visitors, Volume 3 (1853–64), 50, VMI Archives.

275. For more on the Terrill family, see Armstrong, *God Alone*.

276. "Aunt Magdelen" [Reid] to "Dear Dowell." Feb. 1, 1854, Reid papers, Leyburn Library, Washington and Lee University, Lexington, VA.

Chapter 29

277. Morton, *History of Rockbridge County*, 249; Virginia Military Institute, *Register of Former Cadets*, 8–9; Couper, *One Hundred Years*, I, 84, 214, 222.
278. "The Testimony of Miss Anderson."
279. John Howard Sharp to John Anderson, Dec. 12, 1903, VMI Archives, Alumni Files Collection, Thomas Blackburn, Class of 1854.
280. "Aunt Magdelen" [Reid] to "Dear Dowell." Feb. 1, 1854, Reid papers, Leyburn Library, Washington and Lee University, Lexington, VA.
281. Ibid.
282. Ibid.; Lexington *Valley Star* (Feb. 2, 1854).
283. Cook, *The Family*, 84.

Chapter 30

284. Mary Anna Morrison would later marry Thomas J. Jackson.
285. Daniel Harvey Hill to Mary Anna Morrison, Jan. 27, 1854, Jackson-Arnold Collection, Presbyterian College, Clinton, SC.
286. Philip St. George Cocke to John B. Cocke, Jan. 29, 1854, Cocke Family Papers, Special Collections, University of Virginia.
287. Pearson and Hendricks, *Liquor and Anti-Liquor*, 73, 75n., 77, 78, 88n.
288. Philip St. George Cocke to John B. Cocke, Jan. 29, 1854, Cocke Family Papers, Special Collections, University of Virginia.
289. "Aunt Magdelen" [Reid] to "Dear Dowell," Feb. 1, 1854, Reid papers, Leyburn Library, Washington and Lee University, Lexington, VA.
290. Couper, *One Hundred Years*, I, 278.
291. Ibid.
292. W.N. Anderson to F.T. Anderson, Jan. 25, 1854, Anderson Family Papers, Leyburn Library, Washington & Lee University, Lexington, VA.
293. Ibid.
294. Giles Gunn to "Molly," Feb. 1, 1854, VMI Archives, Giles Gunn papers, MS0292.
295. Couper, *One Hundred Years*, I, 123–24.
296. Francis H. Smith, "Death of Cadet Thomas Blackburn," in Minutes of the Board of Visitors, Volume 3 (1853–64), 50, VMI Archives.
297. Couper, *One Hundred Years*, I, 278; Richmond *Dispatch* (April 18, 1854); Francis H. Smith, "Death of Cadet Thomas Blackburn," in Minutes of the Board of Visitors, Volume 3 (1853–64), 50, VMI Archives. Glasgow was most likely the eldest son of Robert Glasgow of "Max Meadows," after whose brother, Joseph, the 1890s boom town of Glasgow, VA, was named. See Miller, *Glasgow*, 12–13.

Chapter 31

298. Richmond *Dispatch* (April 18, 1854); Couper, *One Hundred Years*, I, 278; see also Francis H. Smith, "Death of Cadet Thomas Blackburn," in Minutes of the Board of Visitors, Volume 3 (1853–64), 50, VMI Archives.

299. Richmond *Dispatch* (April 18, 1854).

300. Couper, *One Hundred Years*, I, 279.

301. Ibid.

302. Richmond *Dispatch* (April 18, 1854).

303. Ibid.

304. Couper, *One Hundred Years*, I, 279.

305. Ibid., 278; See also Francis H. Smith, "Death of Cadet Thomas Blackburn," in Minutes of the Board of Visitors, Volume 3 (1853–64), 50, VMI Archives.

306. Ibid.

307. G.W. Turner to Francis Henney Smith, Jan. 23, 1854, Superintendent's Incoming Correspondence Files, 1854, #383, VMI Archives.

308. Couper, *One Hundred Years*, I, 279.

309. G.W. Turner to Francis Henney Smith, Jan. 23, 1854, Superintendent's Incoming Correspondence Files, 1854, #383, VMI Archives.

Chapter 32

310. R.S. Blackburn to Francis Henney Smith, Feb. 8, 1854, Superintendent's Incoming Correspondence Files, 1854, #38, VMI Archives.

311. Robert Ryland to Francis Henney Smith, May 18, 1854, Superintendent's Correspondence, Incoming, 1854, #341, VMI Archives, summarized in William Couper's notes for Couper, *One Hundred Years at VMI*, in William Couper Papers, Mss 053, VMI Archives, Lexington, VA.

312. Hackley, *Faces on the Wall*, 89–91.

313. Ibid.

314. Ibid.

315. Rev. Jeremiah Bell Jeter quoted in Duke and Jordan, *Richmond Reader*, 83.

316. Valentine Museum, "Richmond Portraits," 184–85.

317. Ibid. See also Hackley, *Faces on the Wall*, 89–91; Ward, *Richmond*, 96–97. For a differing view of Ryland, see Franklin, *Negro in Virginia*, 117–18, 274–76. See also Jordan, *Black Confederates*, 116.

318. Valentine Museum, "Richmond Portraits," 184–85.

319. Blanche Sydnor White quoted in Dabney, *Richmond*, 139.

320. Ibid.

321. R.S. Blackburn to Francis Henney Smith, Feb. 8, 1854, quoted in Couper, *One Hundred Years*, I, 278.

Chapter 33

322. William N. Anderson to Francis T. Anderson, Feb. 8, 1854, Anderson Family Papers, Leyburn Library, Washington and Lee University, Lexington, VA.

323. Lexington *Valley Star* (April 20, 1854).

324. Ibid.

325. Daniel Harvey Hill to Mary Anna Morrison, Jan. 27, 1854, Jackson-Arnold Collection, Presbyterian College, Clinton, SC.

326. William N. Anderson to Francis T. Anderson, Feb. 8, 1854, Anderson Family Papers, Leyburn Library, Washington and Lee University, Lexington, VA.

327. Charles S. Taylor to Francis Henney Smith, March 2, 1854, Superintendent's Incoming Correspondence Files, 1854, #384, VMI Archives, Lexington, VA.

328. Ibid.

Chapter 34

329. The best public sources for the Lexington trial are, without doubt, the accounts carried in the Richmond *Dispatch* and the Lynchburg *Daily Virginian*, both of which assigned special reporters to cover it. See "Trial for Murder," Richmond *Dispatch* (April 17–28, 1854) *passim*, and "Trial of C.B. Christian, in Rockbridge, for Murder," Lynchburg *Daily Virginian* (April 18–May 4, 1854) *passim*. The Lexington *Gazette* (April 20, 1854) apologized for lack of early coverage, but promised its readers that "One of the counsel has kindly offered us the use of his notes, so that in our next [issue] we will be enable to present to our readers the most interesting details of the trial." See Lexington *Gazette* (April 27–28, 1854) for an excellent summary. The Lexington *Valley Star* did lengthy stories on the trial in its April 20 and April 27, 1854, editions. Press coverage elsewhere appears to have relied almost entirely on reports from the above-named Virginia press. The Richmond *Whig* did lengthy stories on April 18 and April 24–25, 1854. See also Couper, *One Hundred Years*, I, 279. For unpublished legal records see Rockbridge County Circuit Court. Order Book (1854); Rockbridge County Circuit Court. Judgements (April–June 1854). The best online resource is Roth and Watkinson, "Homicides of Adults in Rockbrige," *passim*.

330. Unless otherwise annotated, the account of the events of April 13–14, 1854, are drawn primarily from the Richmond *Dispatch* (April 17, 1854). See also Cadet John Howard Sharp to Captain John Anderson, Dec. 12, 1903, VMI Archives, Alumni Files Collection, Thomas Blackburn, Class of 1854.

331. Wayland, *Historic Homes*, 279.

332. Lynchburg *Daily Virginian* (April 18, 1854); Richmond *Dispatch* (April 17, 1854).

333. John Howard Sharp to John Anderson, Dec. 12, 1903, VMI Archives, Alumni Files Collection, Thomas Blackburn, Class of 1854.

334. See Bladek, "Virginia is Middle Ground," 47; Holt, *The Rise and Fall*, 528, 927.

335. Couper, *One Hundred Years*, I, 22.

336. Couper, *One Hundred Years*, I, 280.

337. Couper, *One Hundred Years*, I, 82, 92.

338. Krick, *Lee's Colonels*, 105.

339. For more on Sterret, see John Douglas Sterrett, http://awt.ancestry.com/cgi-bin/igm.cgi?op=GET&db=:2556712&id=I136818

340. The newly released 1850 census data was covered in the local press while Christian was still incarcerated. See "Statistics of Rockbridge," Lexington *Gazette* (April 6, 1854).

341. Richmond *Dispatch* (April 17, 1854). Biographical and relationship data for the jury members is drawn from Dooley, *1860 Census*, *passim* and from online

data drawn from the VMI Archives Online, Ancestry.com, Findagrave.com and other resources, compiled and incorporated into a reunion database by the author.

342. Richmond *Dispatch* (April 17, 1854).

343. Richmond *Whig* (April 18, 1854).

344. Richmond *Dispatch* (April 17, 1854).

345. Ibid.

346. Buckley, ed., *"If You Love That Lady,"* xvi, citing Sally C.P. Thomas to R.J. Taylor, Feb. 20, 1842, her "favorite cousin." See also Francis Thomas, *Statement;* Buckley, *Great Catastrophe.*

347. Roth and Watkinson, *Homicides.*

Chapter 35

348. Unless otherwise noted, accounts of day two of the trial are taken from "Trial for Murder," Richmond *Dispatch* (April 18, 1854) and "The Commonwealth vs. Chs. B. Christian," Richmond *Whig* (April 18, 1854).

Chapter 36

349. Unless otherwise noted, accounts of day three of the trial are drawn from the Richmond *Dispatch* (April 19, 1854).

350. Richmond *Dispatch* (April 20, 1854).

Chapter 37

351. Unless otherwise noted, accounts of day four of the trial are taken from "Trial for Murder," Richmond *Dispatch* (April 20, 1854).

Chapter 38

352. Unless otherwise noted, accounts of day five of the trial are drawn from the Richmond *Dispatch* (April 21, 1854).

353. Richmond *Dispatch* (April 21, 1854); Richmond *Whig* (April 25, 1854).

354. Richmond *Dispatch* (April 21, 1854).

Chapter 39

355. Unless otherwise noted, the accounts of day five of the trial are taken from "Trial for Murder," Richmond *Dispatch* (April 22, 1854).

356. See http://en.wikipedia.org/wiki/Alfred_Swaine_Taylor.

357. Richmond *Dispatch* (April 22, 1854).

Chapter 40

358. Unless otherwise indicated, this account of day five of the trial is drawn from "Trial for Murder," Richmond *Dispatch* (April 22, 1854).

Chapter 41

359. Unless otherwise noted, the account of day six of the trial are drawn from "Trial for Murder," Richmond *Dispatch* (April 24, 1854).
360. Richmond *Whig* (April 24, 1854).
361. Ibid.
362. Ibid.
363. Presumably Winn and Morris.

Chapter 42

364. Unless otherwise noted, the account of day seven of the trial is based on "Trial for Murder," Richmond *Dispatch* (April 25, 1854).
365. Stuart paraphrased Romans 12:19.

Chapter 43

366. Unless otherwise noted, the account of the afternoon of day seven of the trial is drawn from "Trial for Murder," Richmond *Dispatch* (April 25, 1854).
367. Emphasis added.
368. See, *inter alia*, Nisbett and Cohen, *Culture of Honor*, 62.

Chapter 44

369. Unless otherwise noted, the account of day eight of the trial is based on "Trial for Murder," Richmond *Dispatch* (April 25–26, 1854).
370. Richmond *Whig* (April 25, 1854); Richmond *Dispatch* (April 25 and April 26, 1854).
371. Ibid.
372. Ibid.
373. Ibid.
374. Richmond *Dispatch* (April 26, 1854).
375. Ibid.
376. Ibid.

Chapter 45

377. Unless otherwise noted, the accounts of this portion of day eight of the trial are drawn from "Trial for Murder," Richmond *Dispatch* (April 26, 1854).

Chapter 46

378. Unless otherwise noted, this account of day nine of the trial is based on "Trial for Murder," Richmond *Dispatch* (April 28, 1854).

379. Richmond *Dispatch* (April 26, 1854).

Chapter 47

380. Unless otherwise noted, this account of day ten of the trial is based upon "Trial for Murder," Richmond *Dispatch* (April 28, 1854).

Chapter 48

381. Unless otherwise noted, the accounts of this portion of day ten of the trial are taken from "Trial for Murder," Richmond *Dispatch* (April 28, 1854).

Chapter 49

382. Unless otherwise noted, this account of day eleven of the trial is derived from "Trial for Murder," Richmond *Dispatch* (April 28, 1854)

383. "A Remarkable Murder Trial," *New York Times* (May 8, 1854).

Chapter 50

384. Richmond *Enquirer* (May 5, 1854).

385. Lexington *Gazette* (May 18, 1854); Harwood, "Law Student," 42.

386. John Howard Sharp to John Anderson, Dec. 12, 1903, in Thomas Blackburn papers, VMI Archives.

387. Lexington *Gazette* (May 18, 1854). See also "Another Letter to the Editor" reprinted in Harwood, "Law Student," 42.

388. Lexington *Gazette* (May 18, 1854).

389. Harwood, "Law Student," 42.

390. Martinsburg *Gazette* (April 19, 1854).

391. Charles S. Taylor to Francis Henney Smith, May 1, 1854, Superintendent's Incoming Correspondence, VMI Archives.

392. Richard Scott Blackburn to Francis Henney Smith, May 5, 1854, Superintendent's Incoming Correspondence, 1854, #40, VMI Archives, Lexington, VA.

393. Lexington *Valley Star* (April 20, 1854).

394. Richard Scott Blackburn to Francis Henney Smith, May 5, 1854, Superintendent's Incoming Correspondence, 1854, #40, VMI Archives, Lexington, VA.

395. Andrew, *Long Gray Lines*, 6–17; For an excellent short summary of the pressures of Whig vs. Democrat politics in Virginia on Francis Henney Smith see Wineman, "Francis H. Smith," 268 and *passim*.

396. Richard Scott Blackburn to Francis Henney Smith, May 5, 1854, Superintendent's Incoming Correspondence, 1854, #40, VMI Archives, Lexington, VA.

397. Ibid.
398. Charles S. Taylor to Francis Henney Smith, May 1, 1854, Superintendent's Incoming Correspondence, VMI Archives.
399. Richard Scott Blackburn to Francis Henney Smith, May 5, 1854, Superintendent's Incoming Correspondence, 1854, #40, VMI Archives, Lexington, VA.
400. Thomas Michie to Francis Henney Smith, May 22, 1854, Superintendent's Incoming Correspondence, 1854, # 237, VMI Archives, Lexington, VA.
401. Ibid.
402. W.D. Stuart to Francis Henney Smith, Superintendent's Incoming Correspondence, 1854, #278, VMI Archives, Lexington, VA.
403. Ibid.
404. William Harvie Richardson to Francis Henney Smith, April 28, 1854, VMI Archives, Lexington, VA, Superintendent's Incoming Correspondence, 1854, #318.
405. Ibid.
406. Brown, *Stonewall Jackson*, 7.
407. Francis T. Stribling to Francis Henney Smith, May 22, 1854, Superintendent's Incoming Correspondence, 1854, VMI Archives.
408. Winemann, "Francis H. Smith," 308.

Chapter 51

409. Lynchburg *Daily Virginian* (Sept. 9, 1854). Judge George Henry Gilmer's manuscript Order Books survive at the Bedford County Court House, and though limited in scope, they appear to be the best official records of the court proceedings extant. Press coverage of the trial in Liberty was banned by Judge Gilmer. The Lynchburg *Daily Virginian* published short pieces on Sept. 9, 12 and 13, 1854. The Richmond *Dispatch* on Sept. 14, 1854; the Richmond *Enquirer* on Sept. 15, 1854. The Lexington *Gazette* (Sept. 21, 1854) noted Christian's acquittal.
410. For Judge Gilmer and his family see Brown, *The Cabells*, 564.
411. Lynchburg *Daily Virginian* (Sept. 9, 1854).
412. Bedford County District Court, Order Book, Sept. 5, 1854, 94.
413. Richmond *Dispatch* (April 28, 1854).
414. Goode, *Recollections*, 177–78.
415. Lynchburg *Daily Virginian* (Sept. 9, 1854).
416. Bedford County District Court, Order Book, Sept. 5, 1854, 94; Lynchburg *Daily Virginian* (Sept. 9, 1854); Goode, *Recollections*, 177–78.
417. Lynchburg *Daily Virginian* (Sept. 9, 1854).
418. Bedford County District Court, Order Book, Sept. 5, 1854, 94.
419. Ibid.
420. Ibid.
421. Bedford County District Court, Order Book, Sept. 5, 1854, 96.
422. Ibid., 99

423. United States Congress. *Biographical Directory of the United States Congress.* Online edition. http://bioguide.congress.gov/scripts/biodisplay.pl?index=G000256

424. Bedford County District Court, Order Book, Sept. 5, 1854, 99.

425. Lynchburg *Daily Virginian* (Sept. 12, 1854).

426. Bedford County District Court, Order Book, Sept. 5, 1854, 101-102.

427. Goode, *Recollections,* 178.

428. Lynchburg *Daily Virginian* (Sept. 13, 1854).

429. Richmond *Dispatch* (Sept. 14, 1854).

430. Charles Town *Spirit of Jefferson* (Sept. 19, 1854).

431. Richmond *Enquirer* (Sept. 15, 1854).

432. William Harvie Richardson to Francis Henney Smith, Sept. 30, 1854, Superintendent's Incoming Correspondence, VMI Archives.

433. "The Richest Man in Virginia," *New York Times* (June 2, 1854).

Chapter 52

434. Charles Sinclair Taylor to Francis Henney Smith, Superintendent's Incoming Correspondence, 1854, #439, VMI Archives, Lexington, VA.

435. Thomas J. Michie to Francis Henney Smith, Oct. 25, 1854, Superintendent's Incoming Correspondence, 1854, #240, VMI Archives, Lexington, VA.

436. Thomas J. Michie to Francis Henney Smith, Nov. 3, 1854, Superintendent's Incoming Correspondence, 1854, # 241,VMI Archives, Lexington, VA.

437. Ibid.

438. Thomas J. Michie to Francis Henney Smith, Dec. 1 1854, Superintendent's Incoming Correspondence, 1854, # 242, VMI Archives, Lexington, VA.

439. "Excerpts from Superintendent's Report dated June 22, 1854," 49.

440. Thomas J. Michie to Francis Henney Smith, Dec. 1, 1854, Superintendent's Incoming Correspondence, 1854, #242, VMI Archives, Lexington, VA.

441. Ibid.

442. Ibid.

443. Thomas J. Michie to Francis Henney Smith, Dec. 1, 1854, Superintendent's Incoming Correspondence, 1854, #242, VMI Archives, Lexington, VA.

444. William W. Mosby to Francis Henney Smith, Nov. 5, 1854, Superintendent's Incoming Correspondence, 1854, #241¼, VMI Archives, Lexington, VA.

445. Ibid.

446. Couper, *One Hundred Years,* I, 280.

447. Joseph Reid Anderson to Francis Henney Smith, Dec. 9, 1854, Superintendent's Incoming Correspondence, 1854, #29, VMI Archives, Lexington, VA.

Chapter 53

448. For an extensive published genealogy of the Blackburn family, see Ranke, *Blackburn Genealogy.* For the relationships between most, if not all, the characters in this story, see the unpublished Reunion software databases, "Blackburn Family File" and "Christian Family File," compiled by the author.

449. Couper, *One Hundred Years*, I, 279.

450. For a list of Blackburns buried at Spring Grove, see Bee Line chapter, *Tombstone Inscriptions*.

451. Richard Thomas Walker Duke, *Recollections*, III: "College Days and After," published online at http://assistive.usablenet.com/tt/www2.lib.virginia.edu/small/collections/duke/recollections/textfiles/vol3text.html.

452. For an extensive published genealogy of the Christian family, see Stacy, *Christian of Charles City*. Also valuable, Ackerly and Parker, *"Our Kin."* For the relationships between most, if not all, the characters in this story, see the unpublished Reunion software databases, "Blackburn Family File" and "Christian Family File," compiled by the author.

453. Hale and Phillips, "History of the Forty-Ninth," 3, 15, 27, 49, 53, 57, 67, 111, 114, 135–39, 200, 285–86, 322.

454. Joslyn, *Biographical Register*, 70.

455. Krick, *Lee's Colonels*, 2nd ed., 77.

456. Richmond *Times-Dispatch* (Aug. 13, 1905), letter to the editor, reprinted as "The Battle At Bethesda Church," Southern Historical Society Papers. Vol. XXXIII (Jan.-Dec. 1905). Serving in the same brigade with Christian, and killed at Bethesda Church, was Colonel James Barbour Terrill, VMI class of 1858, the son of William Henry Terrill, who prosecuted the case against Christian at the second, Bedford County, trial.

457. For an overview of Lee's career, see Houck, "Jack Lee."

458. Lee was expelled from UVA for dueling. There were also unsubstantiated rumors that in 1887 Lee shot and killed a man who slapped him after a trial in Amherst, that a murder trial followed and Lee was acquitted. This could well have been the incident with Christian embroidered over time. For details of Lee's 1877 duel, see Houck, *"Jack Lee,"* 20–21. For his "duel" with Christian in 1887, see Alexandria *Gazette* (July 14, 1877).

459. Richmond *Times* (Aug. 17, 1902); Richmond *Dispatch* (Aug. 17, 1902); Richmond *Times-Dispatch* (May 12, 1903); Amherst County Historical Museum, "The Trial," *The Muse*, No. 82 (Feb. 1990), 1.

460. Commonwealth of Virginia. General Assembly. House of Delegates. Journal of the House of Delegates. Extra Session Beginning July 15, 1902, 601–6.

461. Richmond *Times-Dispatch* (Jan. 10, 1903); Richmond *Times-Dispatch* (May 13, 1903); Richmond *Times-Dispatch* (May 18, 1903).

462. VMI Archives, Alumni Files Collection, J.B. Norvell, Class of 1849. Norvell had served as captain of Company A and later a major in Christian's old regiment, the Forty-ninth Virginia.

463. Mrs. Alma Walker McCarthy (1906–2001), interview with Daniel S. Morrow, Oct. 2, 1998, Westminster/Canterbury Retirement Home, Lynchburg, VA. Mrs. McCarthy was one of the "Walker's Ford" Walkers. She was Charles Burks Christian's fourth cousin, twice removed.

464. VMI Archives, Alumni Files Collection, Thomas Blackburn, Class of 1854.

Works Cited

Primary Sources

Archives and Manuscript Collections

Bedford County Circuit Court
   Bedford County Circuit Court. Order Book, 1854
Letcher/Lyle Family Papers.
   "Evidence at Inquest of Thos Blackburn." Jan. 16, 1854
Rockbridge County Circuit Court
   Rockbridge County Circuit Court. Order Books, 1854
Virginia Military Institute Archives, Preston Library, Lexington, VA
   Alumni Files Collection and VMI Archives Online Roster Database
      Thomas Blackburn
      Alexander Broadnax Bruce
      George Buck
      Hiram C. Burks
      Robert Preston Carson
      Charles Edward Lightfoot
      J.B. Norvell
      John Howard Sharp
      Richard C. Taylor
   William Couper Papers
   Court-Martial Records, 1850–54
   Stonewall Jackson Papers, 1853–54
   Minutes of the Board of Visitors, Volume 3, 1853–64
   Superintendent's Incoming Correspondence, 1853–54
   Superintendent's Order Book, 1850–54

WORKS CITED

Superintendent's Outgoing Correspondence, 1853–54
Washington and Lee University, Special Collections, Leyburn Library, Lexington, VA
Anderson Family Papers
Reid Family Papers

Newspapers

Alexandria *Gazette* and Virginia *Advertiser*
Baltimore *Sun*
Charles Town *Spirit of Jefferson*
Leesburg *Washingtonian*
Lexington *Gazette*
Lexington *Valley Star*
Lynchburg *Daily Virginian*
Martinsburg *Gazette*
New York Times
Richmond *Dispatch*
Richmond *Enquirer*
Richmond *Whig*
Shepherdstown *Register*
Staunton *Spectator*
Williamsburg *Gazette*

Interview

Mrs. Alma Walker McCarthy (1906–2001), interview with Daniel S. Morrow, Oct. 2, 1998, Westminster/Canterbury Retirement Home, Lynchburg, VA.

Published Primary Sources

Buckley, Thomas E., ed. *"If You Love That Lady Don't Marry Her": The Courtship Letters of Sally McDowell and John Miller, 1854–1856.* Columbia: University of Missouri Press, 2000.
Commonwealth of Virginia, General Assembly, House of Delegates. *Journal of the House of Delegates.* Extra Session Beginning July 15, 1902, 601–6.
Goode, John. *Recollections of a Lifetime.* New York and Washington: Neale Publishing Company, 1906.
Jackson, Mary Anna. *Memoirs of Stonewall Jackson by His Widow.* Dayton, OH: Morningside, 1993. Reprint of the 1895 edition.
Jacob, Diane B., and Judith Moreland Arnold, compilers. *A Virginia Military Institute Album, 1839–1910: A Collection of Photographs and Manuscripts from the VMI Archives, Lexington, Virginia.* Charlottesville: University Press of Virginia for the Friends of Preston Library, 1982.

Moore, Sallie Alexander (Mrs. John H. Moore). *Memories of a Long Life in Virginia.* Staunton, VA: McClure Company, 1920.

Moran, Jeannie Blackburn. *Twin Souls.* Boston: Christopher Publishing Company, 1922.

Mosby, John Singleton. *The Memoirs of Colonel John S. Mosby.* Nashville, TN: J.S. Sander, 1995. Reprint of the Little, Brown and Company edition of 1917.

Thomas, Francis. *Statement of Francis Thomas.* MD: George Johnston, 1845.

SECONDARY SOURCES

Articles and Book Chapters

Amherst County Historical Museum. "The Trial." *The Muse*, No. 82 (Feb. 1990): 1.

Bladek, John David. "'Virginia is Middle Ground': The Know Nothing Party and the Virginia Gubernatorial Election of 1855." *The Virginia Magazine of History and Biography*, CVI, No. 1 (Winter 1998): 35–70.

Brown, Katherine L. "Stonewall Jackson in Lexington." *Proceedings of the Rockbridge Historical Society*, IX (1975–79): 197–210.

Coyner, Boyd. "John Hartwell Cocke: Southern Original: An address delivered to the [Fluvanna County History] Society, September 13, 1964, in which the progressive and many-faceted career of General Cocke is examined, along with a descriptive account of his three Fluvanna plantations." *Fluvanna History*, #6 (1968).

Curry, Charles. "Seduction by a Married Man." *Virginia Law Register*, Vol. V, No. 4 (Aug. 1899).

Curry, Charles, Armistead C. Gordon, F.T. Prufer. "The Portraits in the Court House at Staunton." *The William and Mary Quarterly*, 2nd Ser., Vol. 10, No. 1 (Jan. 1930): 64–65.

"Genealogy: The Bruce Family," *Virginia Magazine of History and Biography*, XI (June 1904): 197–200, 328–32, 441–43.

Harwood, Doug, compiler. "Law Student Murdered Cadet—Only the Jury Was Hung." Lexington *Advocate* (March 1995).

Houck, Leighton S. "Jack Lee (1861–1926): Lynchburg's Legend of the Law." *Lynch Ferry: Official Publication of the Lynchburg Historical Foundation* (Spring/Summer 2003): 17–20.

McCulloch, Ruth [Mrs. Charles]. "The Blue Hotel, 1817–1947." *Proceedings of the Rockbridge Historical Society* 4 (1949–54): 18–21.

Walker, Charles D. "An Earnest Christian Soldier: The Work of General Francis H. Smith at the Virginia Military Institute." *Protestant Episcopal Review* 7 (Jan. 1893): 186–200.

Books

Ackerly, Mary Denham and Lula Eastman Jeter Parker, compilers. *"Our Kin"*: *The Genealogies of Some of the Early Families Who Made History in the Founding and Development of Bedford County, Virginia.* Harrisonburg, VA: C.J. Carrier Company, 1976.

Addey, Markinfield. *Stonewall Jackson: The Life and Military Career of Thomas Jonathan Jackson, Lieutenant-General in the Confederate Army.* New York: Charles T. Evans, 1863.

Alley, Reuben Edward. *History of the University of Richmond, 1830–1971.* Charlottesville: University Press of Virginia for the University of Richmond, 1977.

Andrew, Rod. *Long Gray Lines: The Southern Military School Tradition, 1839–1915.* Chapel Hill: University of North Carolina Press, 2001.

Armstrong, Richard L. *"God Alone Knows Which Was Right"*: *The Blue and Gray Terrill Family of Virginia in the Civil War.* Jefferson, NC: McFarland & Company, 2010.

Bean, W.G. *Stonewall's Man: Sandie Pendleton.* Chapel Hill: University of North Carolina Press, 1959.

Bee Line Chapter, National Society Daughters of the American Revolution, compilers. *Tombstone Inscriptions and Burial Lots, Jefferson County, West Virginia.* Charles Town, WV: Bee Line Chapter, National Society Daughters of the American Revolution, 1981.

Boley, Henry. *Lexington in Old Virginia.* Richmond, VA: Garrett & Massie, 1936.

Boney, F.N. *John Letcher of Virginia: The Story of Virginia's Civil War Governor.* Tuscaloosa: University of Alabama Press, 1966.

Bowers, John. *Stonewall Jackson: Portrait of a Soldier.* New York: William Morrow, 1989.

Brown, Katharine L. *Stonewall Jackson: The Christian Soldier.* Lexington, VA: Garland Gray Memorial Research Center, Stonewall Jackson House, 1984.

Buckley, Thomas E. *The Great Catastrophe of My Life: Divorce in the Old Dominion.* Chapel Hill: University of North Carolina Press, 2002.

Carrington, Wirt Johnson. *A History of Halifax County, Virginia.* Richmond, VA: Appeals Press, 1924.

Chambers, Lenoir. *Stonewall Jackson and the Virginia Military Institute: The Lexington Years.* Lexington, VA: Garland Gray Memorial Research Center, 1982 reformat of the 1959 William Morrow edition.

Chambers, S. Allen, Jr. *Lynchburg: An Architectural History*, photographs by Richard Cheek. Charlottesville: University Press of Virginia for the Sarah Winston Henry Branch of the Association for the Preservation of Virginia Antiquities, 1981.

Chambers, William Nisbet. *Thomas Hart Benton, Old Bullion Benton, Senator from the New West: Thomas Hart Benton, 1782–1858.* Boston: Atlantic Monthly Press, Little, Brown and Company, 1956.

Chase, William C. *The Story of Stonewall Jackson: A Narrative of the Career of Thomas Jonathan (Stonewall) Jackson, from Written and Verbal Accounts of His Life.* Atlanta: D.E. Luther Publishing Company, 1901.

Cook, Roy Bird. *The Family and Early Life of Stonewall Jackson*, 3rd ed., revised. Charleston, WV: Charleston Printing Company, 1948.

Coulling, Mary Price. *Margaret Preston Junkin: A Biography.* Winston Salem, NC: John F. Blair, 1993.

Couper, William. *One Hundred Years at V.M.I.* Vol. I. Richmond, VA: Garrett and Massie, 1939.

Crenshaw, Ollinger. *General Lee's College: The Rise and Growth of Washington and Lee University.* New York: Random House, 1969.

Dabney, R.L. *Life and Campaigns of Lieut.-Gen. Thomas J. Jackson.* Harrisonburg, VA: Sprinkle Publications, 1983. Reprint of the 1865 edition.

Duke, Maurice, and Daniel P. Jordan, eds. *A Richmond Reader, 1733–1983.* Chapel Hill: University of North Carolina Press, 1983.

Evans, Clement A., ed. *Confederate Military: History Extended Edition.* Vol. 4, *Virginia.* Wilmington, NC: Broadfoot Publishing Company, 1987. Reprint of the Confederate Publishing Company 1899 edition.

Farwell, Byron. *Stonewall: A Biography of General Thomas J. Jackson.* New York: W.W. Norton, 1992.

Fishwick, Marshall. *General Lee's Photographer: The Life and Work of Michael Miley.* Chapel Hill: University of North Carolina Press for the Virginia Historical Society, 1954.

Franklin, John Hope. *The Negro in Virginia.* Winston Salem, NC: John F. Blair, 1994. Reprint of the 1940 edition.

Hackley, Woodford B. *Faces on the Wall: Brief Sketches of the Men and Women Whose Portraits and Busts Were on the Campus of the University of Richmond in 1955.* Richmond, VA: Virginia Baptist Historical Society, 1955.

Hageman, James. *The Heritage of Virginia: The Story of Place Names in the Old Dominion,* Revised 2nd ed. West Chester, PA: Whitford Press, 1988.

Hale, Laura Virginia and Stanley S. Phillips. *History of the Forty-ninth Virginia Infantry, CSA, "Extra Billy Smith's Boys."* Lanham, MD: S.S. Phillips and Associates, 1981.

Holt, Michael F. *The Rise and Fall of the American Whig Party: Jacksonian Politics and the Onset of the Civil War.* New York: Oxford University Press, 1999.

Jordan, Erwin L., Jr. *Black Confederates and Afro-Yankee in Civil War Virginia.* Charlottesville: University Press of Virginia, 1995.

Joslyn, Mauriel. *The Biographical Register of the Immortal 600.* Shippensburg, PA: White Mane, 1992.

Krick, Robert K., ed. *Lee's Colonels: A Biographical Register of the Field Officers of the Army of Northern Virginia,* 2nd ed., revised. Dayton, OH: Press of the Morningside Bookshop, 1984.

Lankford, Nelson D. *The Last American Aristocrat: The Biography of David K. E. Bruce. 1898–1977.* Boston: Little, Brown and Company, 1996.

Lee, Susan P. *Memoirs of William Nelson Pendleton, D.D., Rector of Latimer Parish, Lexington, Virginia; Brigadier-General C.S.A; Chief of Artillery, Army of Northern Virginia.* Philadelphia: J.B. Lippincott, 1893.

Lyle, Royster, Jr., and Pamela Hemenway Simpson. *The Architecture of Historic Lexington,* photographs by Sally Munger Mann. Charlottesville: University Press of Virginia for the Historic Lexington Foundation, 1977.

Miller, Lynda Mundy-Norris. *Glasgow, Virginia: One Hundred Years of Dreams.* Natural Bridge Station, VA: Rockbridge Publishing Company, 1992.

Morton, Oren F. *A History of Rockbridge County, Virginia*. Baltimore, MD: Genealogical Publishing Company for Clearfield, 1997. Reprint of the Staunton, VA edition of 1920.

Paxton, M.W. *A Judge's School: The Story of John White Brockenbrough*. Lexington, VA: Washington and Lee University, 1971.

Payne, Brooke. *The Paynes of Virginia*, 2nd ed. Harrisonburg, VA: C.J. Carrier Company, 1990. Reprint of the original 1937 edition.

Pearson, C.C., and J. Edwin Hendricks. *Liquor and Anti-Liquor in Virginia, 1619–1919*. Durham, NC: Duke University Press, 1967.

Phillips, Catherine Coffin. *Jessie Benton Fremont: A Woman Who Made History*. Introduction by Christine Bold. Lincoln: University of Nebraska Press, 1995. Reprint of the 1935 edition.

Ramage, James A. *Gray Ghost: The Life of Col. John Singleton Mosby*. Lexington: University Press of Kentucky, 1999.

Randolph, Sarah Nicholas. *The Life of Gen. Thomas J. Jackson*. Philadelphia: J.B. Lippencott & Co., 1876.

Ranke, Vinnetta Wells. *The Blackburn Genealogy with Notes on the Washington Family through Intermarriage*. Washington, D.C.: Vinnetta Wells Ranke, 1939.

Ray, Worth S., compiler. *Tennessee Cousins: A History of Tennessee People*. Baltimore, MD: Genealogical Publishing Company, 1999. Reprint of the 1950, Austin, Texas, edition.

Robertson, Alexander F. *Alexander Hugh Holmes Stuart, 1807–1891: A Biography*. Richmond, VA: William Byrd Press, 1925.

Robertson, James I., Jr. *Stonewall Jackson: The Man, the Soldier, the Legend*. Framingham Hills, MI: Cengage Gale, 1997.

Roosevelt, Theodore. *Thomas H. Benton*. Cambridge, MA: The Riverside Press: 1899.

Schildt, John W. *Jackson and the Preachers*. Parsons, WV: McClain Printing, 1982.

Schwarz, Philip J. *Slave Laws in Virginia*. Athens: University of Georgia Press, 1996.

Siepel, Kevin H. *Rebel: The Life and Times of John Singleton Mosby*. New York: St. Martin's Press, 1983.

Stacy, Eunie V. Christian. *Christian of Charles City: An Account of the Antecedents and Descendants of Charles Christian of Virginia and Allied Families, Mainly Found in the Southern States*. Shreveport, LA: Insty-Prints, 1982.

Takagi, Midori. *"Rearing Wolves to Our Own Destruction": Slavery in Richmond, Virginia, 1782–1865*. Charlottesville: University Press of Virginia, 1999.

Tyler-McGraw, Marie. *At the Falls: Richmond, Virginia, and Its People*. Chapel Hill: University of North Carolina Press for The Valentine: The Museum of the Life & History of Richmond, 1994.

United States, Works Progress Administration. *Virginia: A Guide to the Old Dominion*, compiled by Workers of the Writer's Program of the Work Projects Administration in the State of Virginia, in the American Guide Series. Richmond: Virginia State Library and Archives and the Virginia Center for the Book, 1992. Reprint of the 1940 edition.

Valentine Museum. "Richmond Portraits in an Exhibition of Makers of Richmond, 1737–1860," exhibit catalog. The Valentine Museum, Richmond, VA, 1949.

Vandiver, Frank E. *Mighty Stonewall.* College Station, TX: Texas A&M University Press, 1957.

Virginia Military Institute. *Roster of Graduates of the Virginia Military Institute, 1842–1919, with Brief Biographical Notes,* World War Edition. Lexington: Virginia Military Institute, 1920.

Washington and Lee University. *Washington and Lee University Alumni Directory, 1749–1949.* Lexington, VA: Washington and Lee University Alumni Incorporated, 1949.

Wayland, John W. *Historic Homes of Northern Virginia and the Eastern Panhandle of West Virginia.* Staunton, VA: McClure Company, 1937.

White, Blanche Sydnor. *First Baptist Church, Richmond, 1780–1955: One Hundred and Seventy-five Years of Service to God and Man.* Richmond, VA: Whittet & Shepperson, 1955.

White, Frank E., Jr. *The Governors of Maryland, 1777–1970.* Annapolis: Hall of Records Commission, State of Maryland, 1970.

Wiencek, Henry. *The Hairstons: An American Family in Black and White.* New York: St. Martin's Press, 1999.

Williams, Richard G. Jr. *Stonewall Jackson: The Black Man's Friend.* Nashville: Cumberland House, 2006.

Wright, Alice ("Grace") Moran. *The Moran Family Descendants of Hezekiah, Robert Milton, Franklin Pierce Moran and Alice Grace Moran Wright and Services of George Brinton McClellan for the Preservation of the Union.* N.p.: self-published, 1997.

Web Resources

Ancestry.com

Dooley, Edwin L., ed. *1860 Census: Town of Lexington, Virginia.* (2012). http://www.vmi.edu/uploadedFiles/Archives/Local_History/1860Census.pdf VMI Archives online.

Findagrave.com

Roth, Randolph, and James Watkinson, compilers. "Homicides of Adults in Rockbridge County, Virginia, 1778–1900," Criminal Justice Research Center at The Ohio State University. cjrc.osu.edu/researchprojects/hvd/usa/maryland/rockbridge%20county%20homicides.doc (October 2010).

Washington and Lee University School of Law. John White Brockenbrough. http://law.wlu.edu/faculty/profiledetail.asp?id=354 (accessed May 31, 2013).

Dissertations and Theses

Wineman, Bradford Alexander. "Francis H. Smith: Architect of Antebellum Southern Military Schools and Educational Reform," PhD dissertation, Texas A&M University, 2006.

Index

ABOUT THE AUTHOR

Dan Morrow is a co-founder and principal of the Jamestown Exploration Company, a northern Virginia consultancy specializing in the establishment, growth, expansion and positioning of public/private partnerships.

He also happily serves as publisher, columnist, reporter, copyeditor and general factotum at the *Middleburg Eccentric*, a community newspaper he helped found, serving the very best parts of Loudoun and Fauquier Counties, in the outermost ring of the Washington, D.C., suburbs.

He was the first executive director of the Computerworld Smithsonian Awards Program and served for nearly twenty years as executive director and, later, chief historian of its successor, the Computerworld Honors Program.

He has served as a member of the Board of Directors of the Windy Hill Foundation in Middleburg, Virginia; the Mosby Heritage Area Association for historic preservation; the Loudoun County Public Library Board of Trustees; and the Friends of the Balch Library. He was a founding member of the Loudoun County Science and Technology Cabinet, a member of the Board of Visitors for the University of North Carolina's School of Information and Library Science and a founding member of the Knowledge Trust and the Louis Round Wilson Academy.

In his studies at the University of Virginia in the mid-sixties, Mr. Morrow began an academic career in physics and, as a result of what he describes as a profound personal overestimation of his mathematical talents (and a compensating affinity for German), completed two degrees in modern European history.

At UVA he was an Echols Scholar, a DuPont Regional Scholar, a University Scholar and Fellow and a member of the Raven Society. After leaving the University of Virginia, Dan did post-graduate work under John L. Snell at the University of North Carolina at Chapel Hill and under Karl Otmar Freiherr von Aretin at the German Institute for European History in Mainz.

Mr. Morrow's professional career has spanned executive positions in advertising and publishing at the Village Companies, Chapel Hill, North Carolina; Whitney Communications Corporation; and the *Washington Post.*

Dan remains an avid student of the history of the Weimar Republic, nineteenth-century traditions of duty and honor and the American Civil War. His golf game is deteriorating rapidly from a plateau that wasn't all that high in the first place. He is happily married and an equally happy and lucky stepfather and grandfather.